IMAGES
of America

SAVANNAH RIVER PLANT

On the Cover: A displaced resident drives away from a looming reactor in the background. Once construction of the Savannah River Plant began, the large outer shells of the concrete and steel reactors rose from the ground at a rapid pace. What had once been sprawling farmland and dense forest was quickly transformed into an efficient culture of nuclear materials production and technological innovation. (Courtesy of the Department of Energy.)

IMAGES
of America

SAVANNAH RIVER PLANT

Savannah River Site Museum
Foreword by Walt Joseph

ARCADIA
PUBLISHING

ISBN 978-1-4671-0875-1

Published by Arcadia Publishing
Charleston, South Carolina

Printed in the United States of America

Library of Congress Control Number: 2022941125

For all general information, please contact Arcadia Publishing:
Telephone 843-853-2070
Fax 843-853-0044
E-mail sales@arcadiapublishing.com
For customer service and orders:
Toll-Free 1-888-313-2665

Visit us on the Internet at www.arcadiapublishing.com

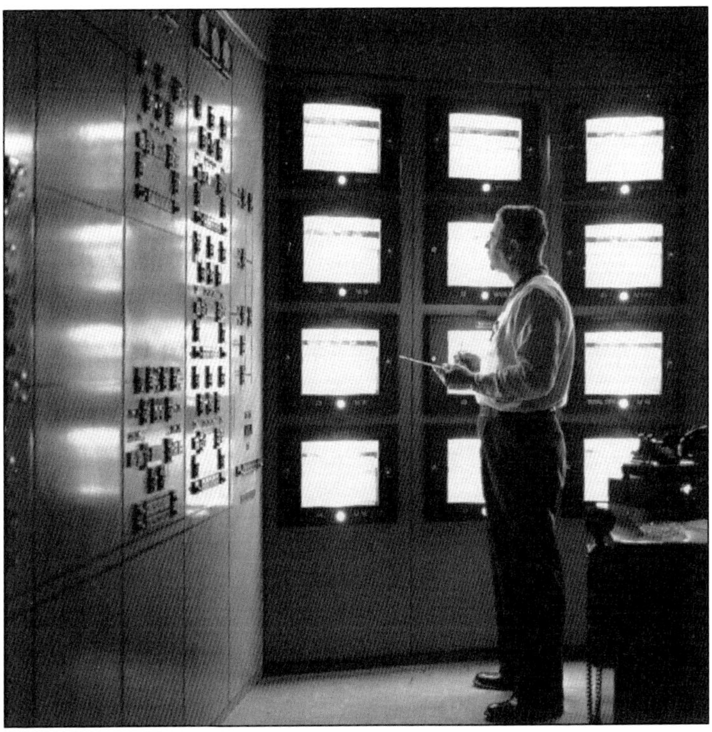

The Savannah River Plant was surrounded by rumors in the earliest years of operation; as soon as plant boundaries were closed to the public, only those with proper access knew the depth and importance of projects going on behind the security fence. The local community gave several nicknames to the plant, the most popular being "the Bomb Plant." The name is still used today, even though bombs were never assembled on-site. (Courtesy of the Department of Energy.)

Contents

Foreword

I am delighted to introduce this new publication complete with early photographs of the Savannah River Plant (SRP). I joined DuPont at the Savannah River Plant in 1954 as an engineer in the Pile Engineering Division of the Savannah River Laboratory. At the time, I was told only that "the site was located near Aiken, South Carolina." I quickly learned that we were a primary source of nuclear materials for the Cold War. Later, I transferred to plant operations where I served with colleagues who held many different job titles ranging from scientists to craftsmen and laborers. Regardless of their job title, these employees were consistently proud of their work and organization.

Many of the early DuPont employees had served in the US military before coming to Savannah River. We veterans understood the need for secrecy about SRP processes and considered that the so-called "Cold War" was an extension of an actual, occasionally "Hot," war between the United States and the Soviet Union. Military experiences reinforced this concern and enhanced our pride in our service. We knew we were on the front line of American defense even though we could not talk about it in public. The requirements for secrecy were particularly onerous to the spouses of employees, who were largely female; security rules prevented families and friends from conversations about work at SRP. I worked at the plant for 25 years before my wife was permitted to see my office.

Employee safety was a corporate mantra for DuPont beginning with the hazardous business of making black powder explosives and continuing through a world-class safety performance during World War II and the Manhattan Project. DuPont management emphasized that employee safety was not only humanitarian but also made good business sense. We were proud of our world-class safety performance and relished showing other organizations how to work safely.

I hope you enjoy the period photography that shows the history of the formerly secret plant as well as those that gave up their homes and land for its creation. Savannah River Site (SRS) Cold War curator Melissa Hanson, SRS museum director Kelly Brown, SRS museum educational specialist Evelyn Berry, and SRS historian Josh Blackmon have put together a great collection of historic images, some well-known, while others have never been viewed before. I hope you can identify with the thousands of workers and families, some of your friends and neighbors, who labored behind the fences to make the SRP a safe and productive cornerstone of our national defense.

—Walt Joseph

Acknowledgments

The publication of this book has been made possible by the Savannah River Site Heritage Foundation and the Savannah River Site Museum. Archival photographs found in this book have been provided courtesy of the Department of Energy as well as the Savannah River Site Archeological Research Program. We would like to thank the SRS Retirees Association, the Citizens for Nuclear Technology Awareness, and New South Associates for providing crucial documentation to help tell the stories of the Savannah River Site. This book, and the mission to preserve and share the legacy of SRS, would not have been possible without the vision and leadership of the SRS Heritage Foundation's former executive director, Walt Joseph.

INTRODUCTION

On September 23, 1949, Pres. Harry S. Truman announced the detonation of the Soviet Union's first atomic bomb. This event brought an end to the United States' short-lived nuclear monopoly after World War II and led to a greater mistrust between the United States and Soviet Russia for much of the remainder of the 20th century. This period, known as the Cold War, lasted from the end of World War II to the fall of the Soviet Union in the early 1990s and prompted a nuclear arms race between the two superpowers. Key to this arms race was a ready supply of nuclear materials that were needed in constructing the next generation of atomic weapons to maintain parity with the Soviet arsenal. In response to this need, the Atomic Energy Commission (AEC) announced the construction of a new nuclear materials production facility in November 1950 to be built along the Savannah River. Comprising one percent of the total land area of the state of South Carolina, the Savannah River Plant (SRP) played a critical role in the national defense of the United States during the Cold War and continues that mission today as the Savannah River Site (SRS). Conceived to produce nuclear materials on an industrial scale, SRS continues to be a vital component of the United States' national defense.

The SRP was a direct heir of the Manhattan Project, a secretive wartime undertaking to develop an atomic bomb that employed thousands at clandestine sites across the country. The Manhattan Project continued after World War II with a core group of atomic bomb project veterans that produced the nation's third and fourth plutonium bombs, Shot Able and Shot Baker, which were tested at Bikini Atoll in the Pacific in July 1946. These tests gave an invited audience of military officers, congressmen, journalists, and scientists firsthand knowledge of the power of the bombs. The high profile of the tests ensured that atomic weapons research and development remained at the forefront of the nation's defense strategy during this uneasy time. The first Soviet nuclear test in 1949 quickened the pace of nuclear research and the development of a new type of bomb, a thermonuclear weapon known as the hydrogen bomb. Preliminary designs for this new hydrogen bomb required large quantities of tritium, a radioactive isotope of hydrogen that was in short supply. The AEC determined that a new nuclear materials production site with reactors of significantly different design was needed to ensure the availability of tritium.

The E.I. du Pont de Nemours and Company Inc. (DuPont) of Wilmington, Delaware, was tasked with site selection, construction, and operation of the proposed plant in 1950. DuPont, the main contractor for the Manhattan Project–era plant in Hanford, Washington, was reluctant to take on the new site, having retired from the field of atomic energy in 1946. However, DuPont agreed and planning began immediately with site selection and reactor design uppermost in mind. DuPont worked closely with the AEC, helping to mold the plant it would operate. A site location in South Carolina's Barnwell and Aiken Counties was chosen out of 114 candidate sites for the new plant. The search that began in June 1950 ended on November 13, 1950, with the search committee's recommendation for the South Carolina site. Water, abundant in supply and low in mineral content; topography; the isolated character of the site; an available labor pool; and military defense all figured into the site's selection.

Between 1950 and 1955, a transformation occurred with breathtaking speed that eradicated small railroad towns, farms, and mill villages typical of mid-20th-century Southern life on the Savannah. These familiar agrarian settings were replaced with a technological complex built and operated by men and women who came from all parts of the country. International events and science had come to South Carolina and Georgia in the form of the SRP.

The US Army Corps of Engineers (USACE) conducted the acquisition program, ultimately acquiring 1,706 tracts of land, totaling 200,742 acres. Seventy-four percent of the acquired properties were farms cultivated in corn, cotton, and peanuts. Small tenant farms were in the majority; the agricultural labor pool was predominantly African American. The plant area was closed to the public on December 14, 1952.

This rapid change was disruptive to those who called the Savannah River Valley home. Residents of Ellenton (population 600), Dunbarton (population 231), Hawthorne, Meyers Mill, Robbins, and Leigh and farmers and tenants within the outlying areas listened sadly and carefully as AEC, US Army Corps of Engineers, DuPont, and local officials outlined what was ahead for them. Eighteen months were allotted for the staged evacuation of 1,500 families. Ellenton residents were to be evacuated by March 1, 1952; Dunbarton residents by June 15. Land appraisers would contact owners, beginning the acquisition process. Those in construction priority areas had six weeks' notice. The many families who rented or sharecropped for their livelihood were also deeply affected. In a month usually filled with warm thoughts of home and the upcoming holidays, "the DPs," those displaced by the federal taking, grappled with future plans under the scrutiny of reporters who told their story to the nation. Some displaced families chose to physically move their homes out of the area, relocating to the new town of New Ellenton, Jackson, or other environs. Others moved to existing neighboring communities.

Construction workers and craftsmen came in droves to participate in an industrial and engineering "event" that ranked with the construction of the Panama Canal. At peak construction in September 1952, a total of 38,582 workers labored 54 hours a week under the direction of DuPont engineers. South Carolina (25,019) and Georgia (13,776) contributed the majority of the project's construction force; however, 49 states and the Panama Canal Zone were also represented in the ranks. At the end of this unprecedented construction effort, the SRP had five heavy water moderated reactors, two chemical separations plants, a heavy water plant, a fuel and target manufacturing area, and laboratories that were joined by over 60 miles of railroad, 230 miles of new roads, the state's first cloverleaf intersection, power plants, and other infrastructure.

Before production could begin, teams of scientists and engineers descended on the plant and worked to develop the various processes needed for a successful start-up. Pilot plants along the Savannah River were some of the first facilities to become active, testing water chemistry and heat exchangers that would cool the giant reactors. Others devised methods of chemical separation that would be used to separate desired nuclear materials from other elements. The Process Development Pile (PDP), a replica of the production reactors at SRP, was a vital component for testing reactor behavior of the five production reactors before plant start-up.

This construction effort and scientific innovation resulted in radioactive operations beginning in December 1953 when R Reactor went critical, followed shortly thereafter by the four other reactors. Two giant remote-controlled chemical processing plants, known as "canyons," dissolved and refined reactor products and brought the final products to form. Reactor fuel and target rods, which fed the massive reactors, were manufactured on-site in facilities in M-Area. Hosts of scientists and engineers working in the state-of-the-art Savannah River Laboratory (SRL) improved and perfected the processes used throughout the plant. These operations were all supported by teams of safety personnel, administration staff, and facilities maintenance crews who kept the plant running.

Production of plutonium and tritium continued throughout the Cold War at SRP. Between 1955 and 1964, all five SRP reactors were online and the overall focus was increasing production for the growing nuclear arsenal of the United States. Demand for weapons material waxed and waned during the Cold War in response to geopolitical influences, which greatly affected production and the research focus at SRP. A greater focus on legacy waste and environmental cleanup began in the 1970s.

By the end of the 1980s, the reactors at SRP ceased operation and the focus of the site turned to stewardship of the nation's nuclear stockpile as well as environmental remediation. DuPont, the site's longtime operator, declined to renew its contract with the Department of Energy (DOE), and Westinghouse took over as operator in 1989. While tritium is still produced at the site today, SRS also provides maintenance of the nation's nuclear stockpile and disposal of excess nuclear material. SRS is committed to the treatment and disposal of legacy waste from Cold War production with the Defense Waste Processing Facility (DWPF).

SRP fulfilled its Cold War mission of producing tritium and plutonium for the US nuclear stockpile. Beyond that mission, SRP contributed to a wealth of scientific knowledge. Laboratories and facilities at SRL were used on various transplutonium programs, which produced radioisotopes for science, medicine, and industry. Plutonium-238 made at SRP powers satellites and deep space missions such as NASA's *Voyager I* and *Voyager II* deep space probes. Other areas of innovation at SRP include electric power from heavy water reactors, the chemical processing of spent power fuels, the recovery of specific fission products, and the manufacture of special radioisotopes.

DuPont, already a leader in the field of industrial ecology, was responsible for bringing a team from the Academy of Natural Sciences in Philadelphia under the leadership of Dr. Ruth Patrick to the plant to perform a biological baseline study of the Savannah River. SRP became the focal point of long-term ecological studies conducted by the University of Georgia's Savannah River Ecology Laboratory (SREL), which forms the basis of much of our modern understanding of ecology. Vast tracts of forests and other ecological zones are managed by the US Forest Service, Savannah River, which planted millions of pine trees at SRP. The Savannah River Archaeological Research Program (SRARP) works to document and protect the site's archaeological resources.

The participants in the making of the Savannah River Plant—construction workers, scientists, engineers, local politicians, community members, and uprooted residents—contributed to the success of the SRP. These people formed new communities in the Central Savannah River Area (CSRA). What coalesced over the years of operation of the SRP was a transformation of a once agrarian landscape to that of a vibrant and growing community, a blending of old and new that forever changed this part of the Savannah River Valley.

One

From Farming to Fission

Nearly 6,000 people sacrificed their homes when displaced by the US government to construct the Savannah River Plant (SRP). In selecting a suitable site for a major nuclear facility, DuPont posed stringent criteria, including a large amount of land, a low population density, nearby cities to support incoming employees, an accessible water source, mild climate, and stable geology. A final evaluation of sites was recommended to the Site Review Committee, and Site No. 5, a rural region along the Savannah River in South Carolina, was agreed upon as the final selection. On November 13, 1950, after months of searching, the location had been chosen: 310 square miles of land covering areas of Aiken, Allendale, and Barnwell Counties.

On November 28, 1950, the residents of Ellenton, Dunbarton, Meyers Mill, Hawthorne, Leigh, and other small communities learned through a radio broadcast, repeated throughout the day, of the decision to acquire the area. A meeting, led by the US Army Corps of Engineers, followed on December 6, 1950, to discuss the process of land acquisition and appraisal. Residents were afforded three to eighteen months to move, depending on their proximity to the center of the plant. Landowners who accepted compensation had the option to purchase their buildings back at salvage price and to move with them. The corps also assisted in the relocation of nearly 6,000 graves.

By the end of that year, the former inhabitants, nearly 1,500 families, had vacated beyond the plant boundaries. The newly displaced struggled to move on, ensure the livelihood of their families, and remain connected to their scattered communities. Savannah River Plant's complex history includes this story of displacement, a sacrifice that contributed to the achievement of technical milestones, the employment of thousands of people, and the future security of the United States during the Cold War nuclear arms race.

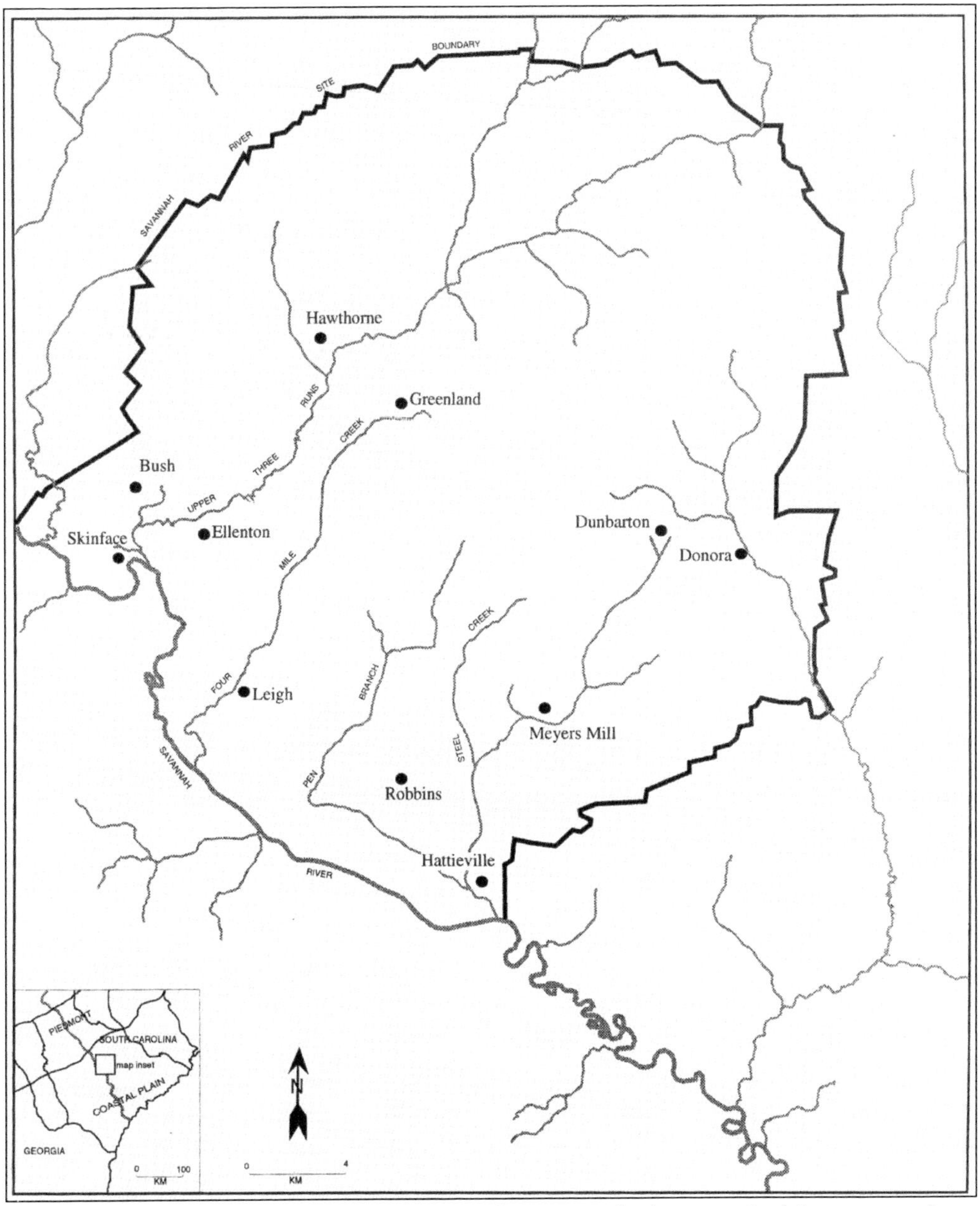

DuPont, contracted to construct and operate the tritium facility, searched for a site with an appropriate topography to construct a manufacturing area as well as additional space to provide a buffer between the reactors and the site boundaries. After several rounds of rigorous evaluation, DuPont decided that Site No. 5, located 22 miles southeast of Augusta, Georgia, would become the future Savannah River Plant (SRP).

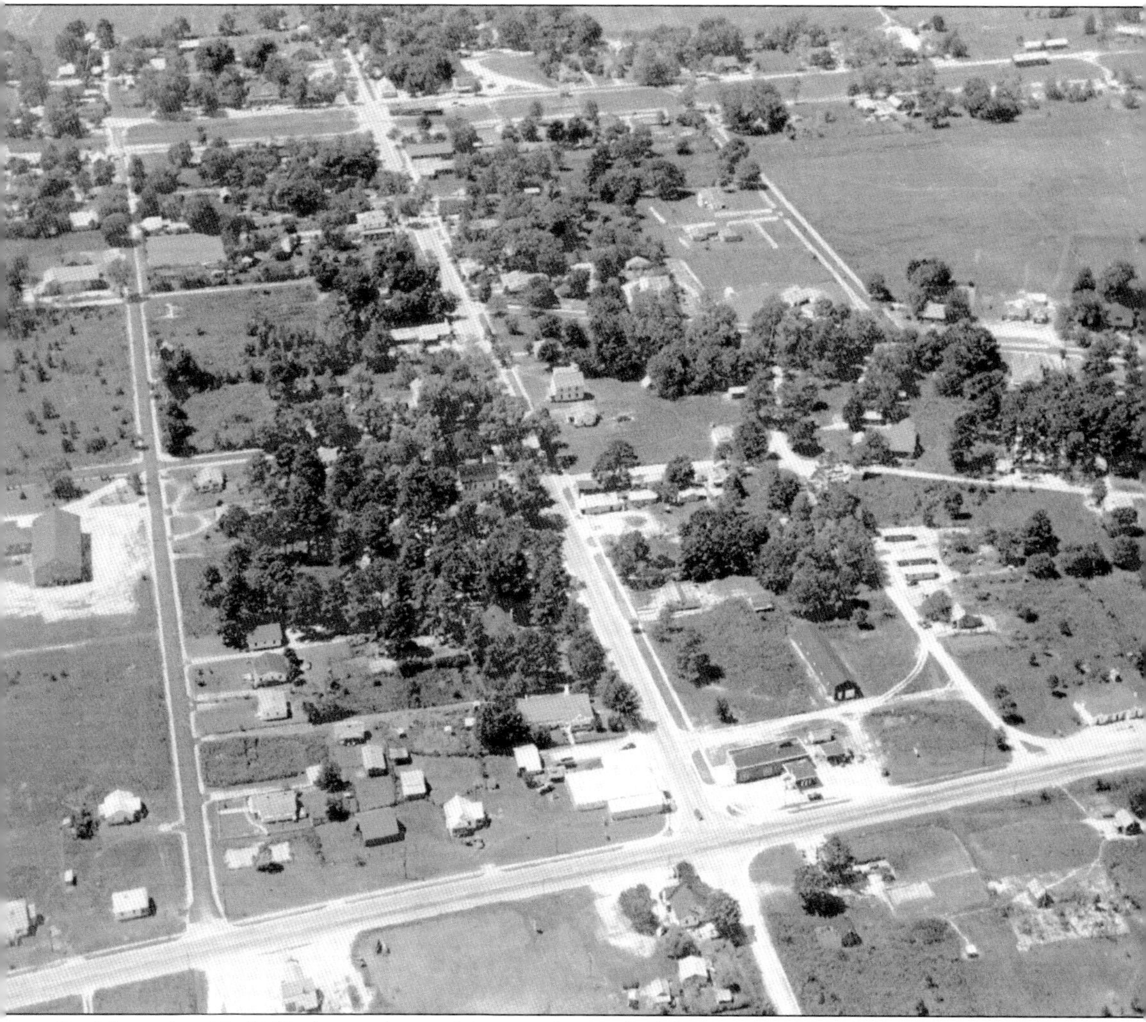

On November 28, 1950, the residents of this area learned of the government's decision to acquire the land. Although tenant farms occupied much of the land, the area was also home to small towns, including Ellenton, South Carolina, a railroad town incorporated in 1880 with a population of 740 people until it was closed to the public in 1952. The town developed around the train depot.

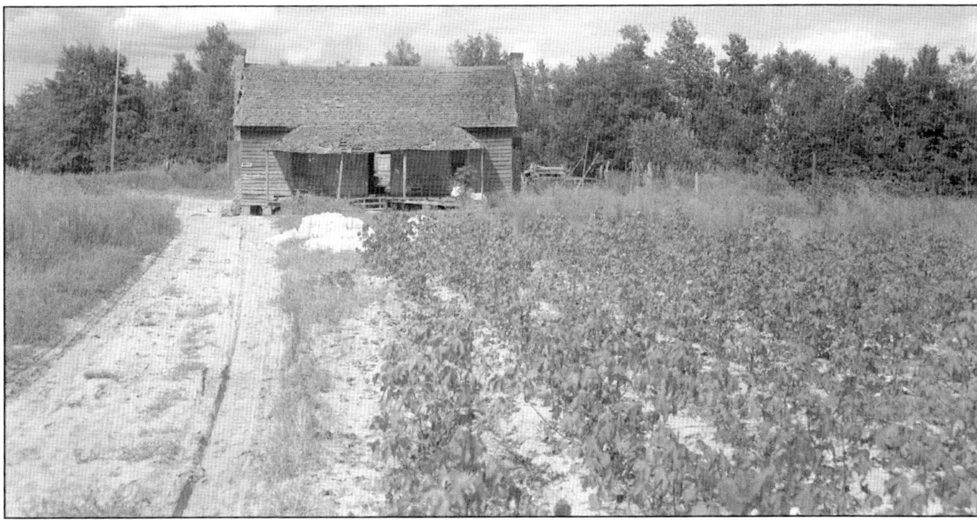

Farming, the region's primary economic engine, kept many busy throughout the year. Landowners, tenant farmers, sharecroppers, and field hands worked in the spring to till the soil, and in the autumn, they harvested, their staple crops feeding local families and cash crops shipped off on the Western & Carolina Railroad. The farmers brought their cotton to the local gin, where they spun it into 500-pound bales.

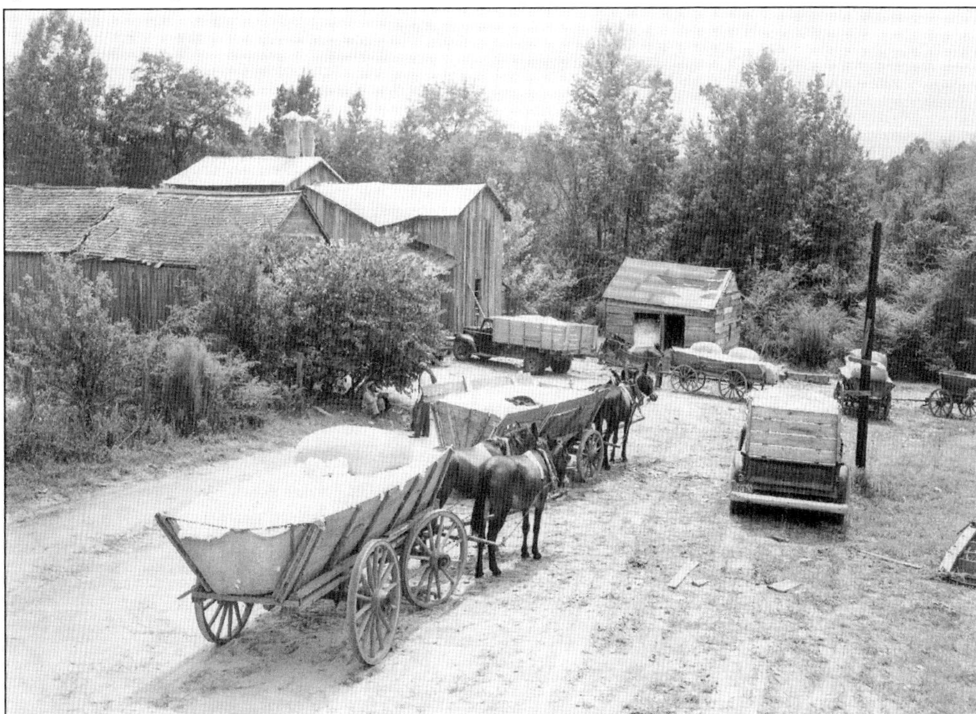

Daily life in this agrarian landscape usually began at daybreak with daily chores of lighting the wood stove, feeding livestock, and collecting eggs. These residents were largely self-reliant, raising their own livestock and smoking their own meat, trading staple crops, and sewing their own clothes. They ventured into the nearby towns to visit the general stores, where they bought their sugar, flour, rice, and coffee.

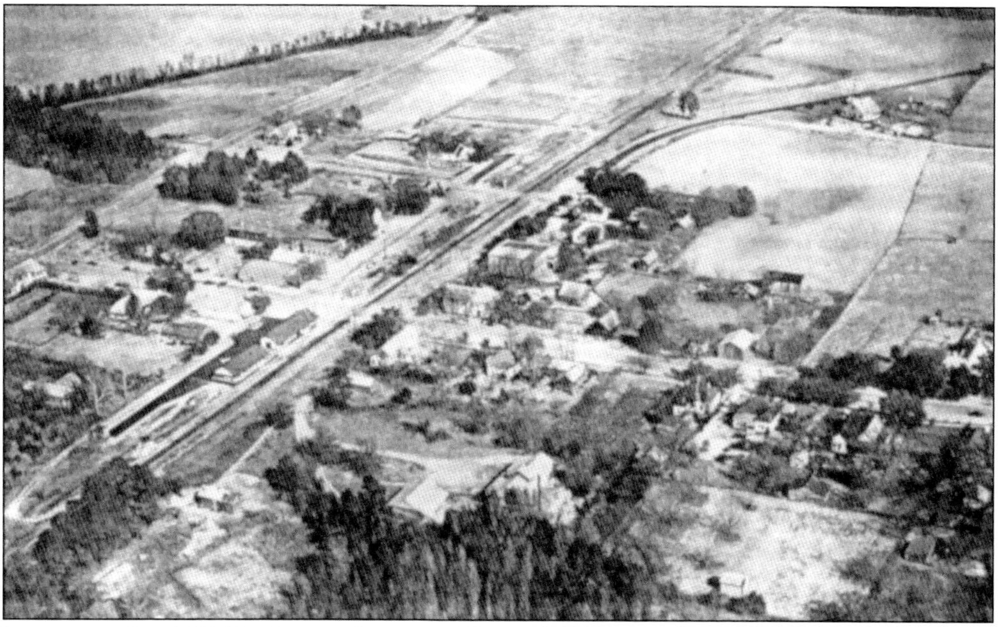

Incorporated in 1910, Dunbarton, home to 462 people, also served as a stop along the Western & Carolina Railroad. Passengers and workers often stopped at the Western Carolina Trading Store or Dean Rountree's general store as well as other local businesses. Dunbarton was also home to the Dunbarton Grammar School and the Four Mile School.

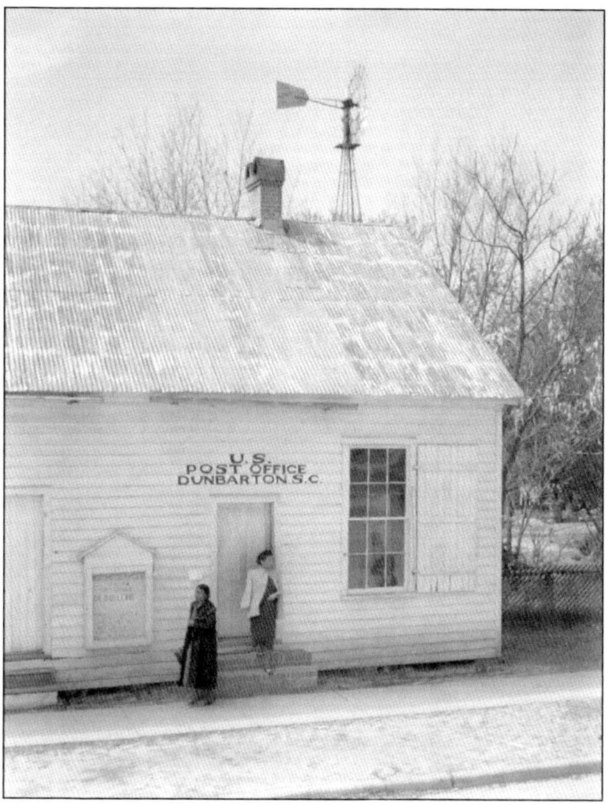

The Dunbarton Post Office was centrally located on Main and Railroad Streets. The town's structures also included churches; several general stores, such as the Western Carolina Trading Store and B.F. Anderson Store; Dicks Garage; and a small brick jail. The Dunbarton Post Office's last day of service was April 15, 1952.

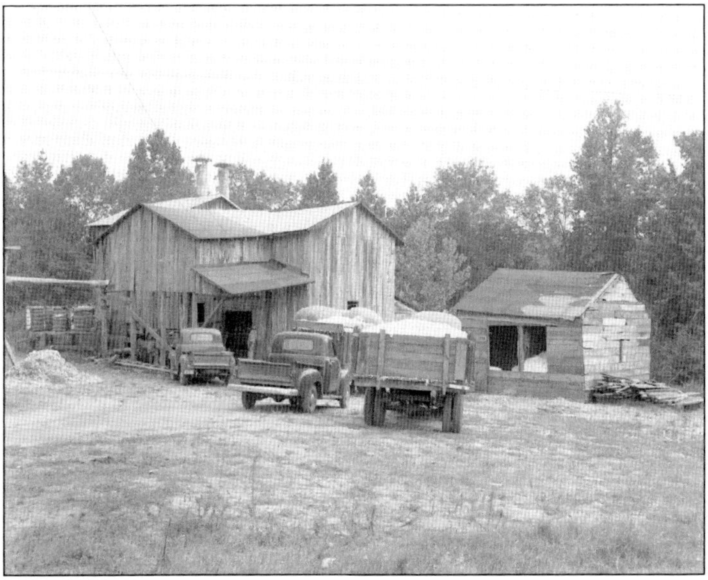

Meyers Mill, a smaller community, included three businesses, Bob Peeple's store, ten homes, two churches, and a post office. Olan Meyer's cotton gin, pictured here, was one of the larger businesses in the area. In addition to staple crops, most farms grew cotton for textiles, the primary industry in the area.

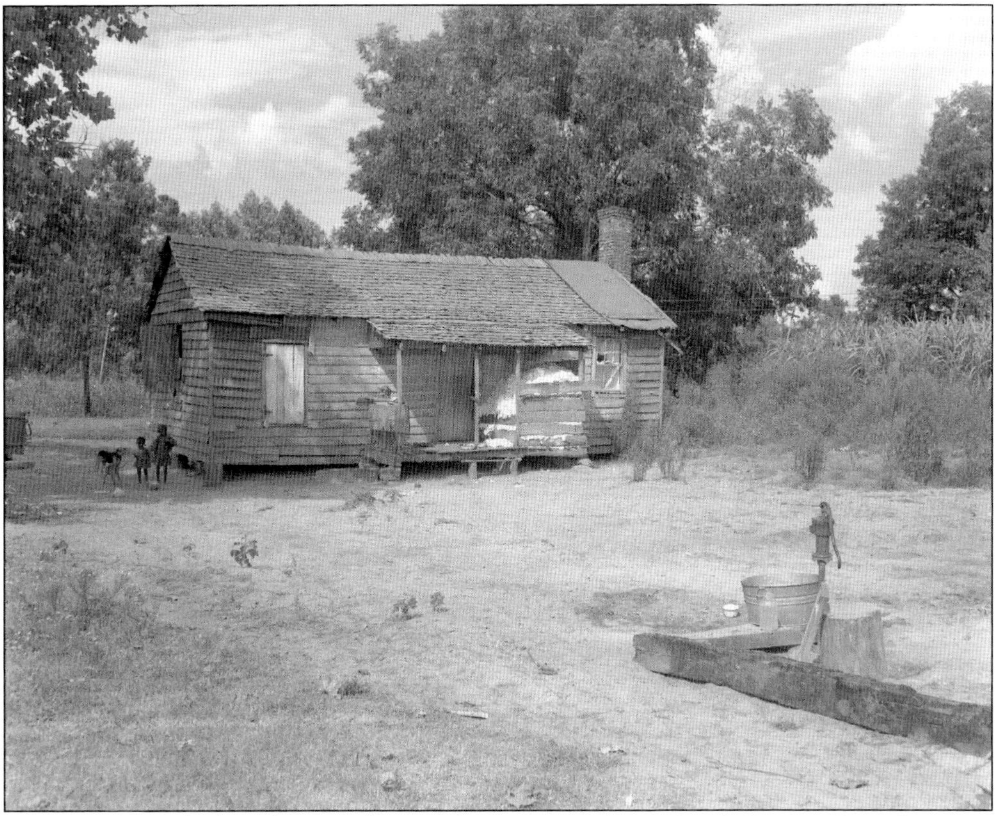

Children play with their dog outside a Leigh community home. Leigh Banana Case Company employed many of the locals, some of whom lived in homes provided by the company with free utilities. The village also included a church, a hotel, and a commissary built by the company. Leigh Banana Case Company manufactured wooden crates from pine, gum, and cypress trees, which were used to ship vegetables and fruits.

Ellenton schools were segregated in the 1950s; African American students attended one, and white students attended the other. The school for white students was known as Ellenton School and offered specialized programs in agriculture and home economics. Before it became accredited in the late 1920s, students went to Dunbarton High to graduate. The Ellenton School facility also served as a community gathering place for dances, festivals, and other celebrations.

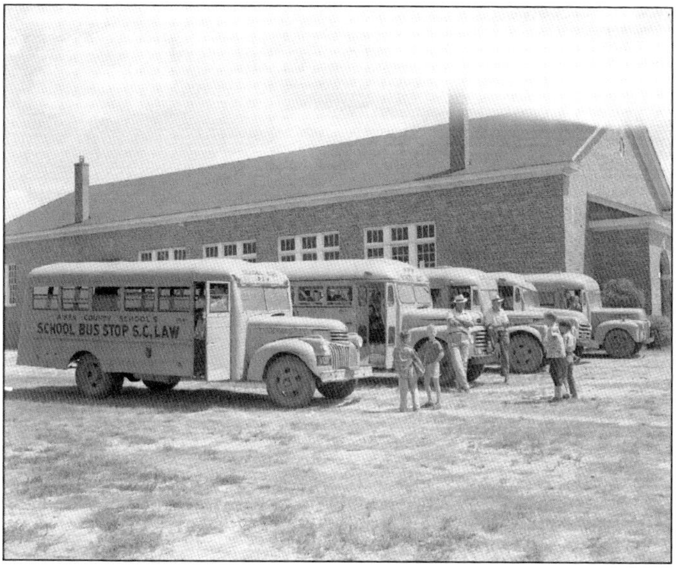

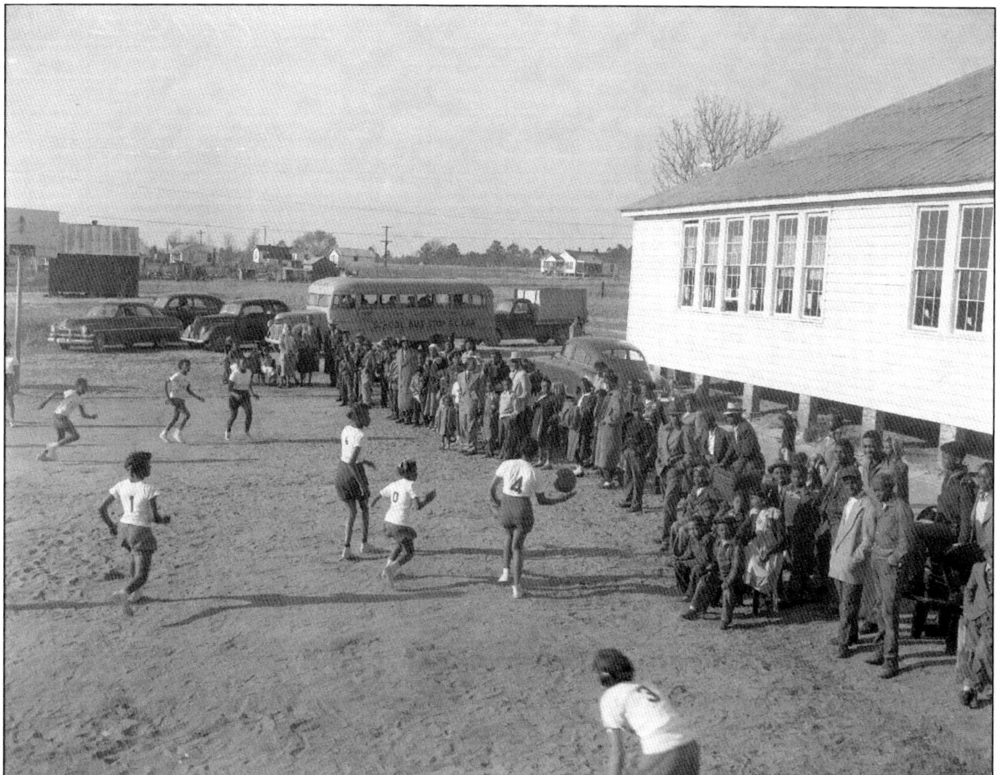

African American students in Ellenton attended the Brinkley School, founded by Dr. Fred Brinkley, up to ninth grade. Students could pursue further education at Four Mile School in Dunbarton. Four Mile was a Rosenwald school with dormitories so children could stay during the week and return home on the weekends. African American students wanting to attend college traveled to Bettis Academy in Graniteville, South Carolina.

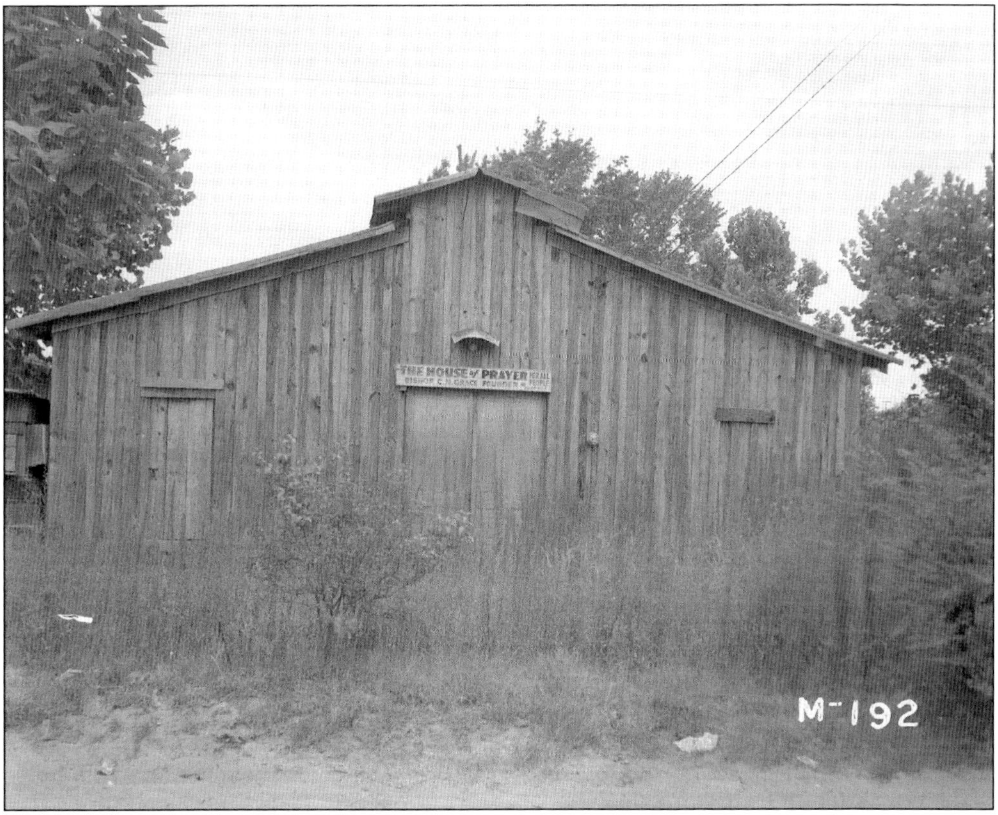

The House of Prayer, built in 1920, hosted several intermingled congregations from across the region. Churches played a major role in the social and spiritual lives of the displaced. Several denominations—Methodist, Christian, and House of Prayer—offered regular services as well as social activities like picnics, potlucks, and cakewalks. Churches also sponsored school events like plays and fundraisers.

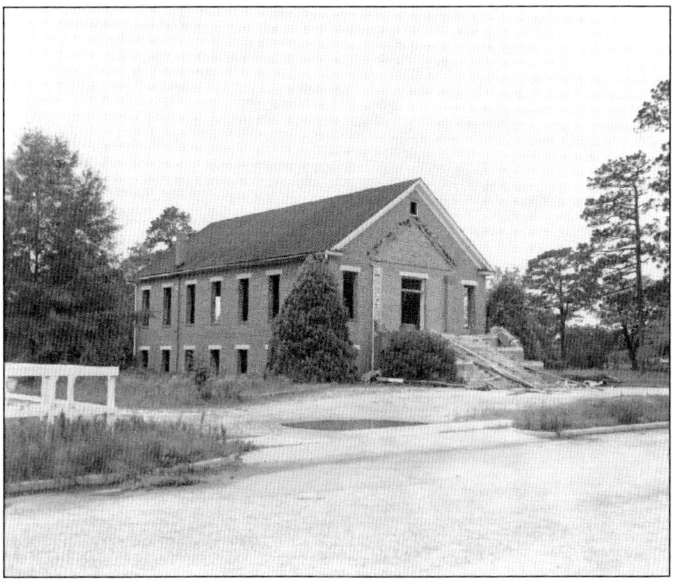

Residents gave up not just their land but a sense of community, especially church congregations. Constructed in 1868, Dunbarton Baptist Church, pictured mid-demolition, held its final service on January 20, 1952, during which the congregation voted on how to dispose of church property and where to donate church furnishings.

Social life centered around the home and churches. Churches hosted large community events, while families often visited each other's homes. They sat on porches or inside homes to talk for long hours and sometimes listen to the radio. Children spent time swimming and fishing in local creeks. On special occasions, families traveled to local movie theaters in Ellenton, Aiken, and Augusta.

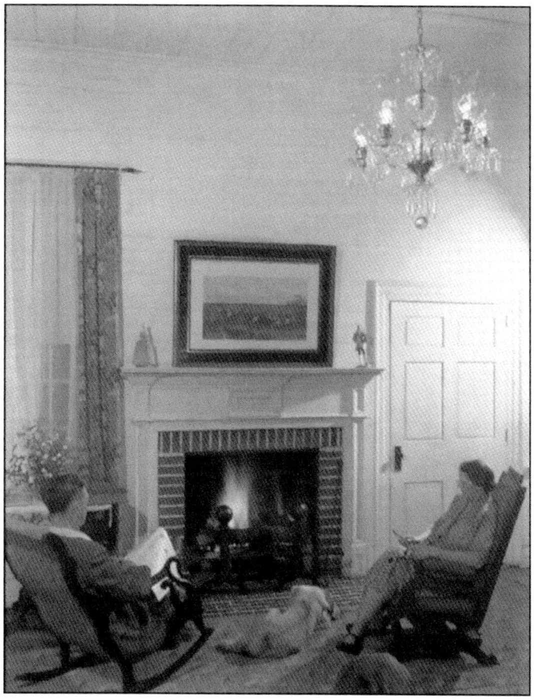

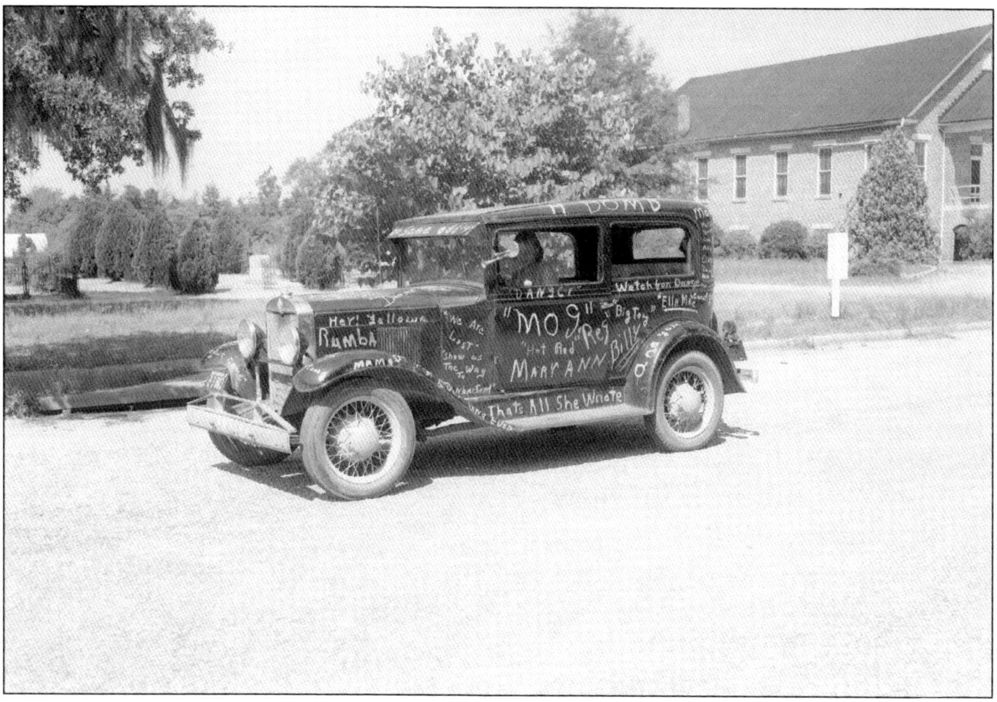

While still preparing to move, Margaret Rountree of Dunbarton, then a teenager, often drove this car around Savannah River Plant. The Ford was decorated with her friends' names and sayings, including her own nickname, "Mog," on the door and "H Bomb" on the roof. Young people often gathered in houses with jukeboxes for private dance parties or attended public dances at regional churches and schools.

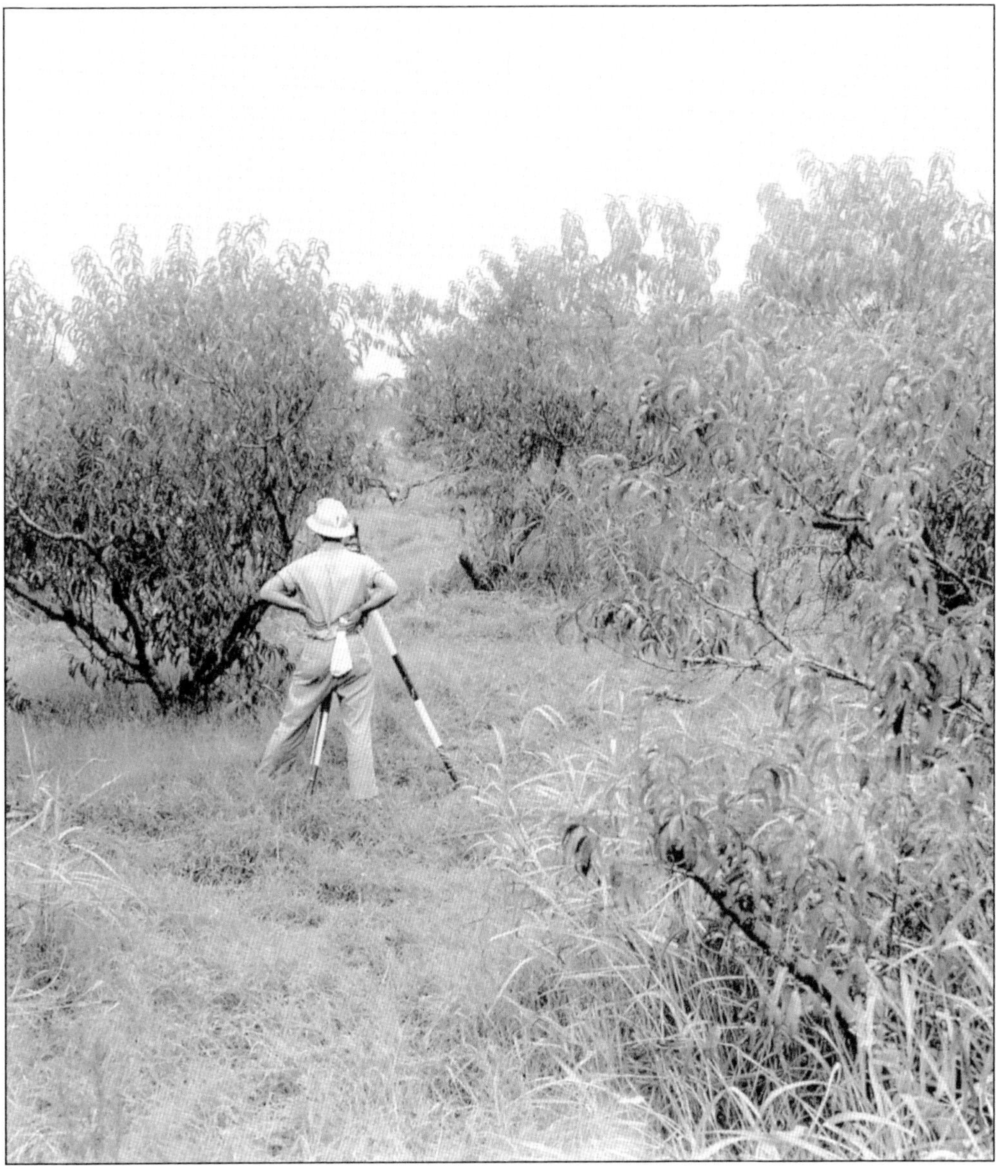

In determining property values, the Army Corps of Engineers appraised the houses, businesses, and structures that families owned, which the US government then purchased. Seen here, a surveyor uses a level meter to measure property boundaries in a peach orchard. Surveyors drew detailed plat maps of each property and placed appraisal number signs near each building, a common sight on everything from tenant homes to chicken coops and even outhouses.

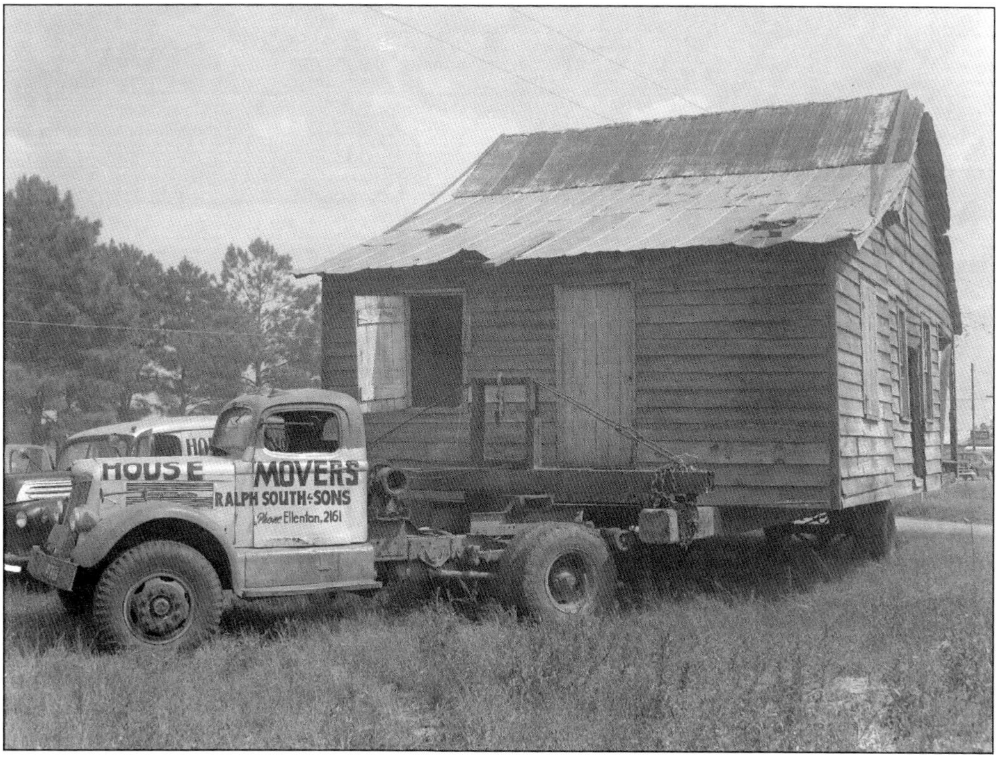

While some contested the appraisals of their properties and negotiated higher compensation in court, other residents signed contracts to accept the initial price, then used the funds to purchase land or housing elsewhere. Many residents chose to buy back their houses and other buildings at salvage value and in doing so accepted the responsibility for moving them. Dozens of moving companies set up shop to help this relocation effort.

In the spring of 1951, a parade of houses migrated away from the communities these families called home. For many, the journey required several days. Crumbling roads, low power lines, and obstructive tree limbs posed serious obstacles on the highways. Some families camped on the side of the road or slept inside their houses perched on the backs of moving trucks.

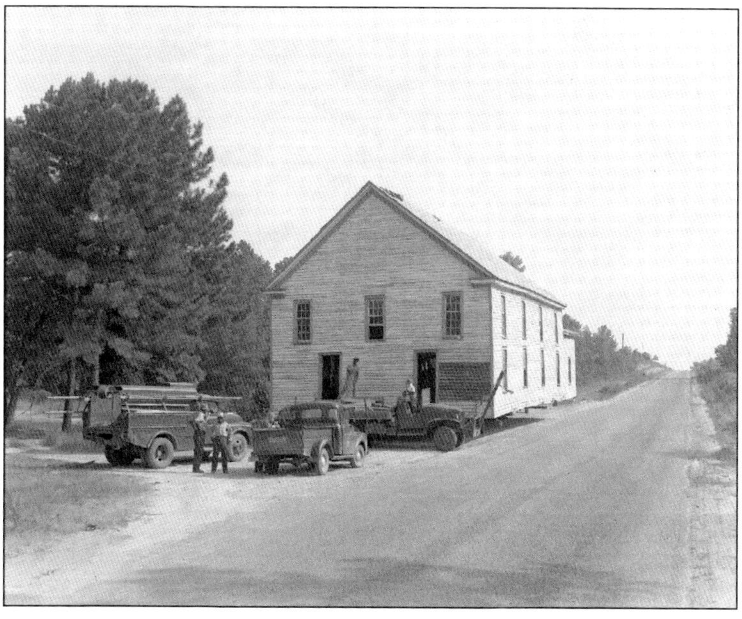

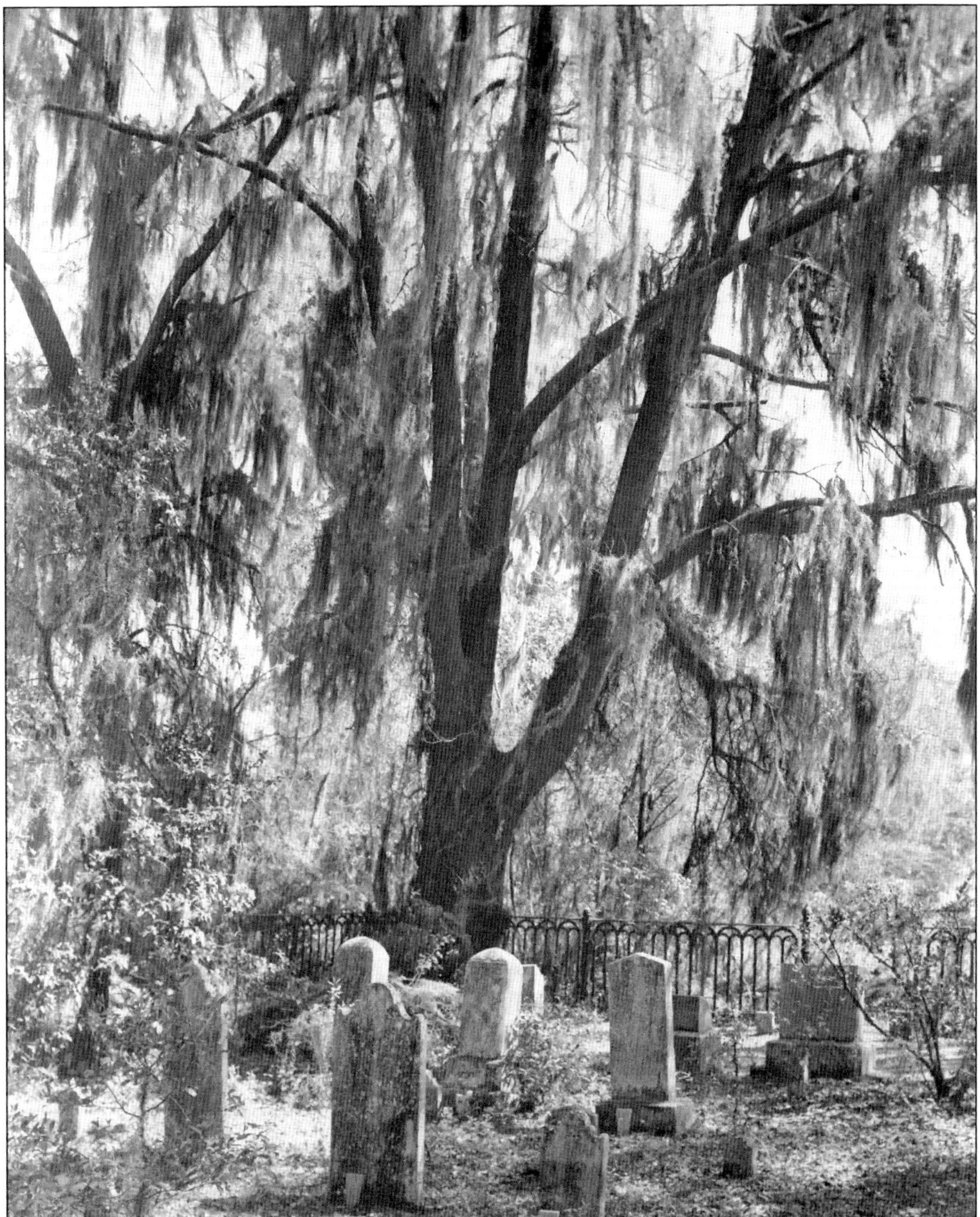

Churches, in coordination with the US government, moved nearly 6,000 graves buried on the land selected for Savannah River Plant. Families too helped move the graves to new locations, and some of the graves unaffected were left behind. Approximately 681 people remain buried on-site, and families of the deceased can still arrange escorted visits.

Workers prepared to move Thorne's Department Store, run by Cecil and Reba Thorne, away from Ellenton. Thorne's Department Store sold a variety of items from groceries to furniture. Ellenton's main street was home to several businesses, including Thorne's, Sanders General Store, Wise Chevrolet, and the O'Berry Movie Theater. The Blue Goose restaurant is visible on the far left.

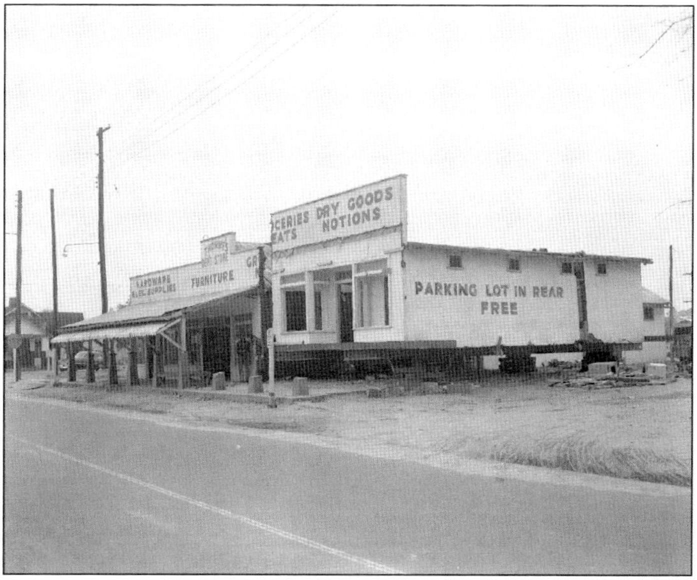

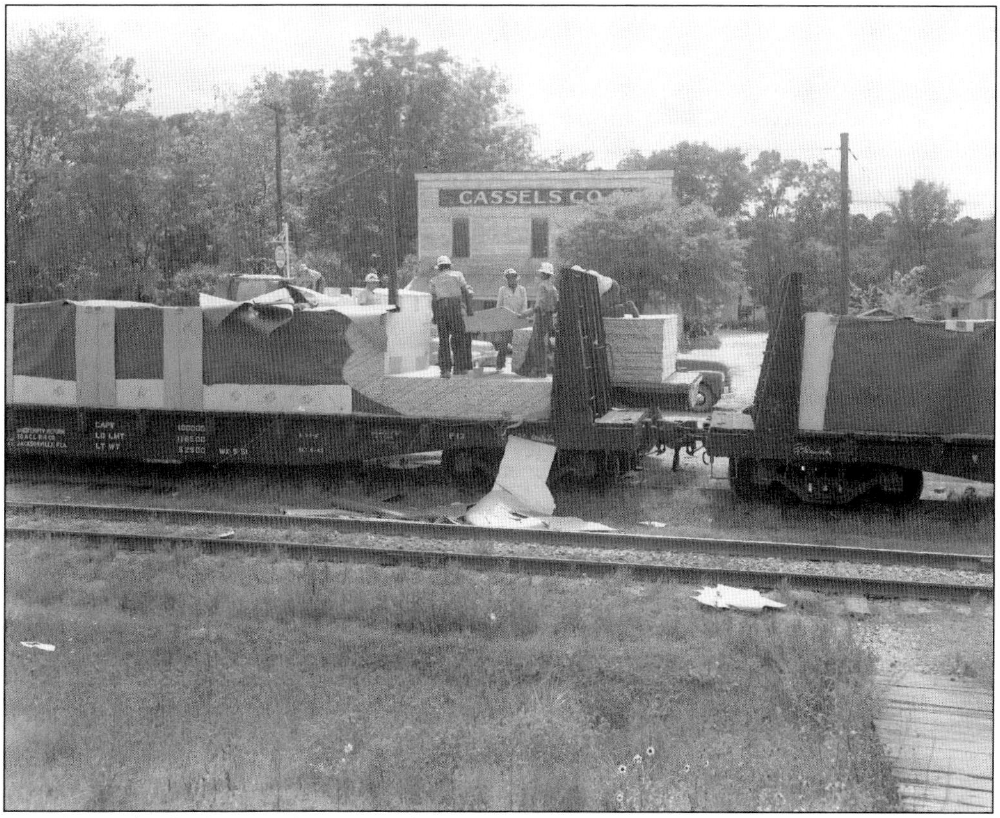

Storefronts that had not yet been moved or razed remained for several months. The Cassels Store in Ellenton, seen in the background of this photograph taken in the fall of 1951, served as an early cafeteria for construction workers. Even as railroads expanded and sheetrock, lumber, and other supplies were delivered during construction, some families continued living in the area.

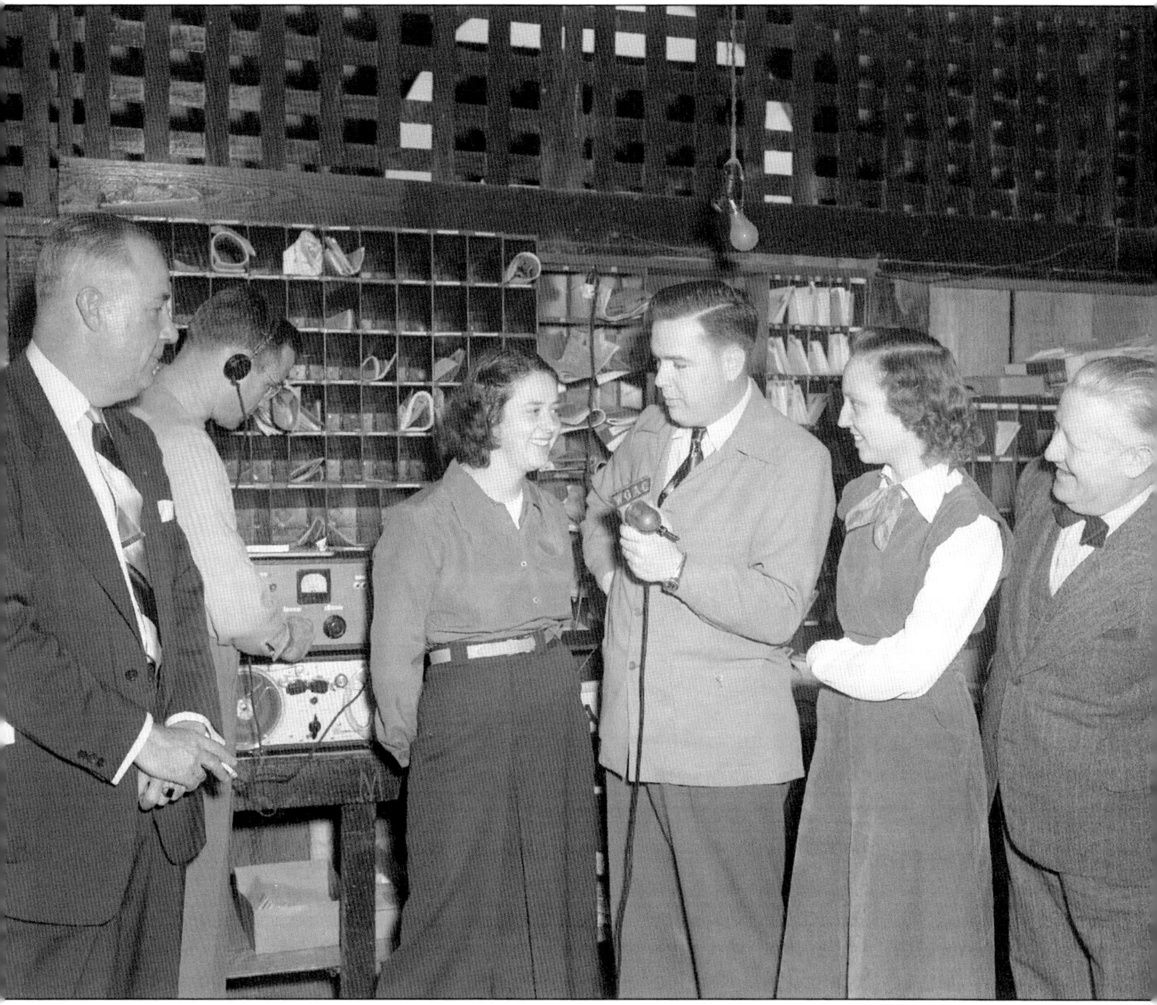

Local radio WGAC interviewed Margaret Brinkley at the Ellenton Post Office on the post office's last day of operation. She speaks about her experience leaving her hometown. The post office remained open during the first year of Savannah River Plant construction. Pictured left to right are Scott Nixon (Augusta Chamber of Commerce), Jack Joplin (WGAC), Margaret Brinkley, Warren Hites, Mary Brinkley, and Hillary Mangum (Augusta Chamber of Commerce).

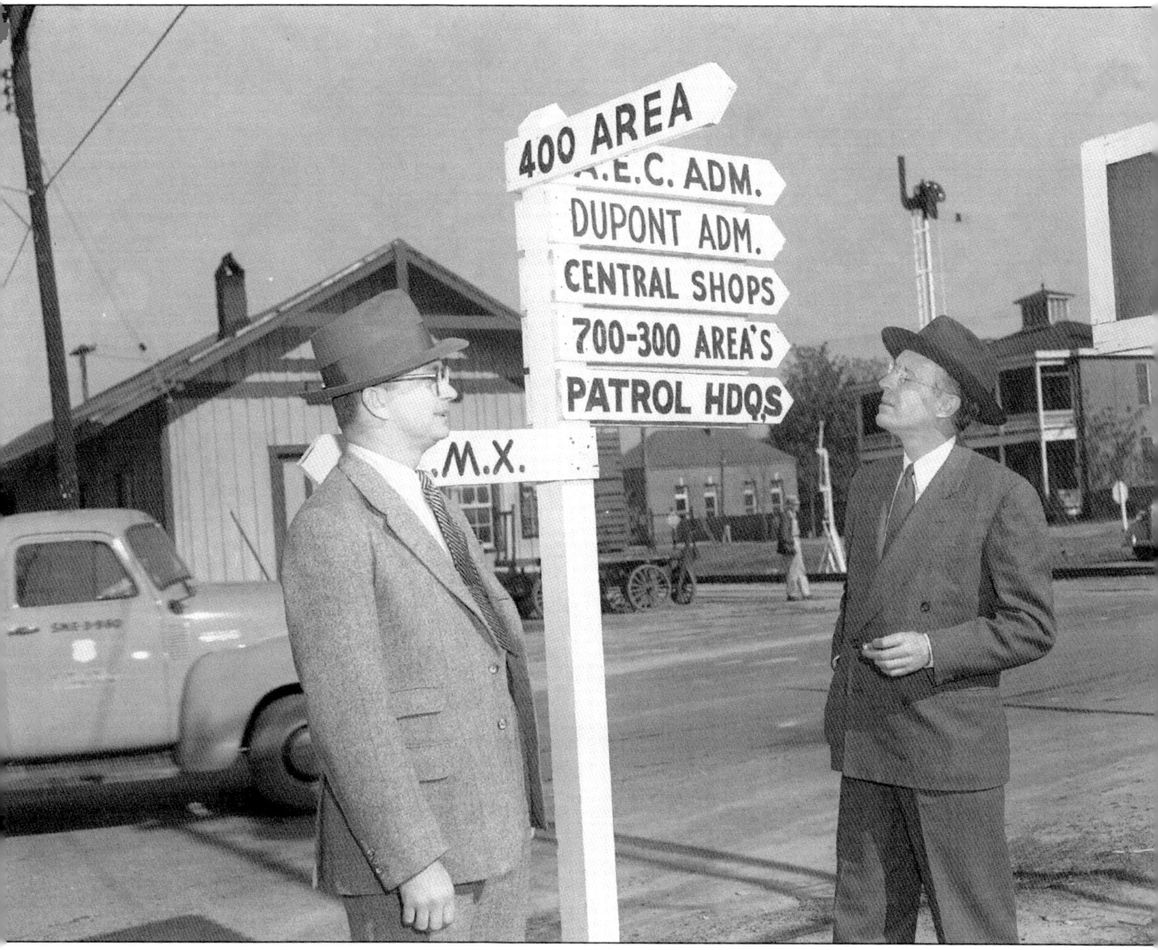

Howard Miller and James Q. DuPont visited Ellenton from Wilmington's DuPont Headquarters. Miller (left) was formerly a special assistant to the SRP field project manager. DuPont (right) worked in the family business in the public relations department. White directional signs point to plant areas, many with purposefully cryptic names. The Ellenton train depot and center of town can be seen in the background.

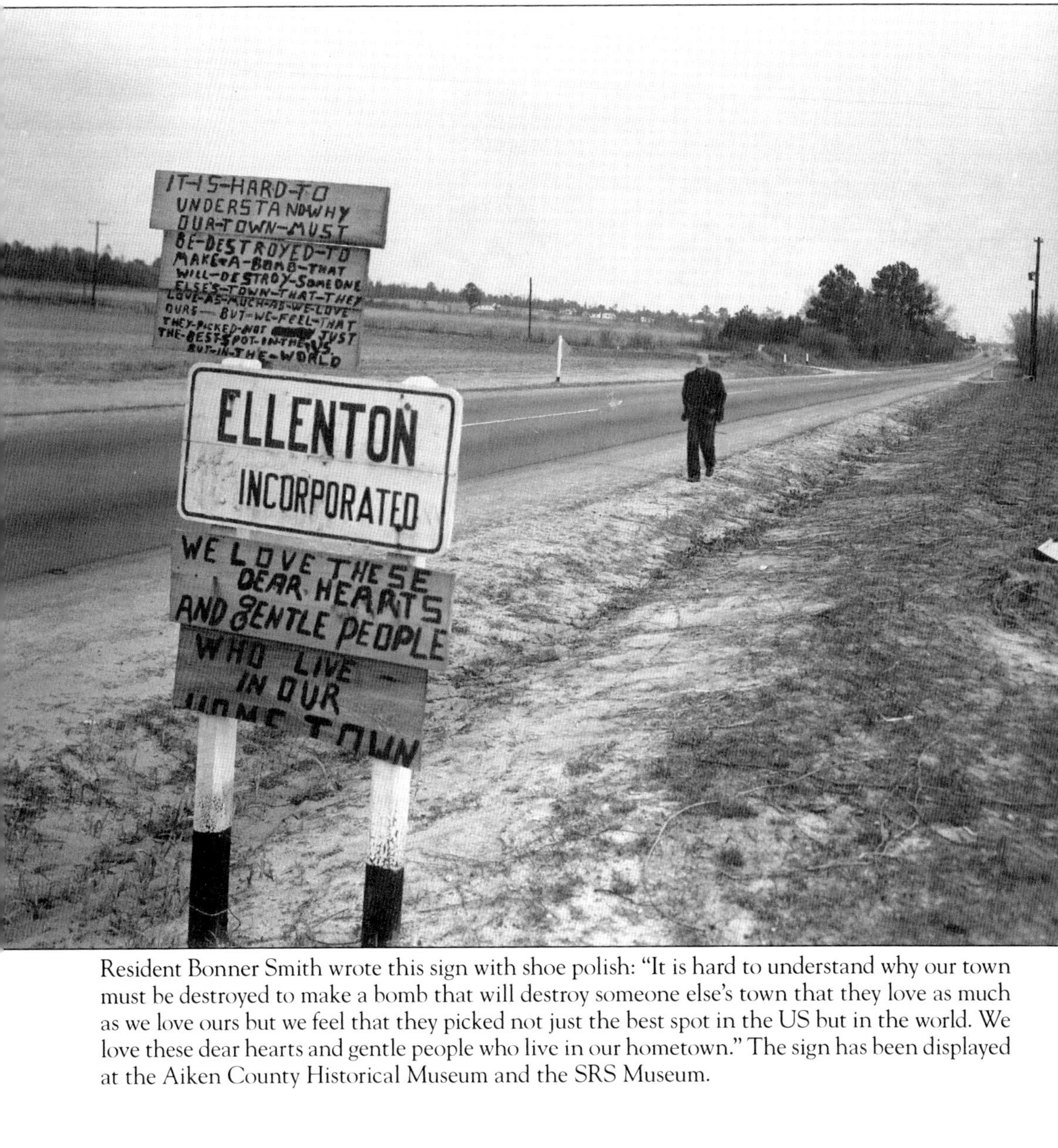

Resident Bonner Smith wrote this sign with shoe polish: "It is hard to understand why our town must be destroyed to make a bomb that will destroy someone else's town that they love as much as we love ours but we feel that they picked not just the best spot in the US but in the world. We love these dear hearts and gentle people who live in our hometown." The sign has been displayed at the Aiken County Historical Museum and the SRS Museum.

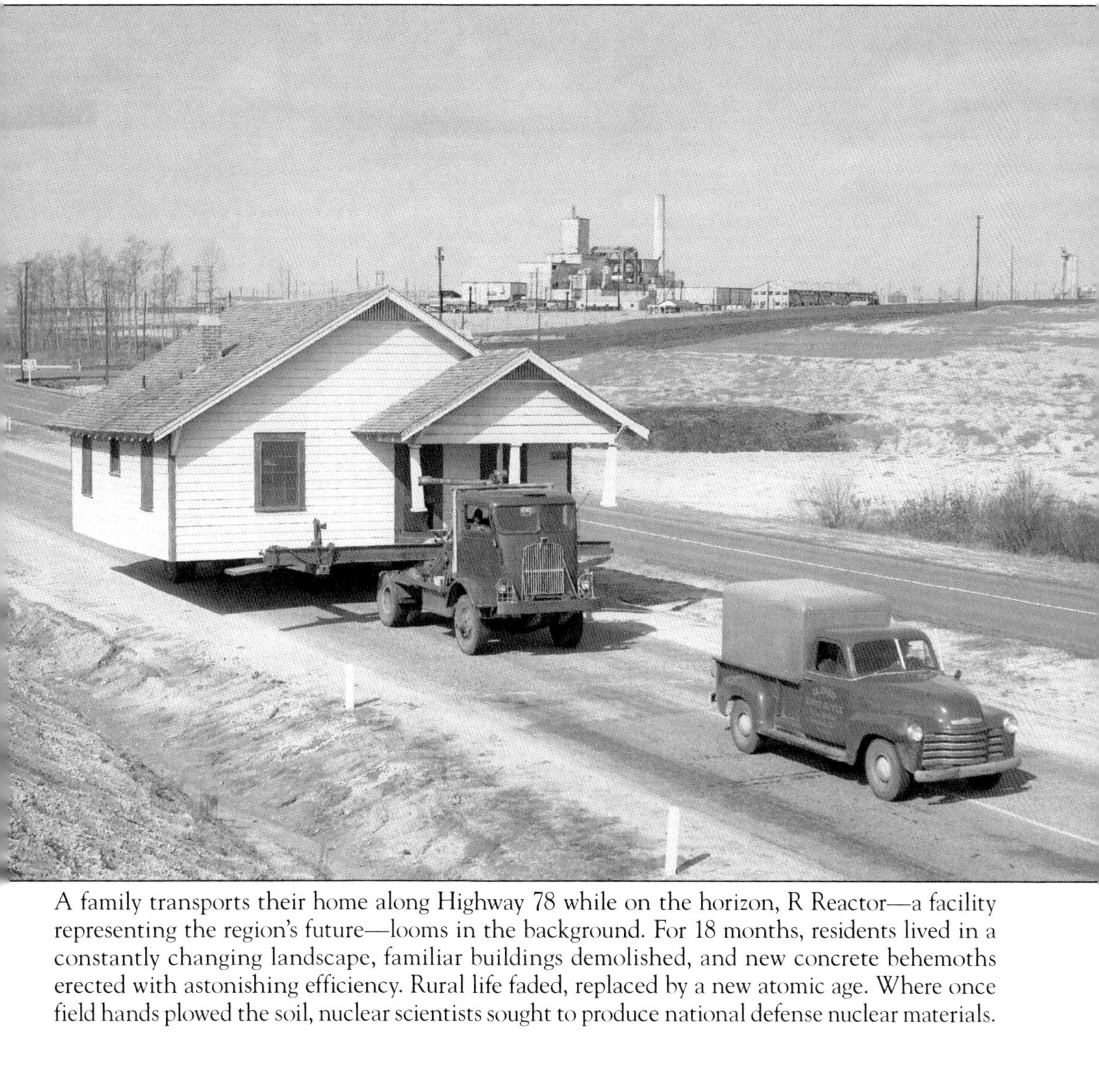

A family transports their home along Highway 78 while on the horizon, R Reactor—a facility representing the region's future—looms in the background. For 18 months, residents lived in a constantly changing landscape, familiar buildings demolished, and new concrete behemoths erected with astonishing efficiency. Rural life faded, replaced by a new atomic age. Where once field hands plowed the soil, nuclear scientists sought to produce national defense nuclear materials.

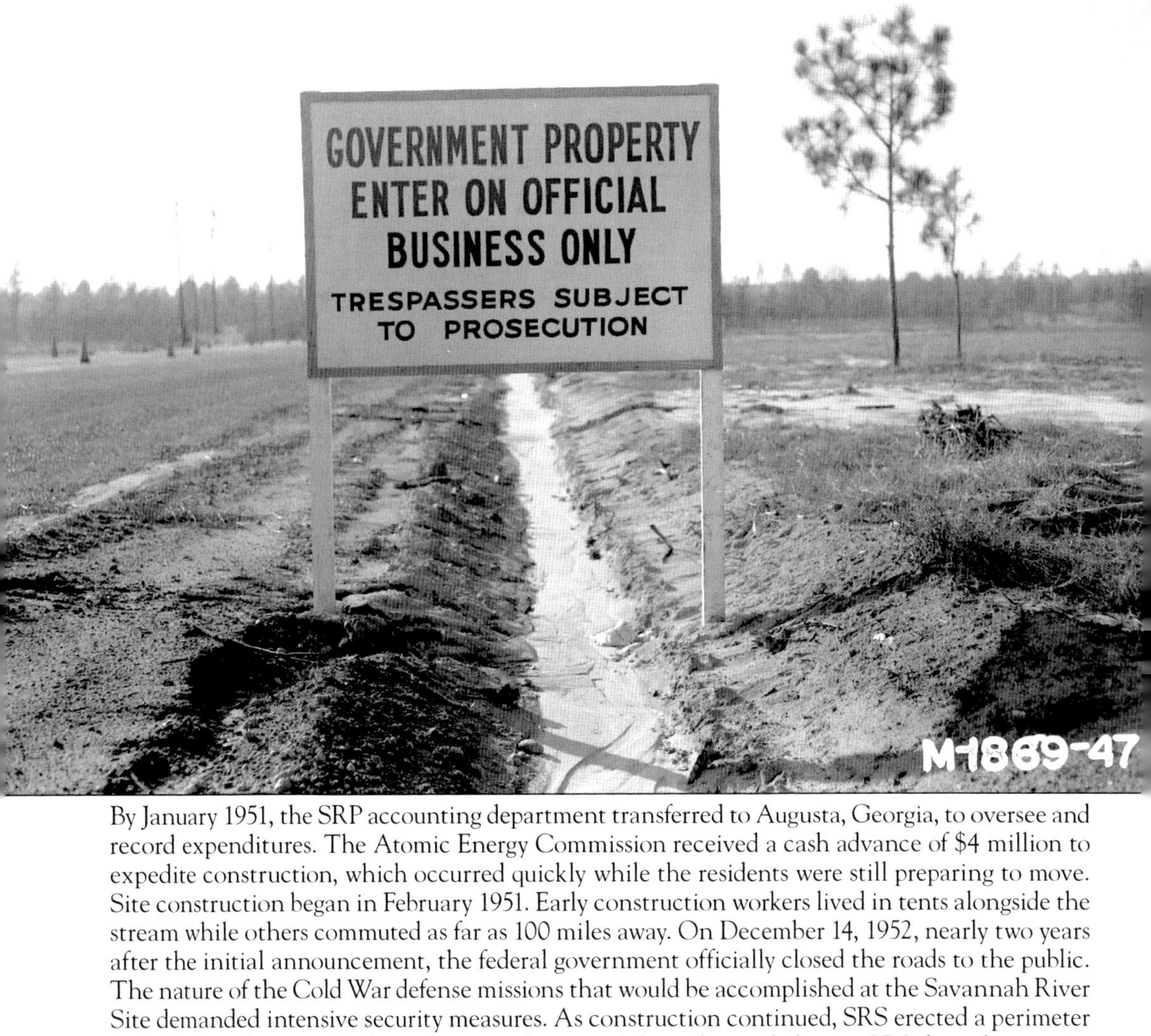

By January 1951, the SRP accounting department transferred to Augusta, Georgia, to oversee and record expenditures. The Atomic Energy Commission received a cash advance of $4 million to expedite construction, which occurred quickly while the residents were still preparing to move. Site construction began in February 1951. Early construction workers lived in tents alongside the stream while others commuted as far as 100 miles away. On December 14, 1952, nearly two years after the initial announcement, the federal government officially closed the roads to the public. The nature of the Cold War defense missions that would be accomplished at the Savannah River Site demanded intensive security measures. As construction continued, SRS erected a perimeter surrounding the site, which employees only entered through guarded gates. SRS shaped a security culture and constructed a physical boundary that prevented Soviet spies from accessing the secrets of the hydrogen bomb.

Two

Building the Savannah River Plant

The urgent construction of the Savannah River Plant lasted from 1950 until 1955. The Atomic Energy Commission contracted DuPont, a company with previous work experience at the nuclear facility Hanford, to construct and operate the weapon materials production plant. DuPont designed and erected the process and support buildings critical to the site mission, which included five reactors, two separations facilities, a heavy water distillation facility, a waste tank farm, expanded infrastructure, administration buildings, and hundreds of other auxiliary facilities.

Much of the research and design occurred while construction was underway, a process DuPont called "flexible design." They recruited several subcontractors and hired thousands of construction workers. In March 1955, four years after construction began, Savannah River Plant produced its first nuclear defense materials.

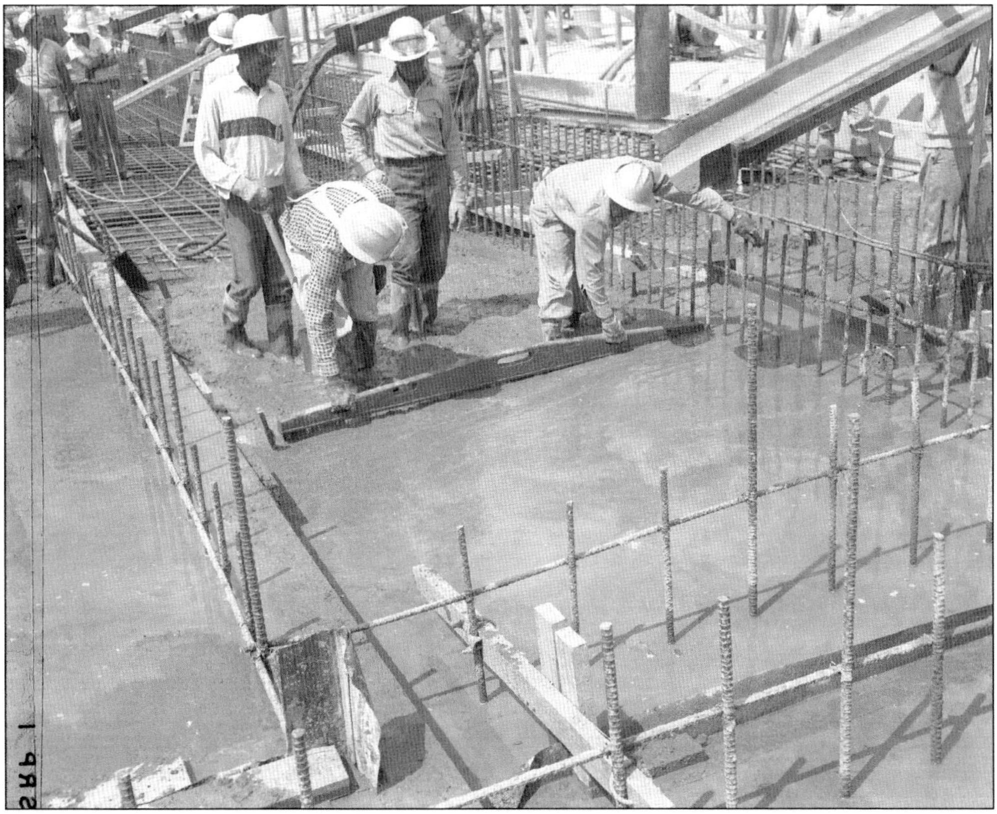

Savannah River Plant construction included five reactors, two separation buildings called canyons, a heavy water extraction plant, a reactor rod manufacturing area, administration buildings, and hundreds of support structures. In an effort to produce product as quickly as possible to support the nation's nuclear needs, much of the site was built with cost-efficient, industrial materials, like concrete, and reinforced steel. To help construction move swiftly, a concrete batch plant was located on-site during the building process. The separations canyon located in H Area was longer than 10 football fields and so the concrete had to be poured in sections.

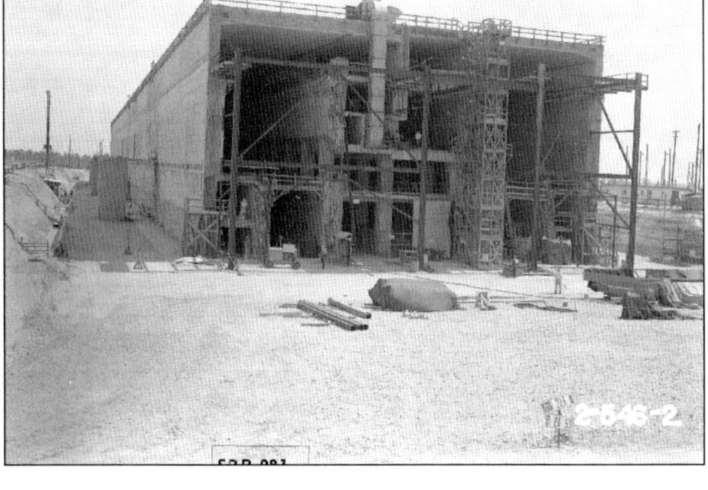

Crawford Greenwalt, president of DuPont, and Bob Mason, SRP field project manager, were photographed during Greenwalt's visit to SRP in September 1951. Greenwalt was a key negotiator in settling DuPont's contract with the Atomic Energy Commission, and Mason was credited with finding innovative construction solutions that kept the project on time and within budget.

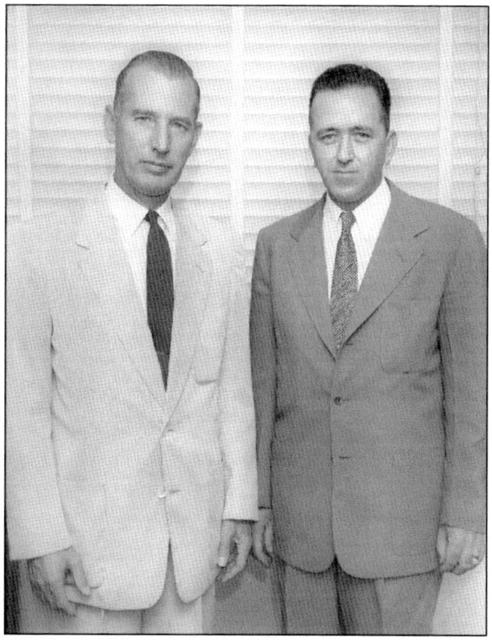

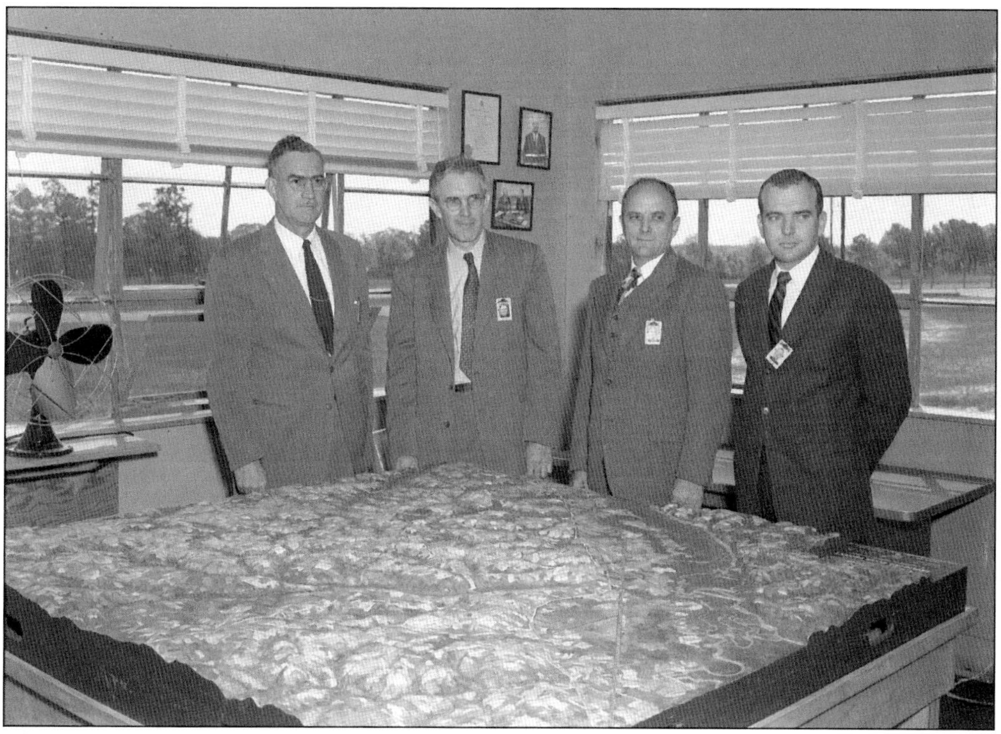

There were several key figures of the Atomic Energy Commission Savannah River Operations Office. Pictured are, from left to right, deputy manager Robert Blair, Dr. Henry Smyth, Curtis Nelson, and John Gray. Each member offered a variety of experiences. Curtis Nelson was assigned as the first local Savannah River Operations Office manager. Nelson's background came from supervising large US Army Corps of Engineer construction projects and nuclear work at Manhattan Project's Oak Ridge as well as Chalk River, a Canadian nuclear facility.

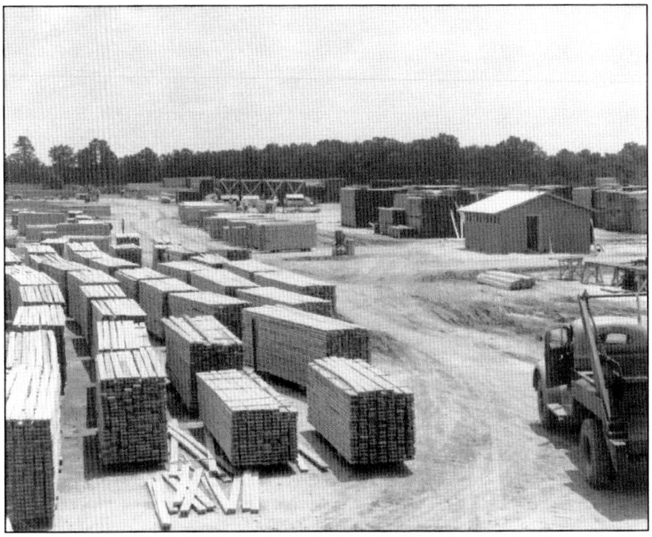

Central shops (CS) was one of the first permanent facilities to be set up at SRP. Most construction materials were transported by railroad and sorted and processed through the receiving and stores department at CS. The storage yards contained machinery, electrical equipment, reinforcing steel, pipes, and quantities of lumber to be used for concrete forms.

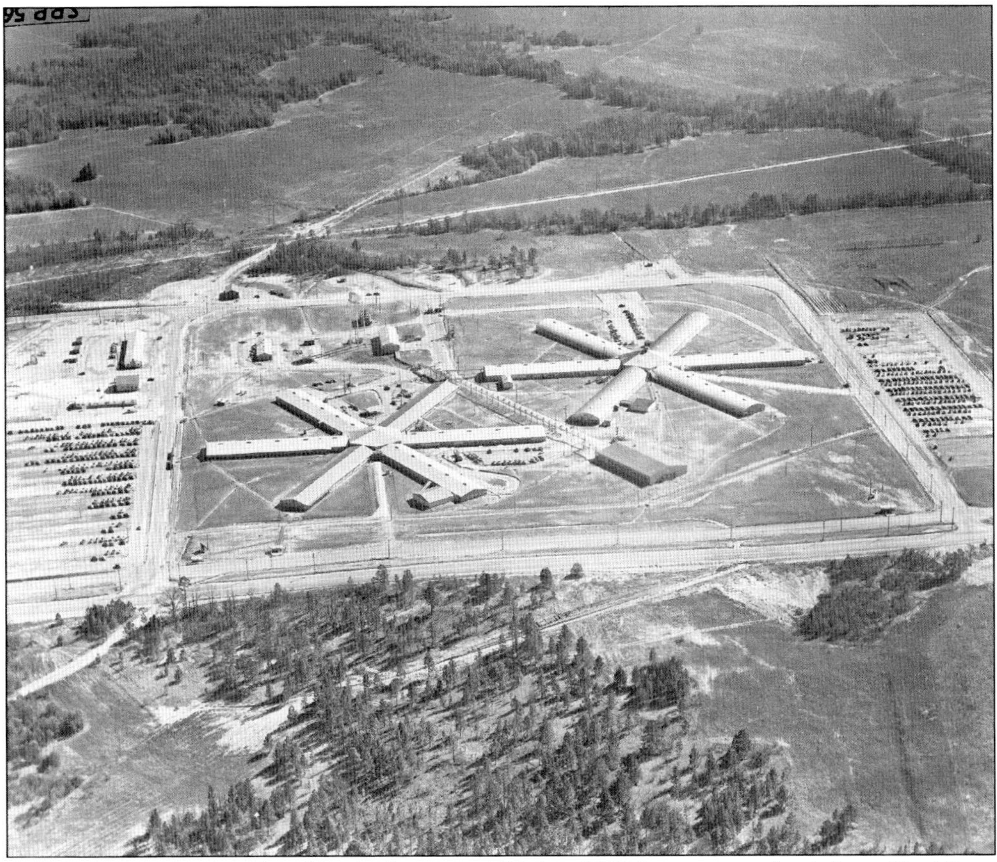

Temporary construction 1 and 2, also known as TC-1 and TC-2, were cartwheel-shaped buildings used as early construction headquarters. Designed by the Augusta-based architectural firm Patchen and Zimmerman, these buildings housed many departments, including accounting, timekeeping, medical, and DuPont and AEC management. After the construction of SRP's main administration building (703-A) in late 1953, many of these departments were relocated.

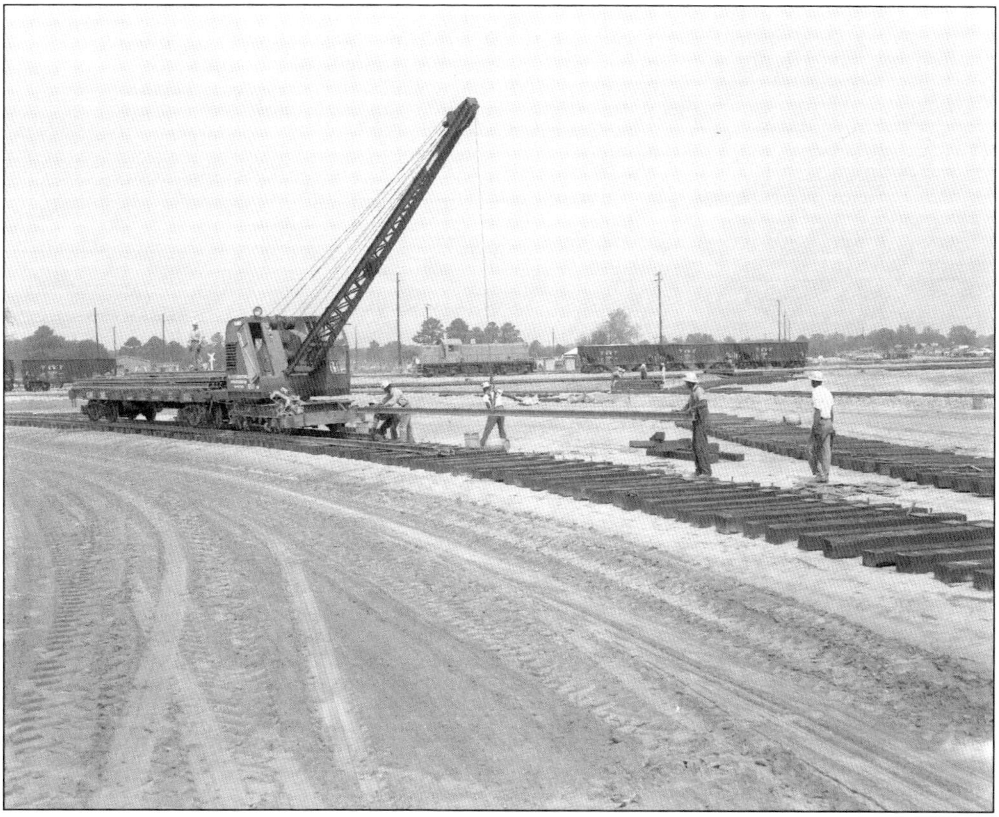

Land acquired from the former towns for the building of the Savannah River Plant included basic infrastructure needs. Early construction steps included the addition of roads and railroads across the 310-square-mile site. The layout of the plant included several site areas, each with a distinct task, that would work together to achieve the overall weapons production goal. Infrastructure was important to operations running smoothly over such a large land area.

Approximately 160 miles of additional roads were built along with at least seven new bridges and the replacement of original wooden structures. Establishing roads and railroads was necessary for supply distribution during construction and the delivery of nuclear materials and coal as a power source during operations. This crew is working on a bridge at Four Mile Creek, located in the bottom southeast side of SRP.

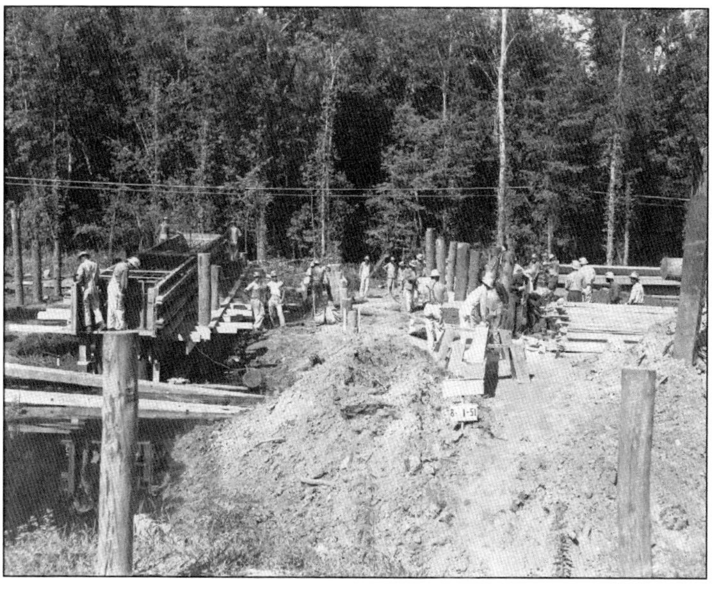

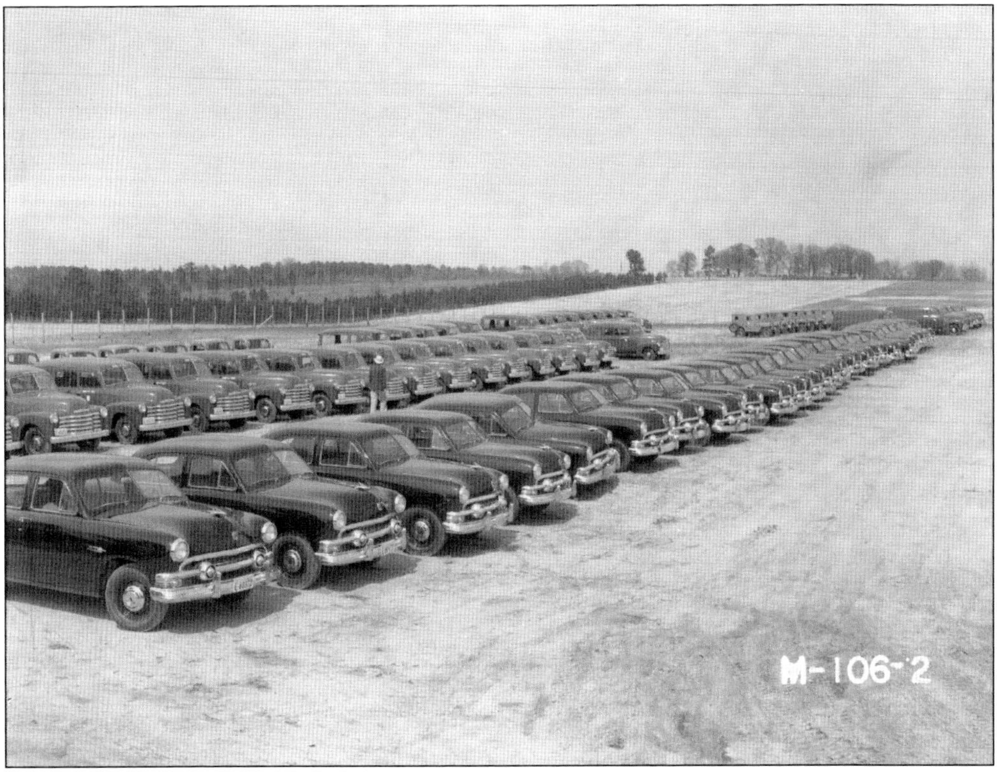

Traffic and Transportation, known as T&T, supported the site through five divisions—traffic, railroad, automotive, equipment maintenance, and labor and heavy equipment. This storage yard shows a fleet of government cars managed by T&T. Government vehicles traveled 835,000 miles per month, equivalent to 33 trips around the world, and used 800,000 gallons of gasoline and 50,000 quarts of oil.

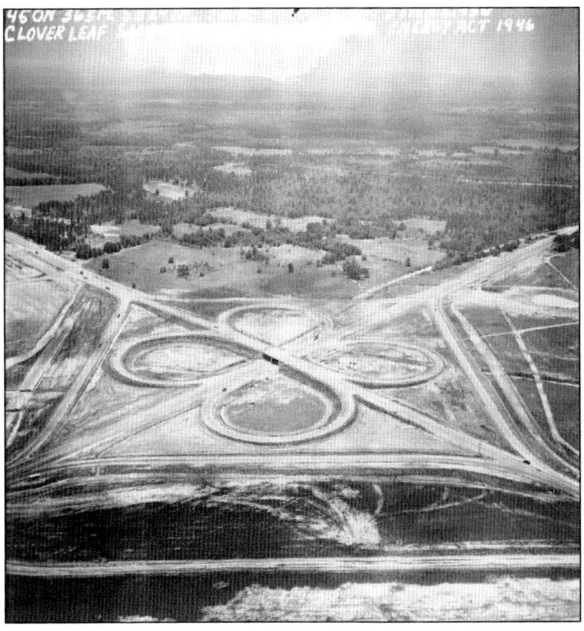

With approximately 38,000 employees at its peak, carpooling was encouraged to minimize the number of vehicles, and SRP roads were planned to handle a large amount of traffic. Heavily traveled areas made use of four-lane roads, and to ensure traffic moved smoothly in a particularly dense area, South Carolina's first cloverleaf was built at SRP to direct traffic flow.

Water pumped from the Savannah River was used to support the power needs of the plant. In powerhouses located throughout the plant, generator units would convert steam to produce electricity. Coal was often brought to the powerhouse directly by railroad cars. The P Area powerhouse in this photograph had two boiler units and produced both electricity and steam for industrial and heating uses.

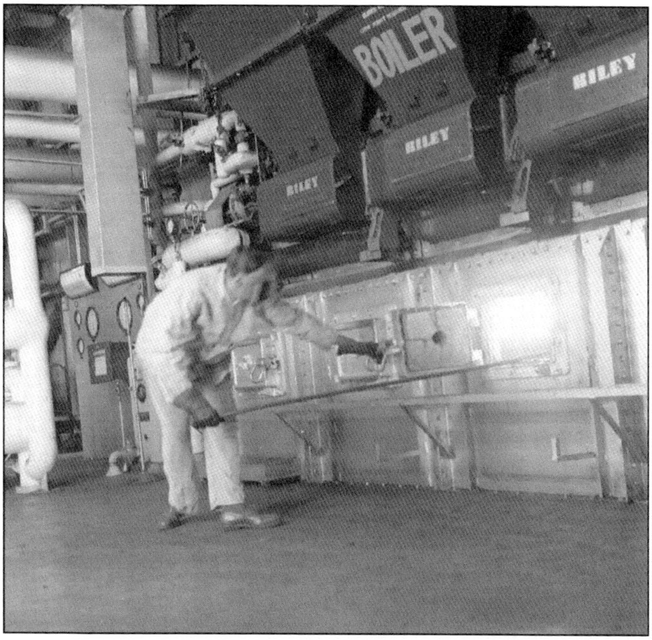

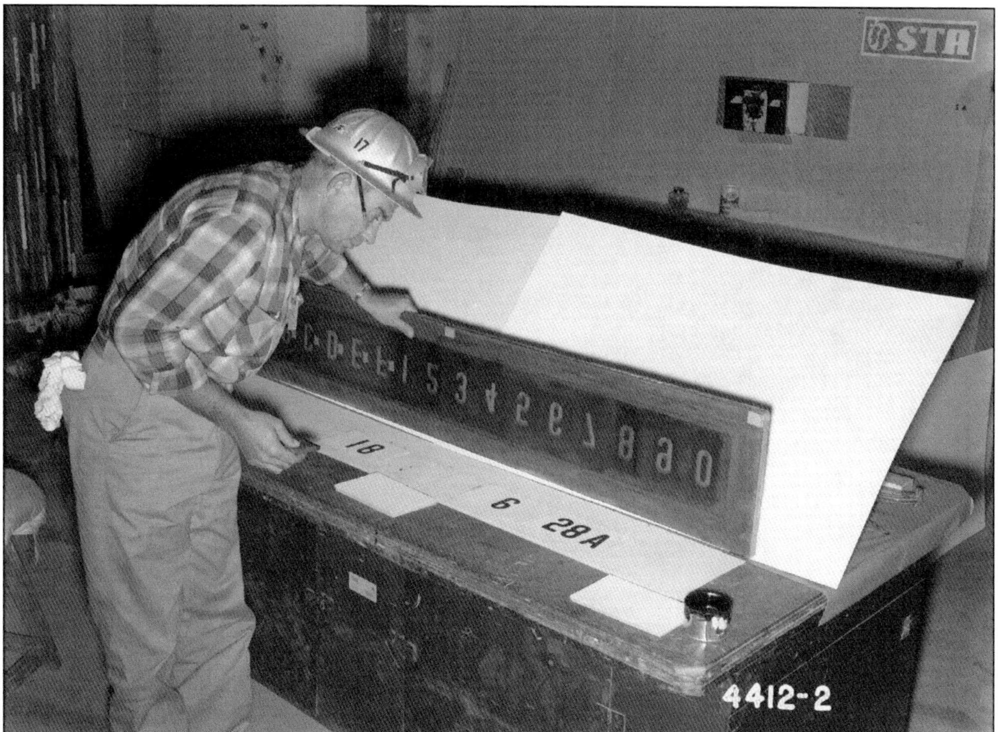

SRP construction included hundreds of buildings, and each structure was given a unique identification number. For example, all reactor buildings were assigned the number 105. The reactor building in C Area was named 105-C and so on. Handmade signs were produced on-site for all buildings. One technique used to produce these signs was the silk-screening process, as seen in the photograph.

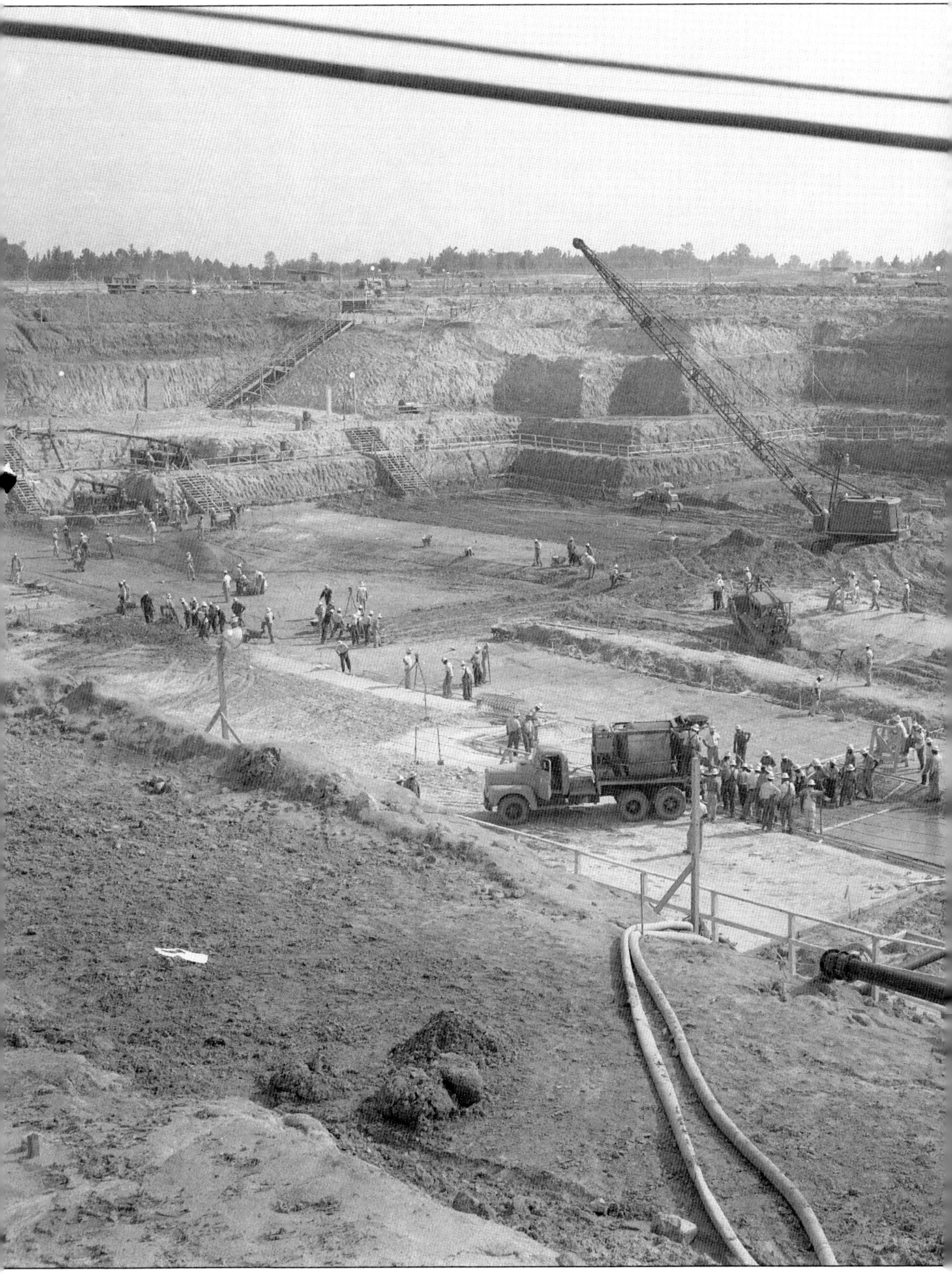

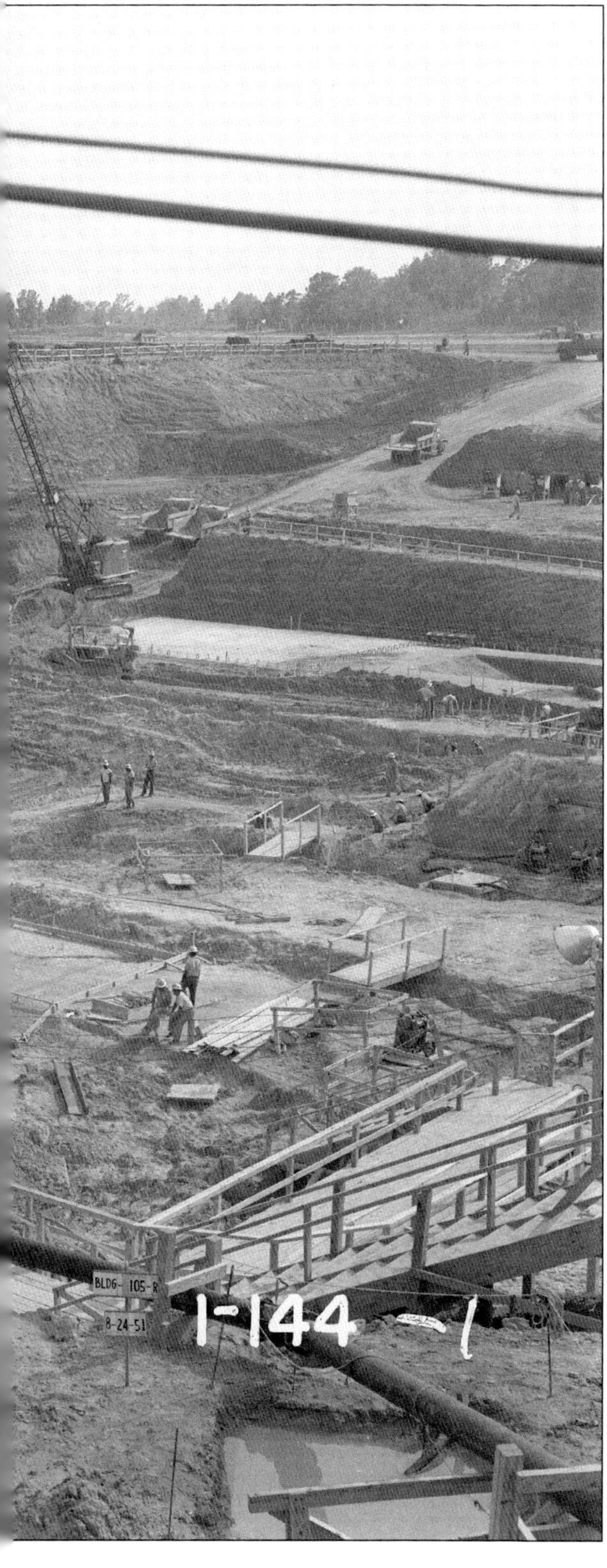

Construction of the plant's five reactors required large-scale excavation. For R Reactor, it involved moving nearly 2.3 million cubic yards of earth. It was ultimately decided that the reactor areas should be arranged in a horseshoe curve with no permanent facilities located inside the pattern. Atomic Energy Commission requirements also stipulated that each reactor be positioned 2.5 miles away from the next reactor, at least 6 miles from the site perimeter, and 3 miles from any passenger-carrying rail line. All five reactor areas share the same basic layout with a "clean" side and a "dirty" side. The clean side of the reactor area included the gate area, the main personnel buildings, and the electrical substations. The "dirty" area, located at the opposite end, included the reactor building's disassembly area and area power plant. The main water facilities and reactor were located in the center of the area. A perimeter fence surrounded the entire area, while a second interior fence further secured the reactor building.

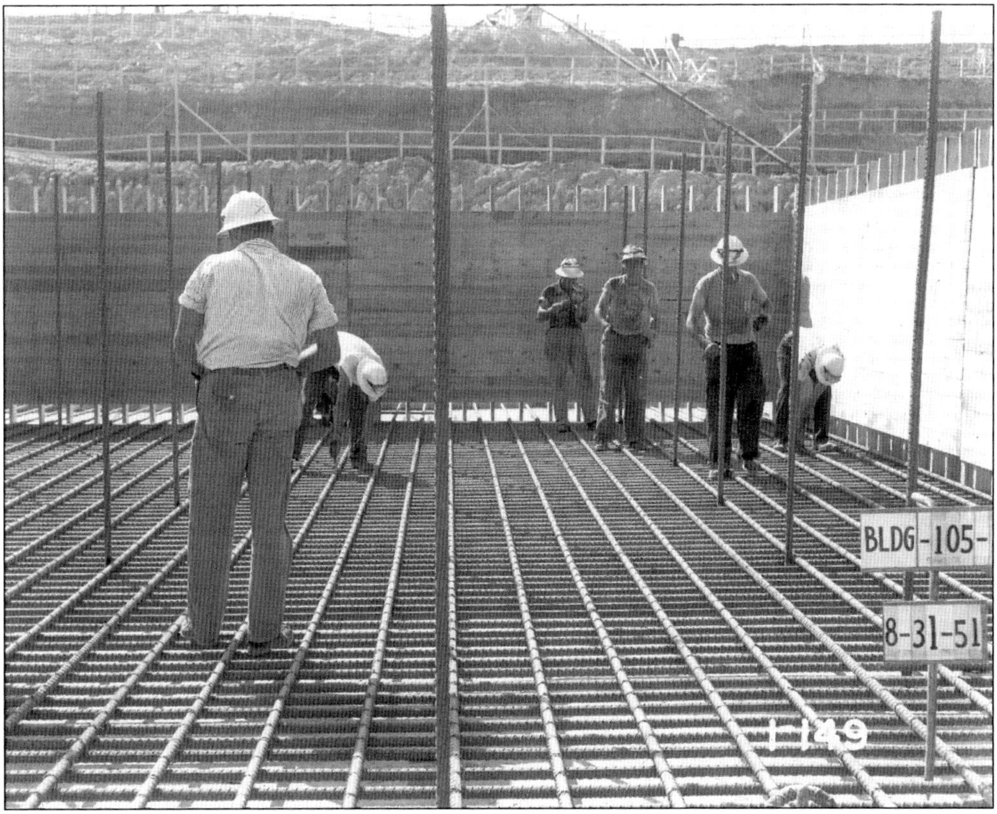

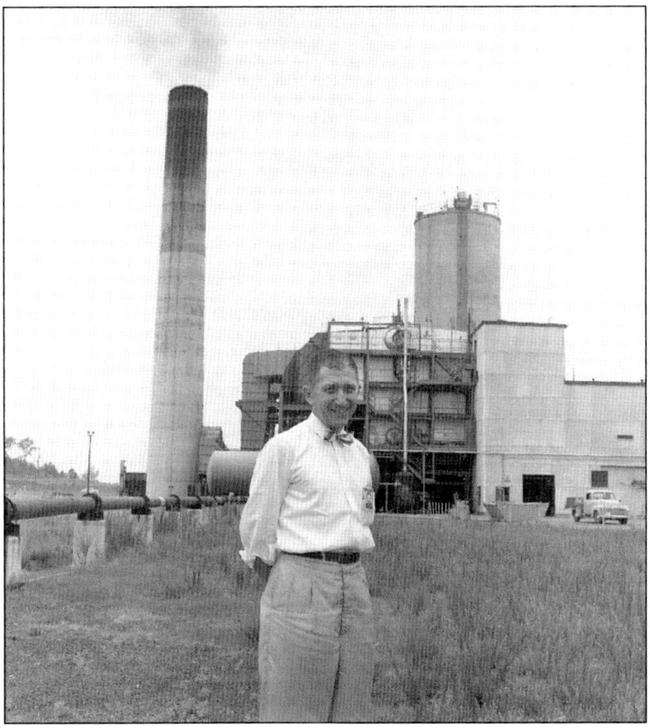

At over 12 million cubic feet, R Reactor was the first and largest of the five reactor buildings constructed at the Savannah River Plant. Critical process structures, like the reactor buildings, were constructed with blast-proof materials and reinforced concrete. Construction of 105-R began in June 1951 and reactor startup came in the fall of 1953 when the critical reactor went online. The reactor reached criticality by December 1953. Pictured in the photograph at left on June 6, 1956, are R Reactor and Doc Shideler just a few years after their combined "debut." In March 1952, as the new reactor tank came online, Shideler became the first production employee and power supervisor in R Area.

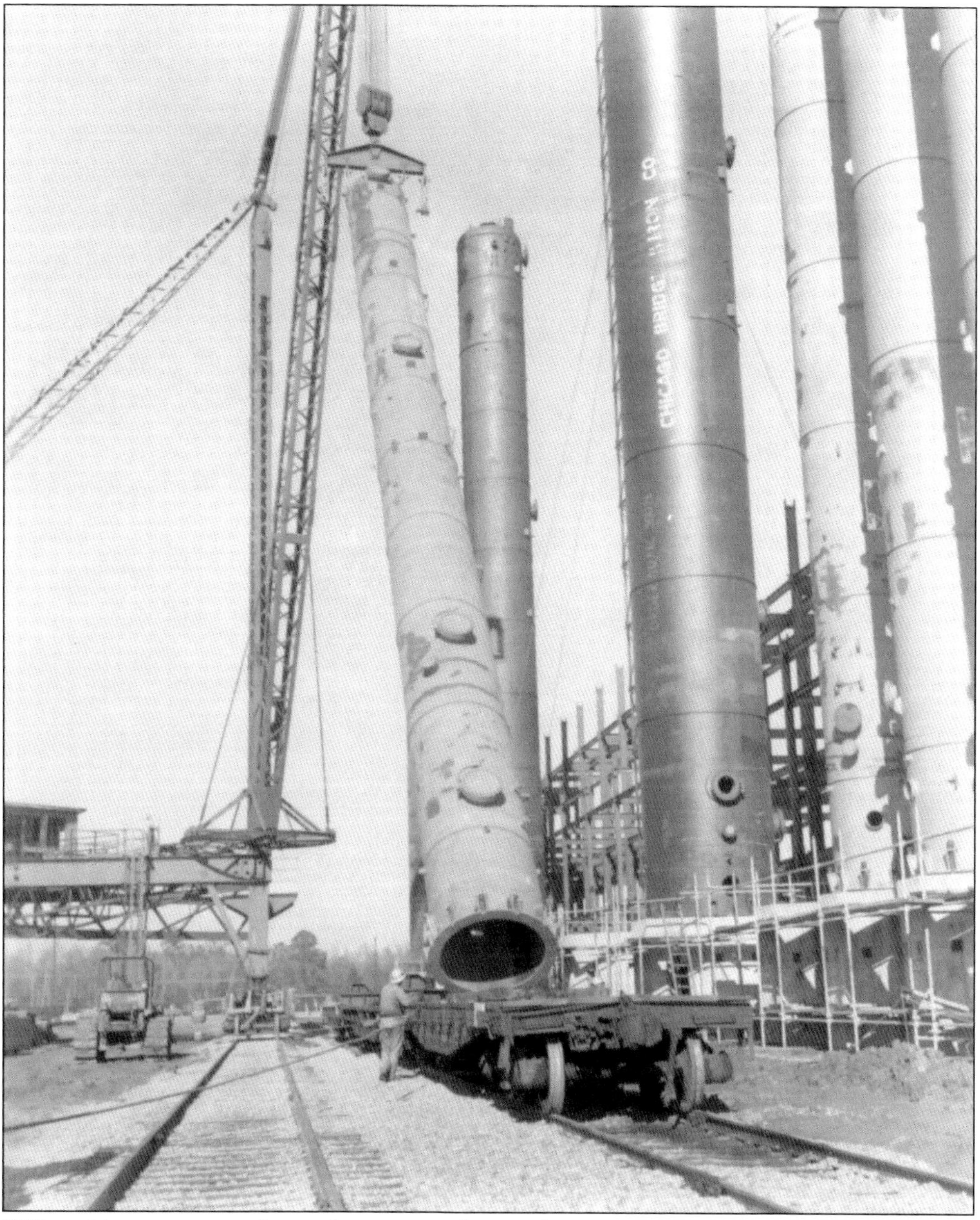

SRP used heavy water as the moderator in its five production reactors. Heavy water was extracted from the Savannah River using the Girdler Sulfide (GS) process of hydrogen sulfide-water exchange. Approximately 140 heavy water extraction towers, at 120 feet each, created D Area's distinct look. To assist in raising the heavy towers, a 200-ton stiff-legged derrick was used. The process began in October 1951 and was completed in November 1952.

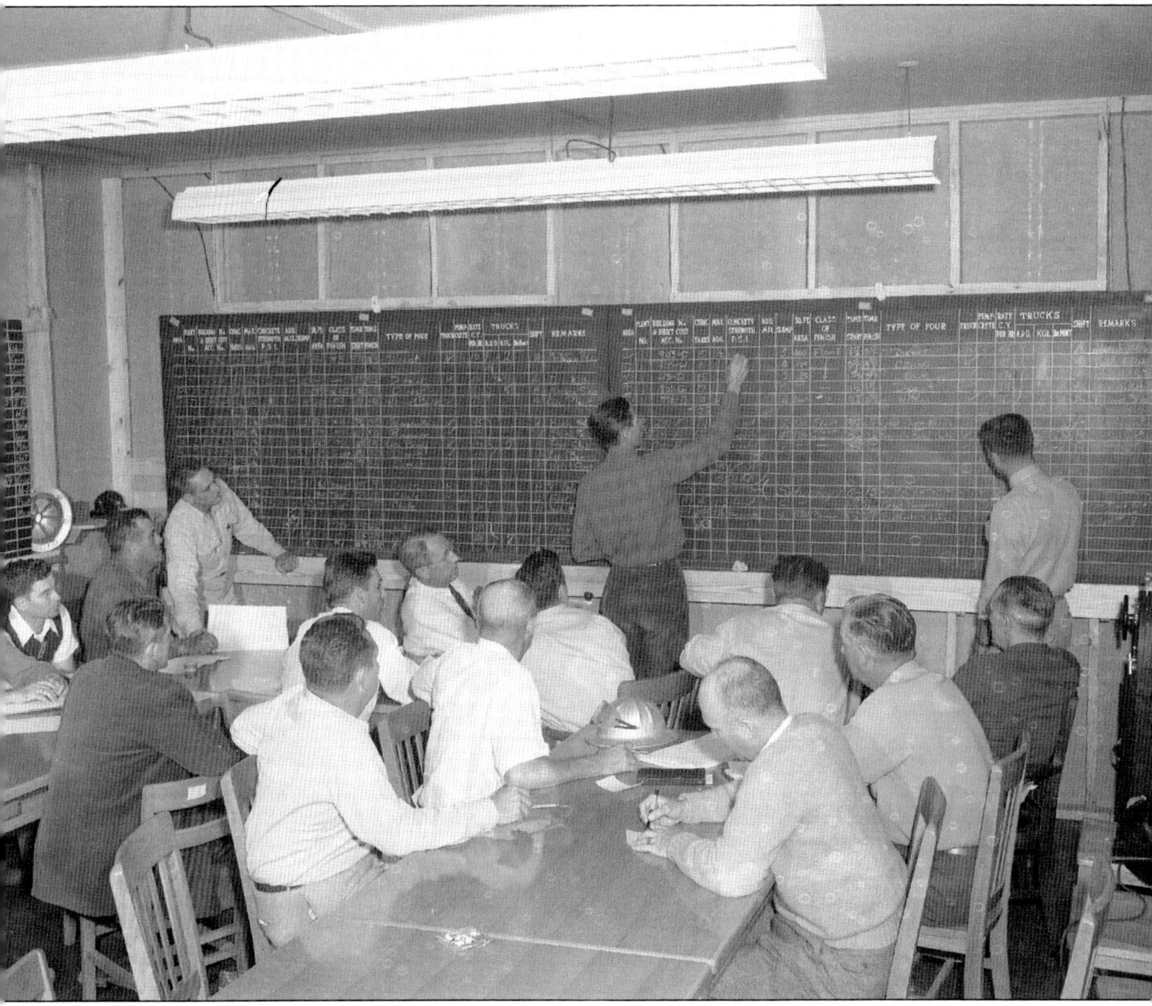

Planning meetings happened frequently in field skid shacks during the construction phase of the project. The DuPont design team used a "flexible design" approach to keep construction on task, addressing both the urgency of the project as well as new technological developments. The approach postponed design decisions until the best option was researched and also factored in the potential for future design changes to be made.

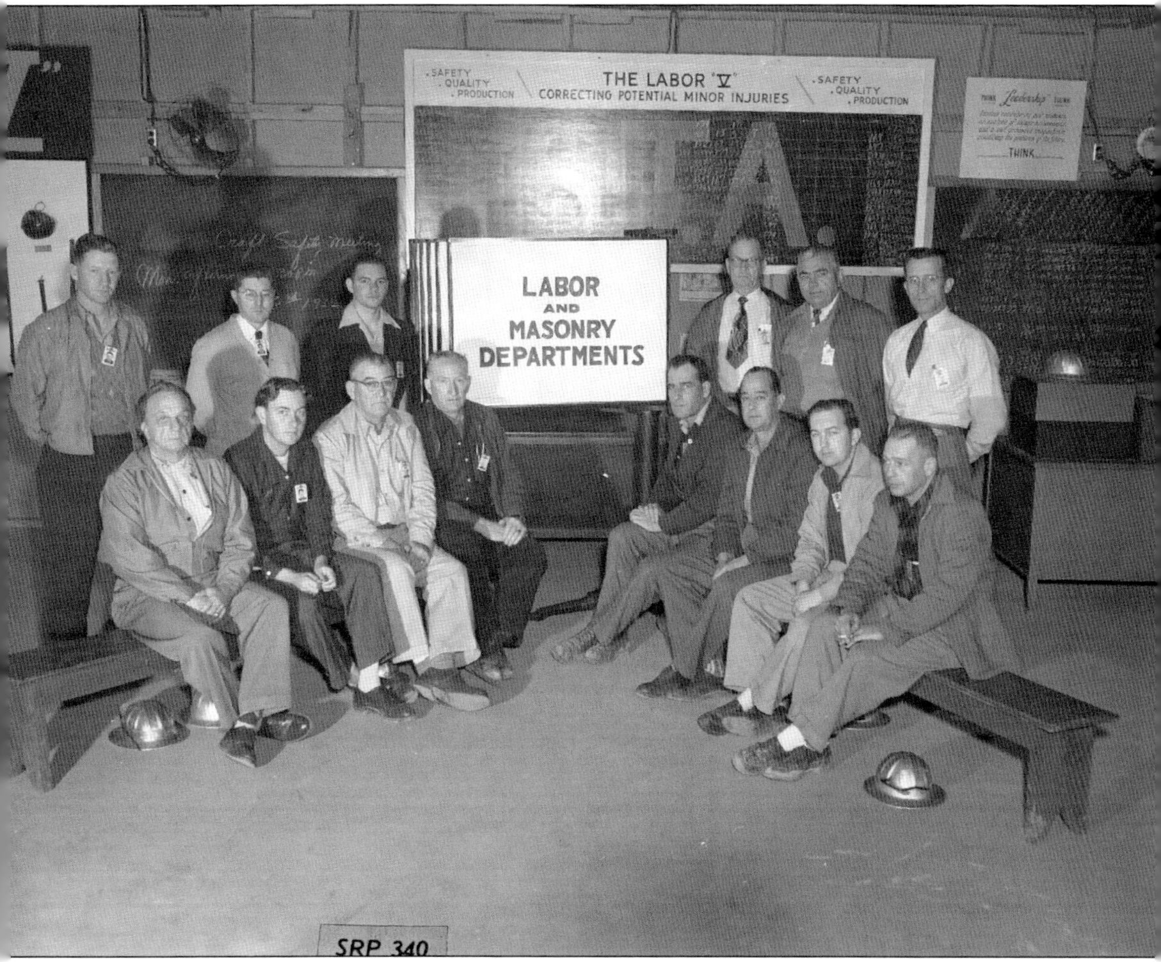

The goal of construction was to build quickly, safely, and cost-efficiently. Each Savannah River Plant area and department had cost reduction goals and an ideas program. This December meeting of the construction labor and masonry groups was a 1952 review of cost savings, employee suggestion participation, and job training.

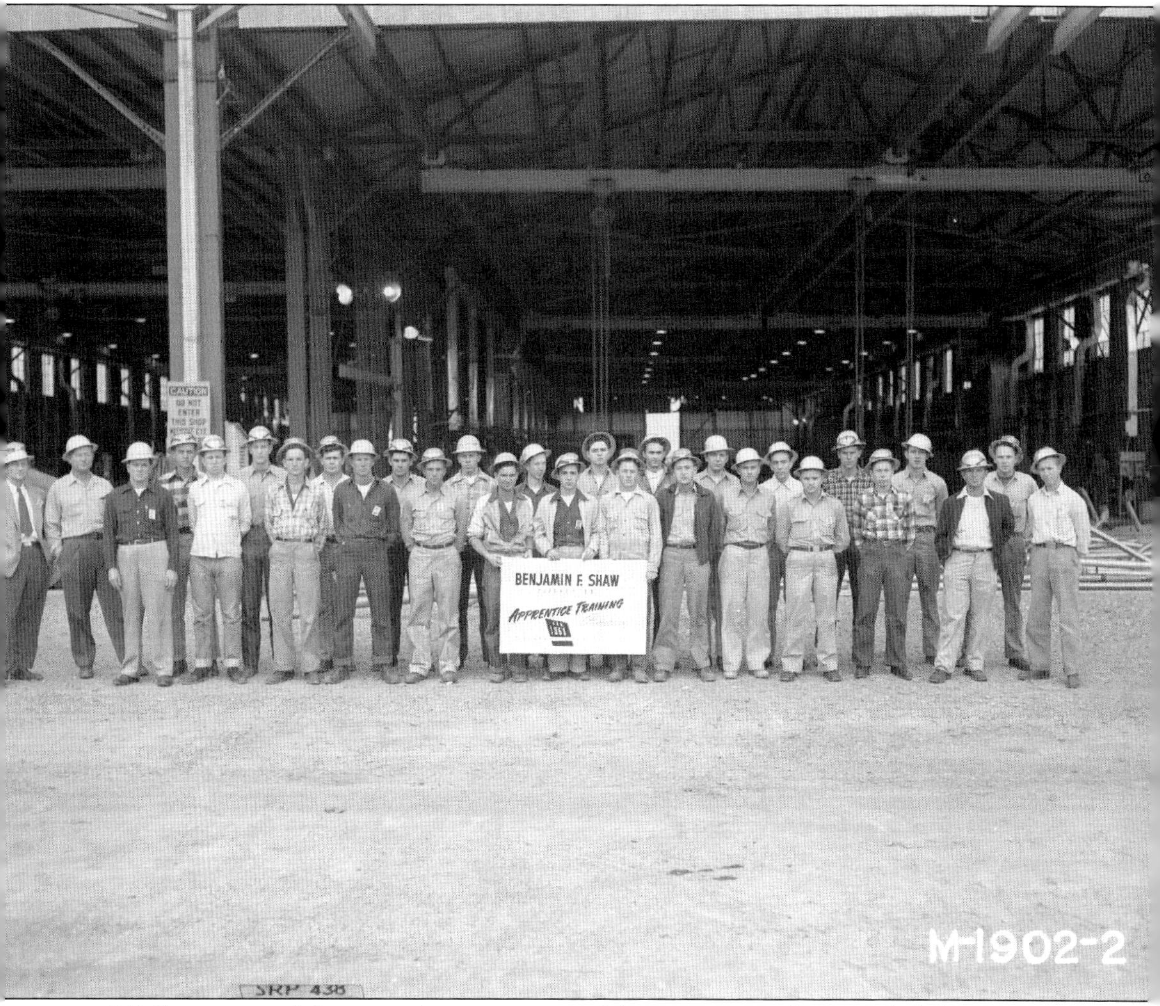

B.F. Shaw managed the piping department, one of the many groups that provided job opportunities for apprentices through training programs. *SRP News and Views* often featured these apprentices during their five-year programs. Piping was based in central shops, alongside other departments of the DuPont Construction Division such as ironworks, layout, electrical, sheet metal, and carpentry.

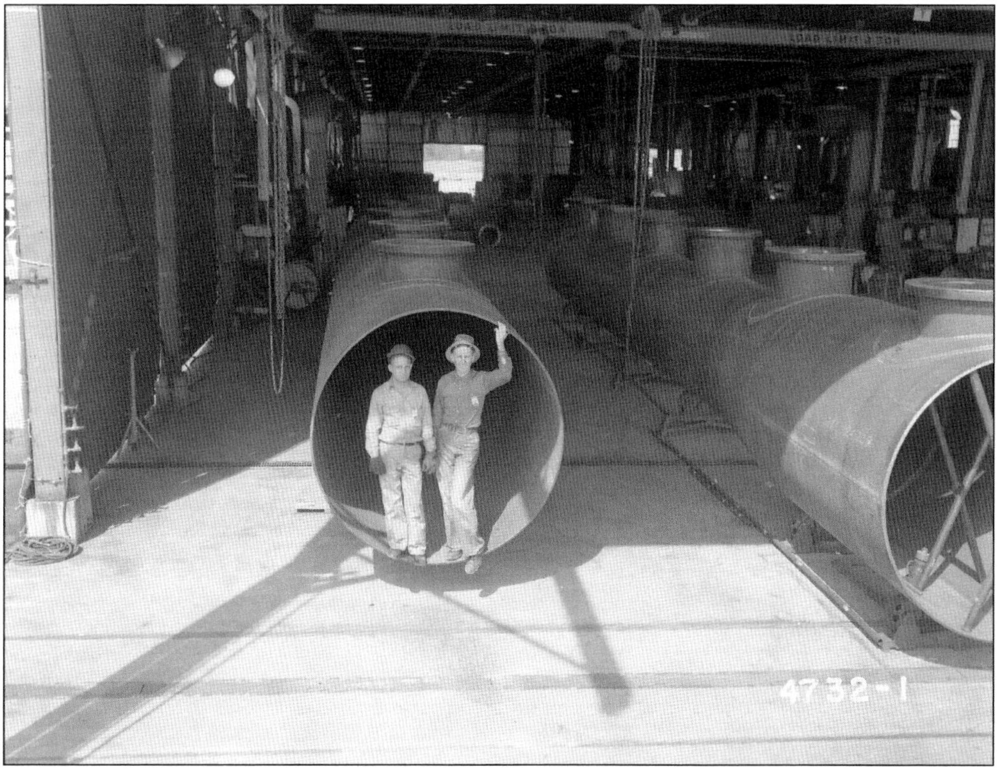

Two men stand comfortably inside one of the water pipes during installation, putting into perspective the immense scale of equipment at SRP. These pipes diverted water from the Savannah River to cool reactor fuel during operation. These 78-inch pipes were most likely part of the pipeline connecting the Par Pond Pumphouse to P and R Reactors.

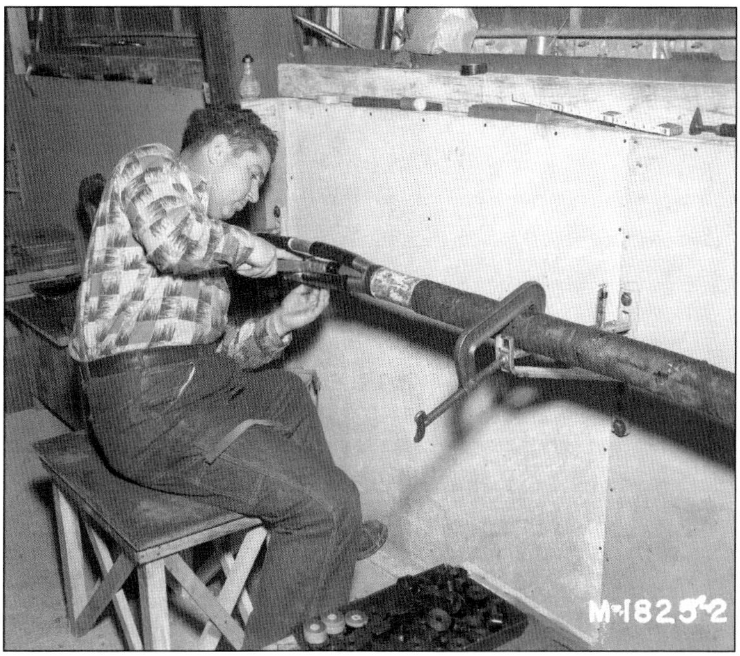

Construction workers moved into the area, but many local employees were also hired. In addition to apprenticeship trade programs, on-the-job training was common. One example of this was a group from the SRP electrical craft department. Fourteen trainees went through full-time 10-week training to master the skill of cable splicing when the site had an urgent need for the skill in the early 1950s.

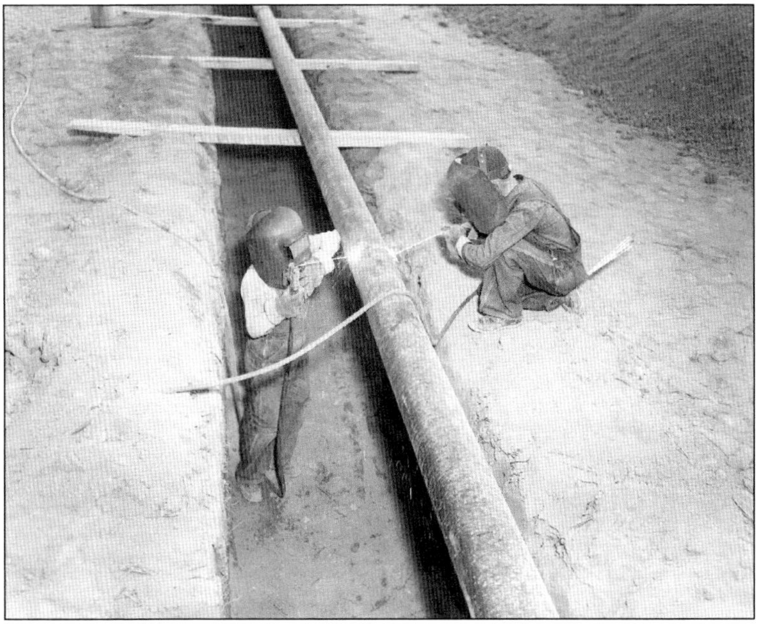

Among the newly hired crew were two brothers, Eugene and Eulie David, two little people who worked as pipefitters at SRP. They became locally famous for their roles in the 1939 MGM classic film *The Wizard of Oz*, as a fiddler and a soldier, respectively. The David brothers' small size allowed them to reach inaccessible spots inside pipes to weld.

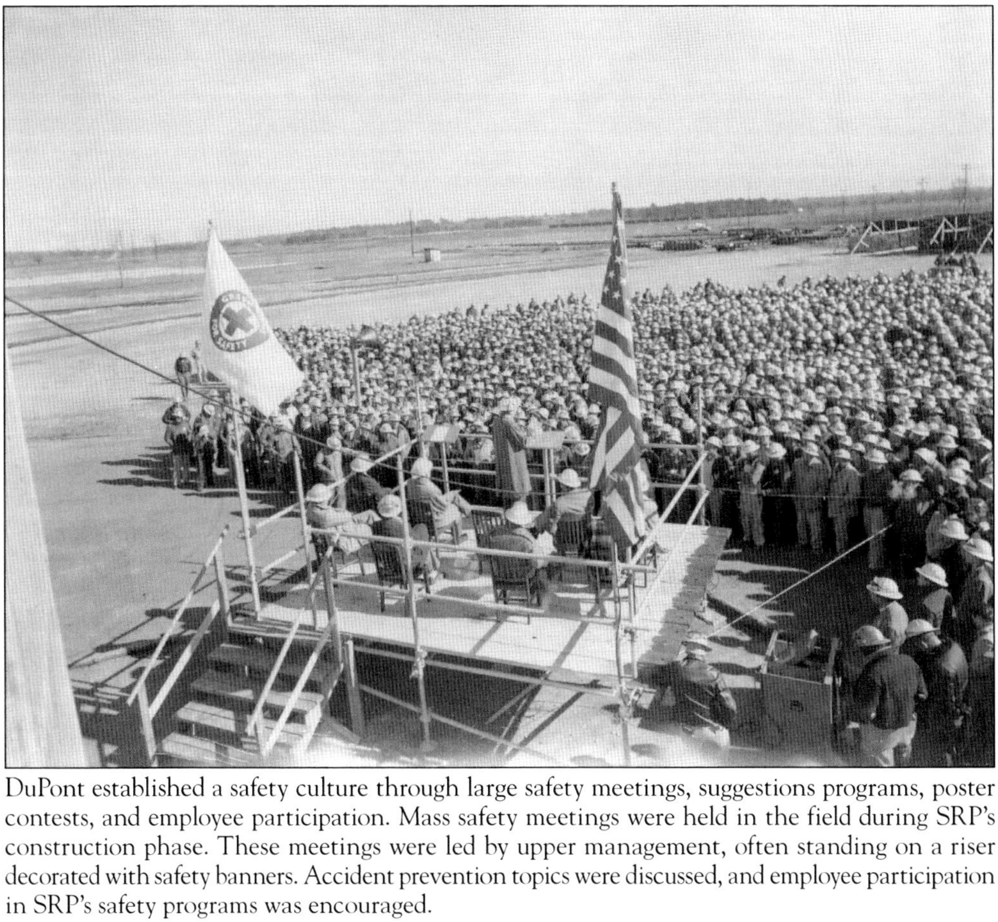

DuPont established a safety culture through large safety meetings, suggestions programs, poster contests, and employee participation. Mass safety meetings were held in the field during SRP's construction phase. These meetings were led by upper management, often standing on a riser decorated with safety banners. Accident prevention topics were discussed, and employee participation in SRP's safety programs was encouraged.

Three

Operations

In December 1953, R Reactor went critical, and by 1955, all five reactors were in operation. From 1955 until 1989, the acronym SRP stood for Savannah River Plant. SRP produced defense material to provide for a more robust nuclear stockpile. Although the reactors remain the most well-known facility across the site, it took a collaboration of workers across multiple areas to ensure the quality of the final product.

Uranium arrived first in the M Area, where, using hot crucibles and extrusion presses, workers encased the uranium slugs in layers of alloy and manufactured reactor rods. These rods were transported to the reactors, where they were remotely inserted into reactor tanks. Inside these tanks, a new element was made; over the course of hours or days, the uranium became either plutonium or tritium. Once the rods were extracted from the reactor, they cooled in water basins, were disassembled, and then sent to be purified.

The product traveled on rails from the reactors to one of two separations facilities. These facilities (called canyons) were long buildings where operators used chemical and mechanical processes to separate the necessary product from the waste. SRP produced both plutonium, a small, capsuled button, and tritium, a gas stored in a reservoir. Once the product was ready, it was temporarily stored in a large storage vault until the AEC collected and shipped it across the country to Colorado, New Mexico, and Texas to be used to assemble hydrogen bombs.

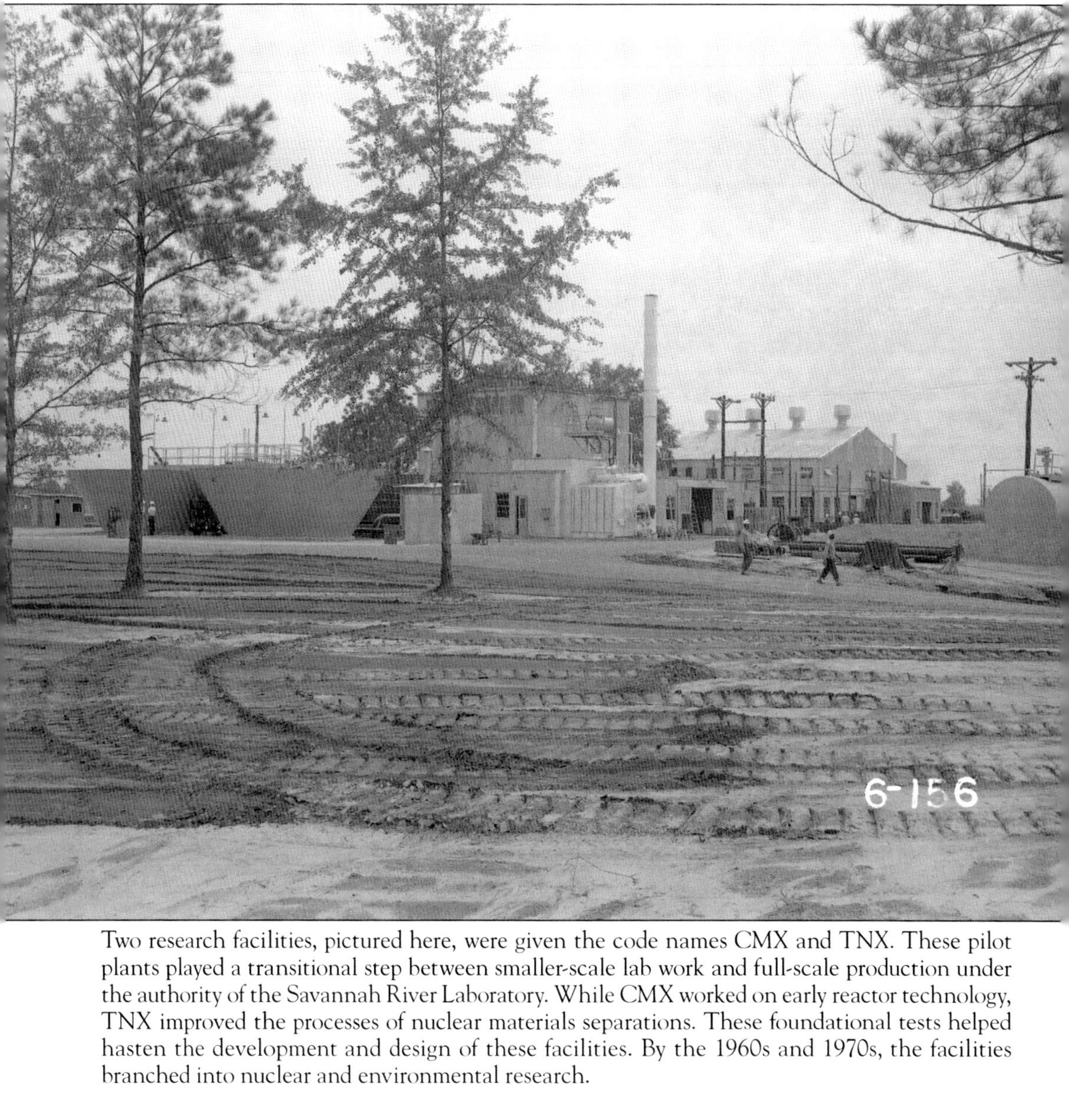

Two research facilities, pictured here, were given the code names CMX and TNX. These pilot plants played a transitional step between smaller-scale lab work and full-scale production under the authority of the Savannah River Laboratory. While CMX worked on early reactor technology, TNX improved the processes of nuclear materials separations. These foundational tests helped hasten the development and design of these facilities. By the 1960s and 1970s, the facilities branched into nuclear and environmental research.

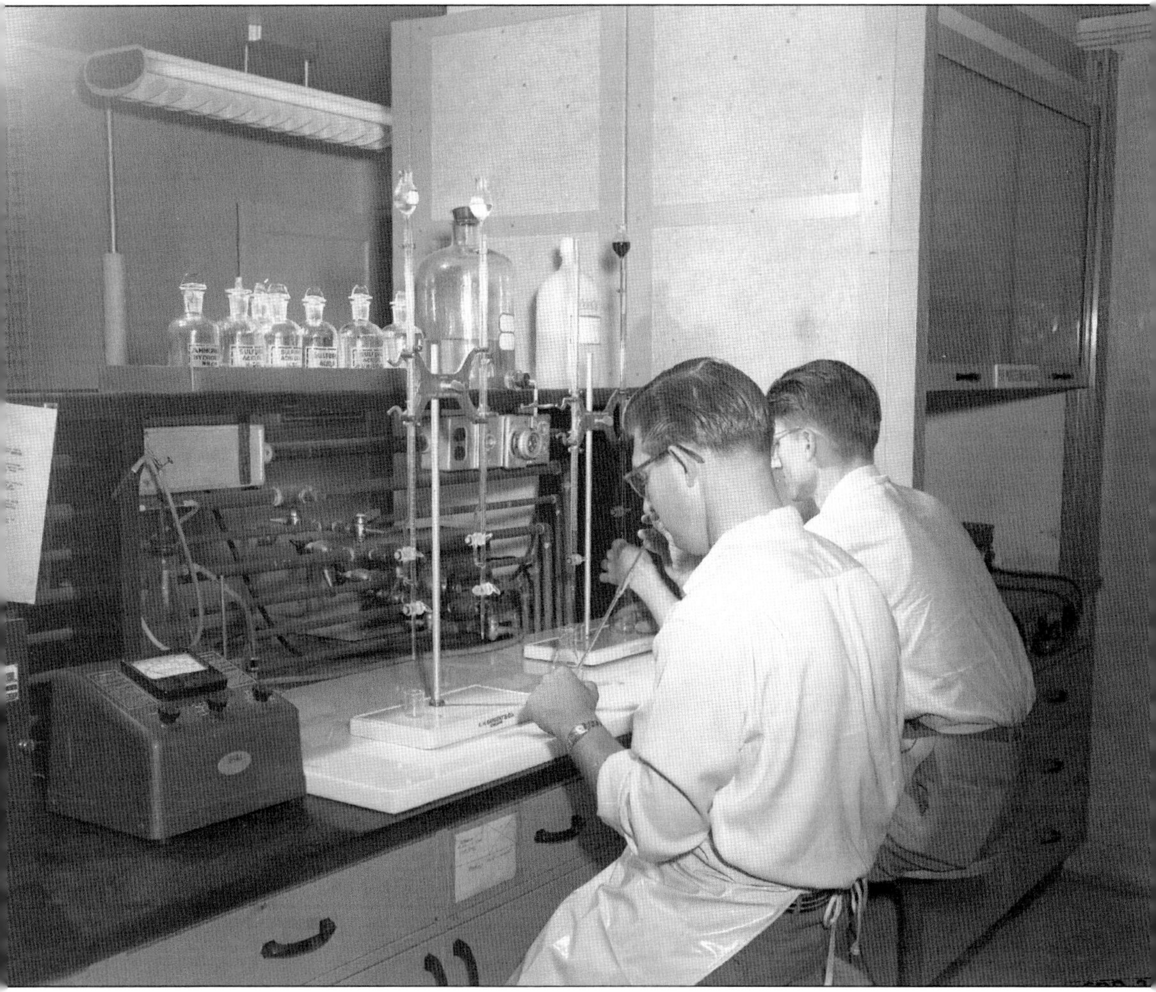

Savannah River's CMX took after its Hanford predecessor located at the Manhattan Project site where the atomic bomb had been developed. Both the Hanford CMX facility and the SRP facility researched reactor cooling water. Cooling water is circulated around a reactor tank to keep the temperatures controlled. Through Hanford's CMX testing, a water treatment building that was necessary at Hanford was found to be unnecessary at SRP, which saved time and money.

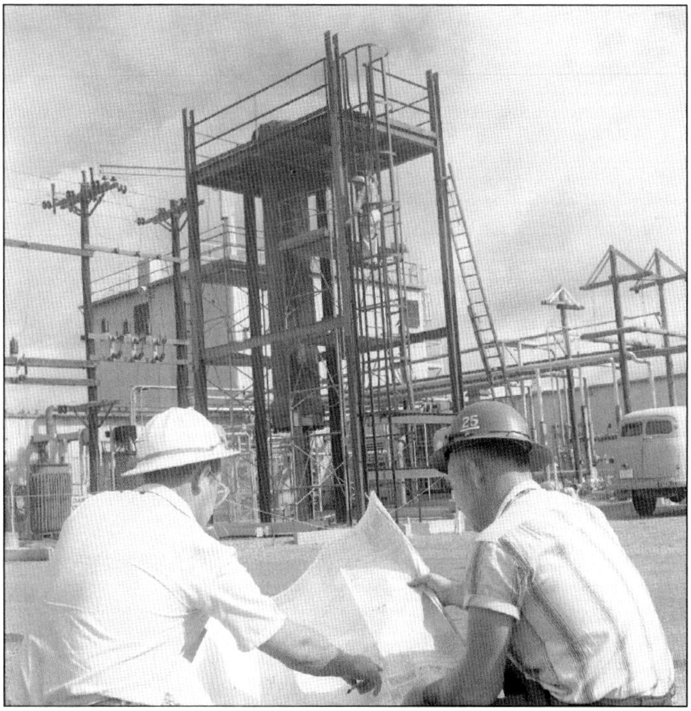

CMX, also known as 679-T or 679-G, was built close to the river for ease of research. It was also built near Ellenton, which had the most infrastructure at the beginning of construction. CMX's early research focused on using the Savannah River as SRP's cooling water source. Later research sought to improve reactor functions through different experiments, such as this power reactor program in 1957.

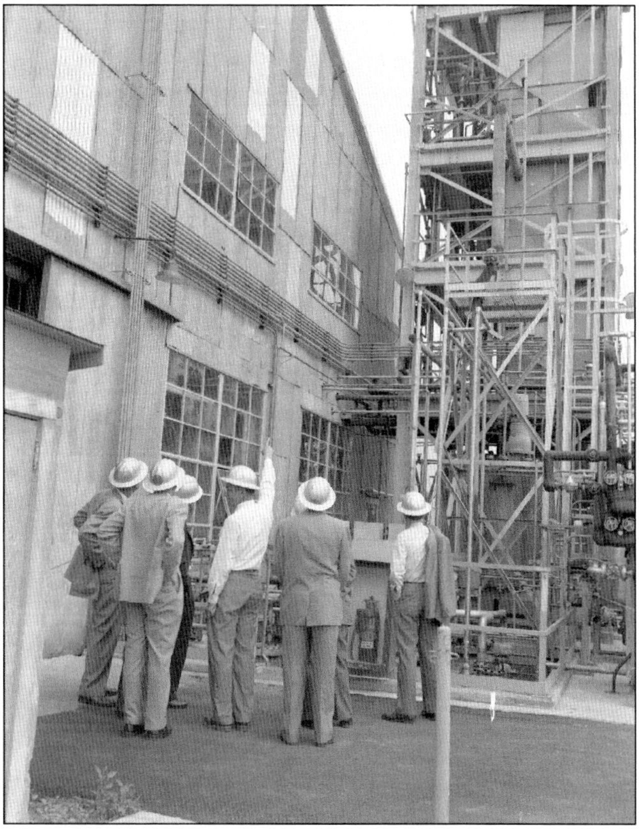

TNX, like CMX, had a connection to the Hanford site. Hanford's separations methods helped develop SRP's Purex process. Irradiated reactor rods are processed through equipment vessels and chemicals to form the final product. Work at TNX, 678-T or 678-G, refined the process and improved canyon processes over the years. It was also essential in waste management development at the Defense Waste Processing Facility.

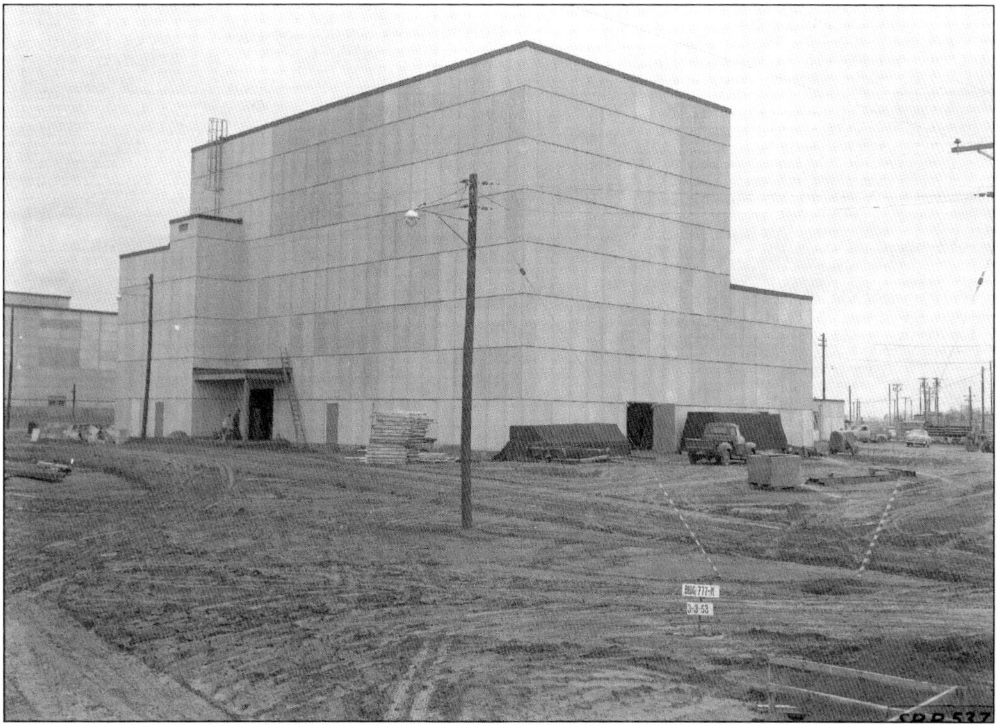

The Savannah River Laboratory managed building 777-M and the research conducted, which supported reactor operations. Building 777-M was significant to decisions in the early SRP reactor planning. The test reactors at 777-M were also used when newly designed reactor rods needed to be tested before going into a full-scale reactor. Building 777-M was constructed in early 1952 and was used until 1979 when computers led to the test reactor's phase out.

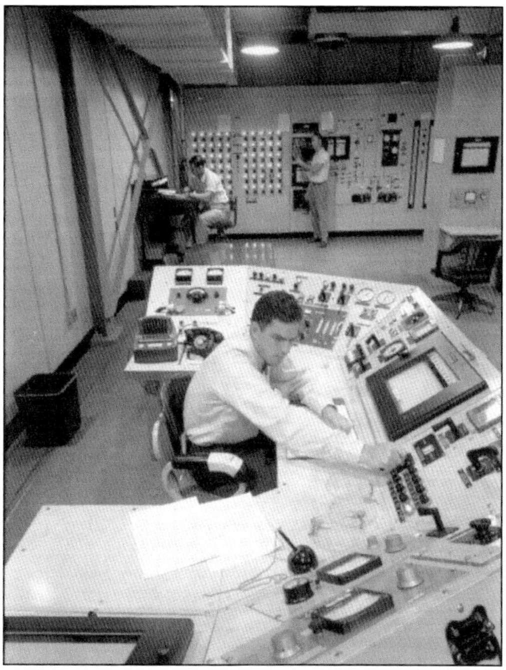

The Physics Assembly Laboratory, 777-M, housed several test reactors used for research, calibration, and testing of reactor rods. Before computers were common, these test reactors were useful in assessing how reactions would occur in the full-sized reactor. Heavy water, for instance, was known to be a successful reactor moderator, but SRP's reactors were the first large-scale production reactors to test and use heavy water.

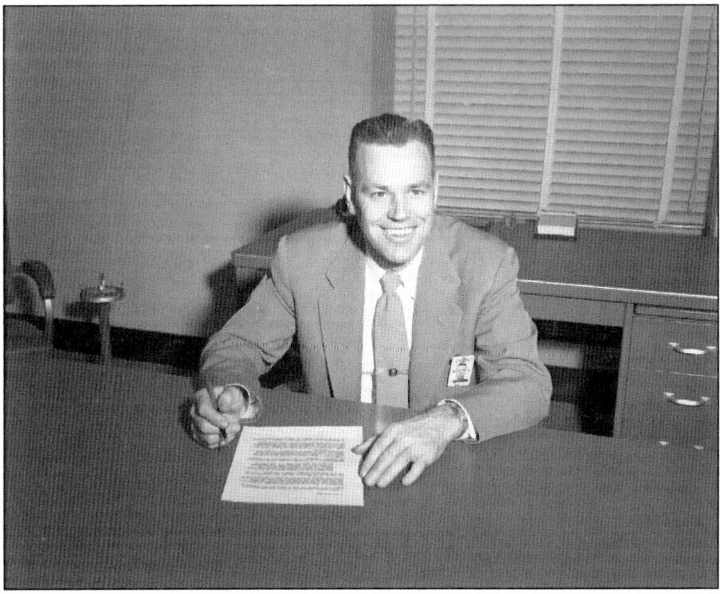

Don Miller was the Savannah River Plant manager from 1952 to 1957. During a long career with DuPont, Miller served at several other locations, including the Hanford site in Washington and the Dana Plant in Indiana.

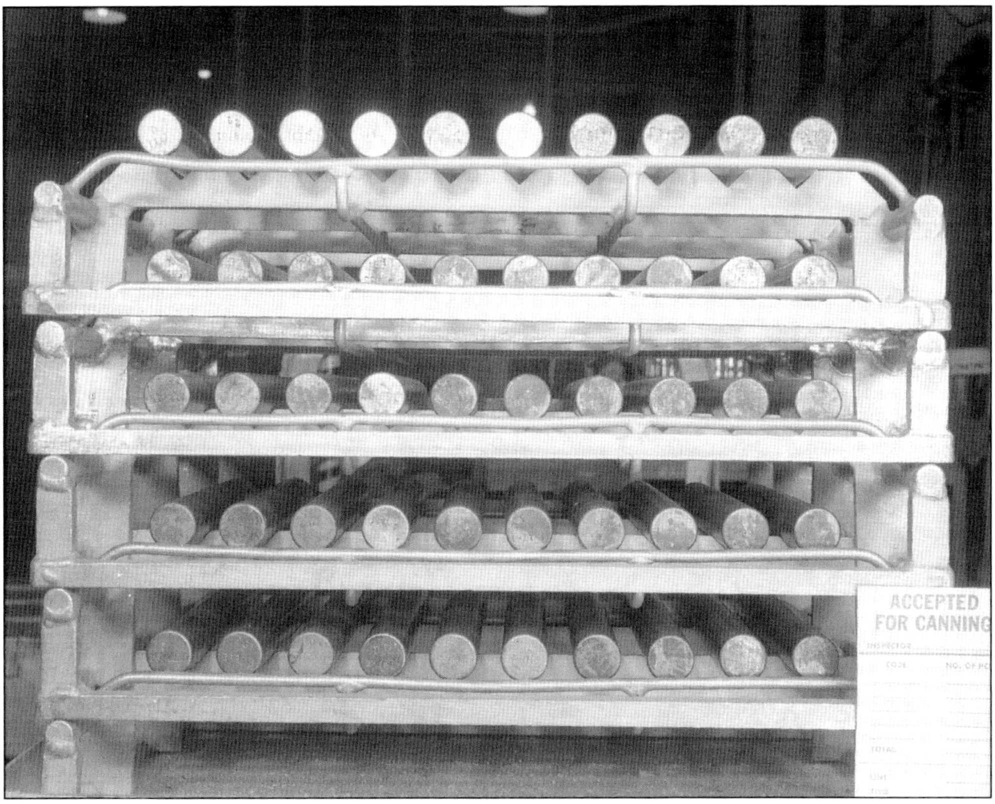

The Atomic Energy Commission network included multiple production areas across the country. The uranium "slugs" photographed here were received from a different Atomic Energy Commission site and are awaiting inspection before being used in SRP reactor rods. After being irradiated and processed at SRP, the final product would then be sent to another Atomic Energy Commission location to go into a nuclear weapon.

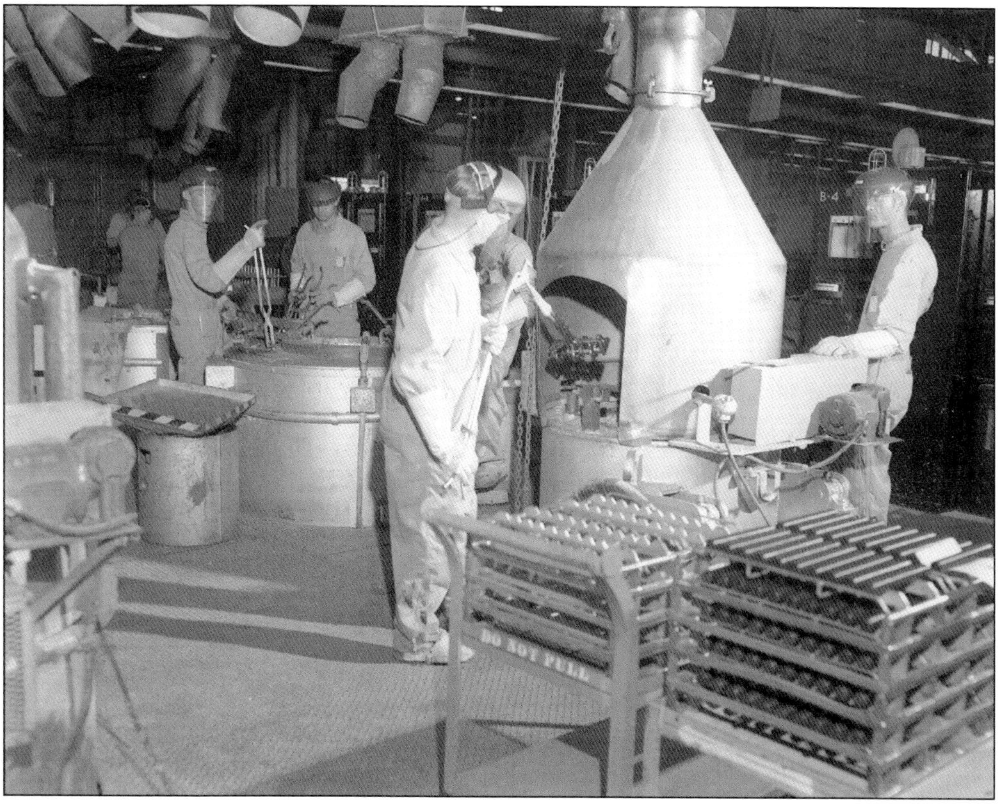

Uranium slugs were used in reactor rods to produce plutonium. The slugs were inspected and canned before being inserted into the rod. Canning the slugs with an aluminum metal coating before irradiating the rods protected the final product and prevented contamination of the valuable heavy water moderator used in the reactor. The canning step took place in SRP's building 313-M.

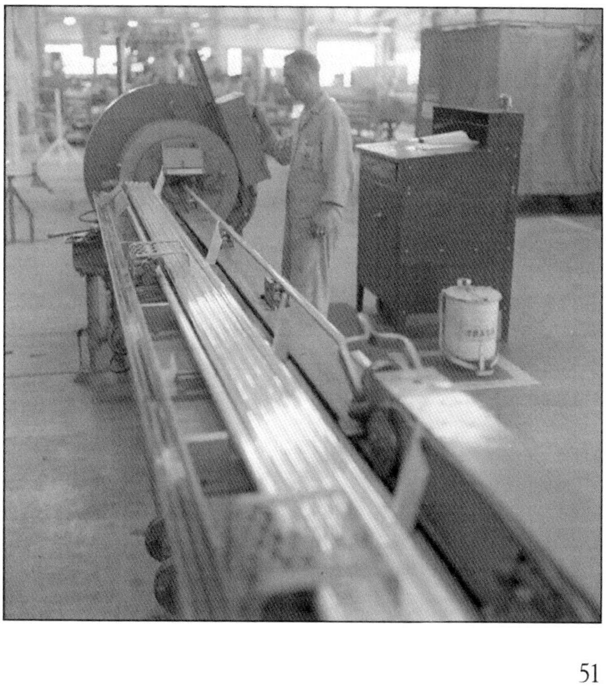

SRP manufactured reactor rods in M Area, or the fabrication area. Fuel rods kept the reaction running, control rods were used to speed or slow the reaction, and target rods contained the material that when irradiated would become the desired product. All three types of rods were made at SRP. Producing the rods on-site gave the flexibility for new designs to be developed and researched for effectiveness.

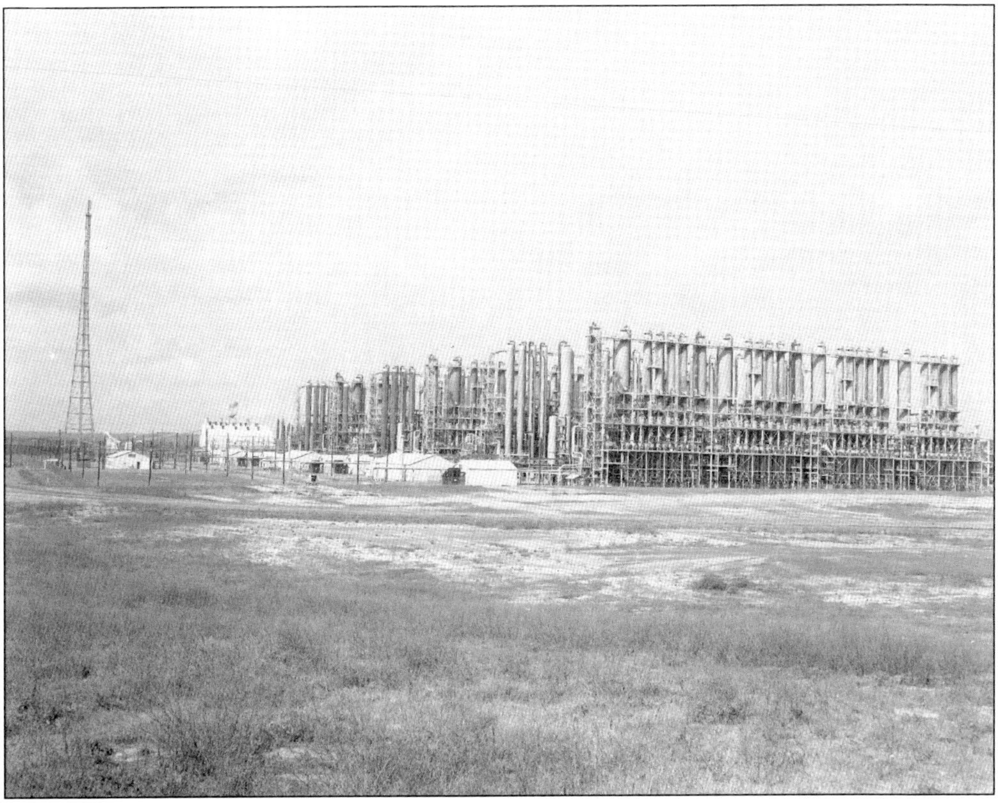

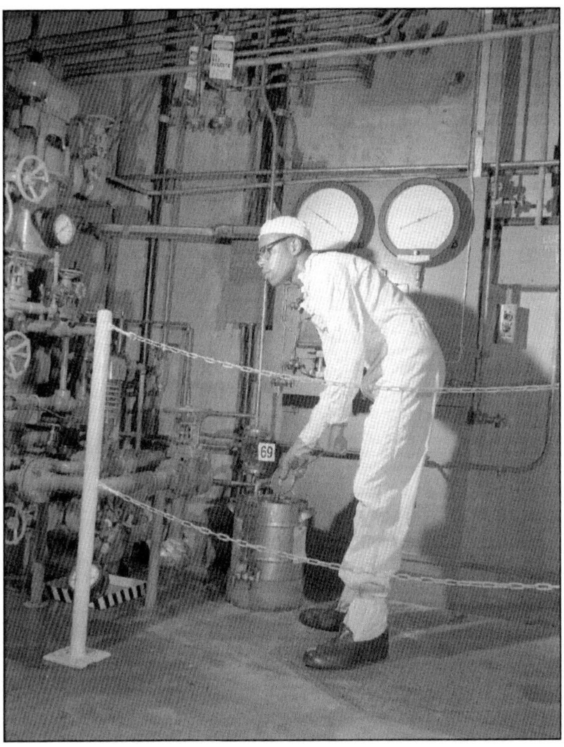

Most reactors before SRP used a graphite moderator to slow the reactor's reaction. SRP used heavy water, or deuterium oxide. Heavy water was extracted at Savannah River's D Area using the Girdler Sulfide process. One ounce of heavy water could be extracted from 52 gallons of river water. Over 140 process towers, approximately 120 feet tall, were used to produce more than 6,000 tons of heavy water from 1952 until 1982.

The heavy water extraction process was expensive and time-consuming, which made it a valuable commodity. Efforts were focused on recovering and reprocessing the water so it could be continually used as a reactor moderator. Every reactor on the plant had a purification area (pictured) to purify the heavy water for reuse.

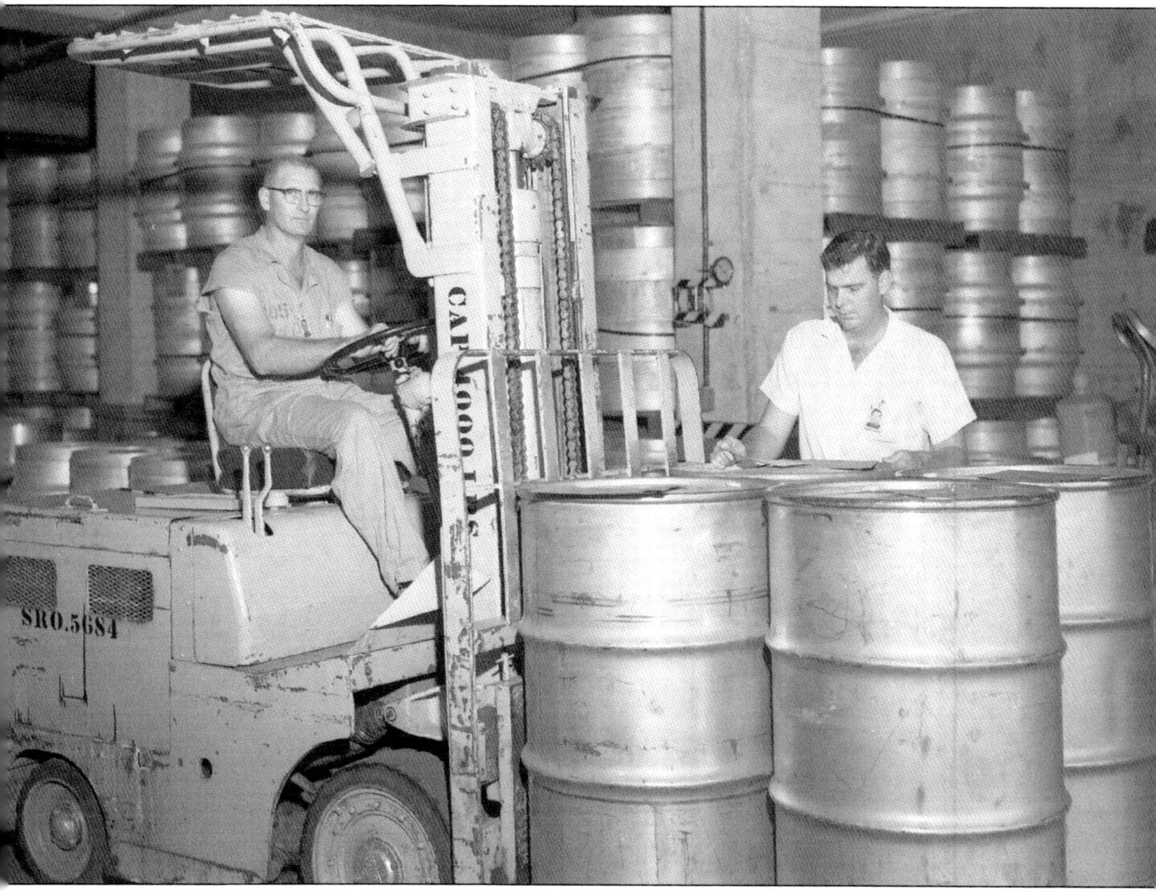

Heavy water produced on-site for reactor moderator use was also a valuable stream of revenue for SRP. The world's market value in 1962 was $24.50 per pound. Over 3,000 tons of heavy water netted more than $170 million in profit for the government between 1956 and 1971. Heavy water was stored in metal drums and inventoried regularly.

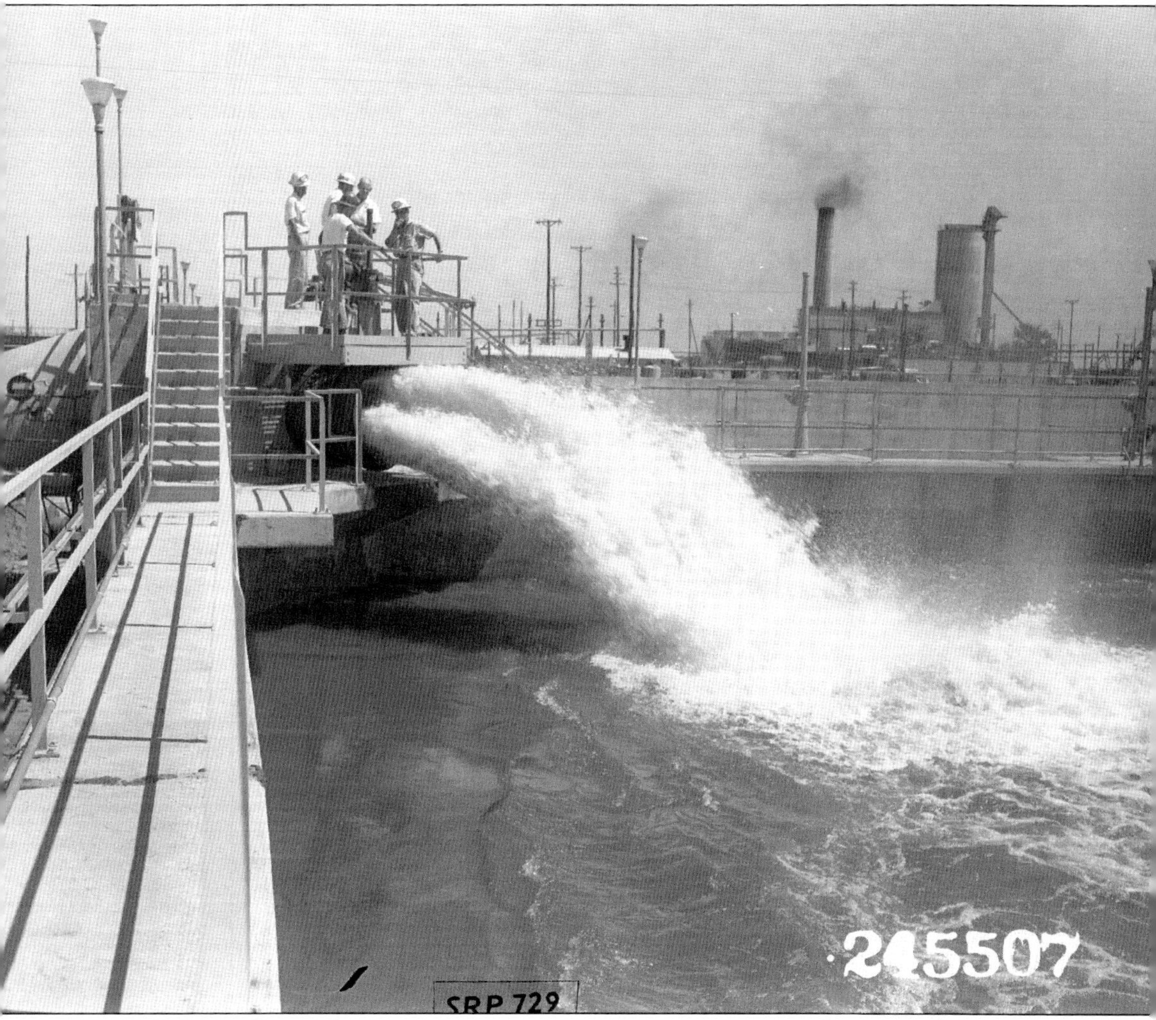

Beside each of SRP's five reactors were open reservoirs containing about 25 million gallons of river water. Here, P Reactor's cooling water pumps are being tested. The river water was pumped directly into the reactor building to cool the reactor's heat exchangers during operations. The large amount of water ensured continuous flow; backup measures were installed in case of malfunction to keep the reactors running safely.

Reactor rods produced in M Area were taken to an assembly area within one of the five reactors for final preparation. The assembly area's high ceilings allowed for rods to be loaded, tested for proper water flow, and stored on hangers. A monorail system aided in moving the rods to the process room through a narrow opening called the "presentation point."

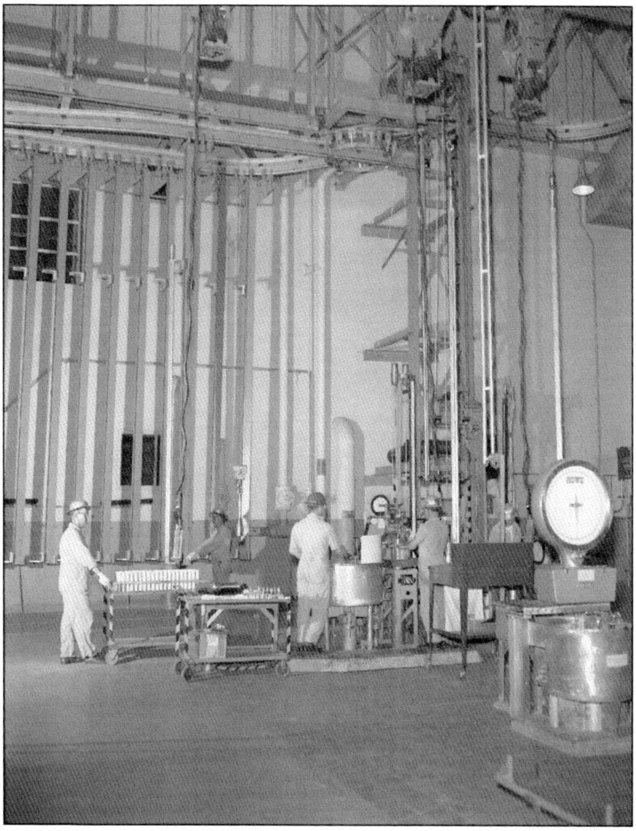

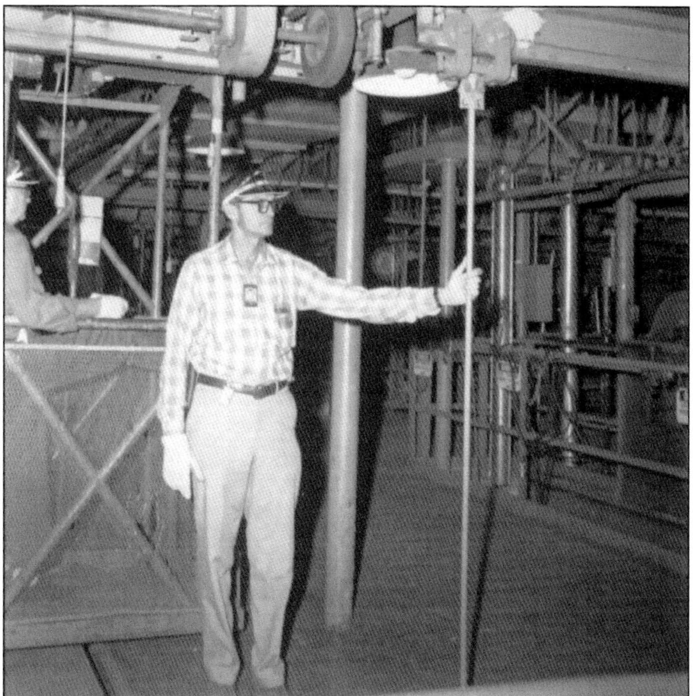

After being irradiated in a reactor tank for several weeks, reactor rods were relocated to the disassembly basin in the reactor building. To cool the rods, they were moved underwater in large basins using a monorail system. Following the cooling procedure, they were then shipped to canyons by rail for the separations and purification process.

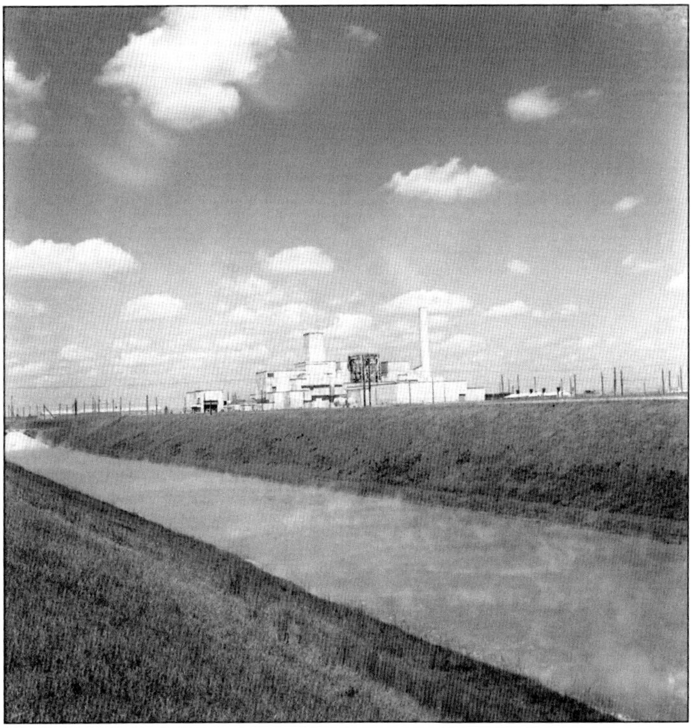

Lessons learned during early reactor construction led to modifications in C Reactor's design. C Reactor was the smallest reactor building—just under 9 million cubic feet versus R Reactor's 12.4 million—but contained the largest reactor tank of the five SRS reactors. It went critical in March 1955 and would reach SRS's highest power performance in 1967.

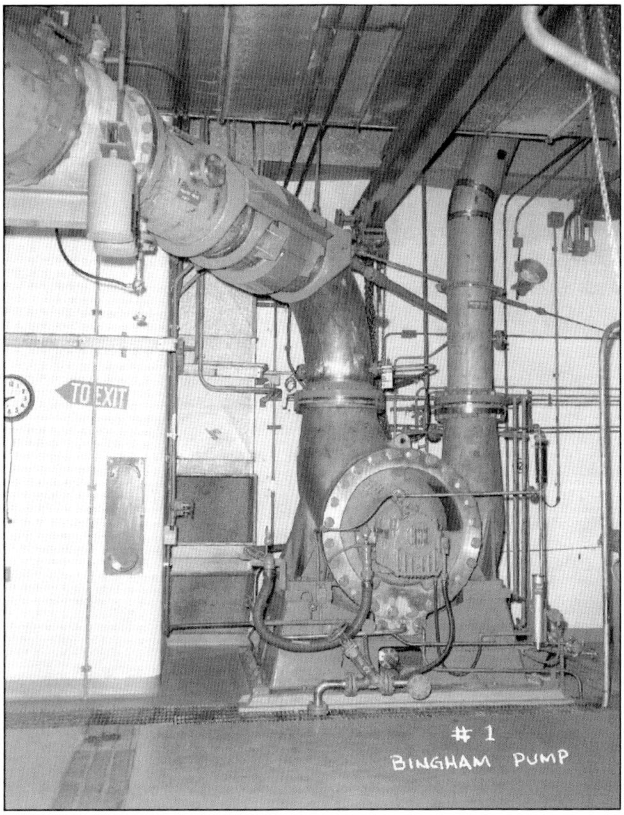

Six pumps circulated heavy water through a reactor tank. A closed circulatory system helped preserve the purity of the heavy water. Byron-Jackson pumps were originally installed in 1951, but those were replaced by Bingham pumps in 1956. The improvement increased the flow rate which meant that the reactor's power levels could be raised.

The technology to operate the five reactors of SRP was duplicated at R, P, K, L, and C Areas. This meant workers trained to run one reactor could run any of the reactors. The main control room's walls were covered with panels that controlled every operation of the reactor process room. This behind-the-scenes view of the reverse of the panels shows the organized intricacy of wires, lights, and alarms and was taken on September 18, 1956.

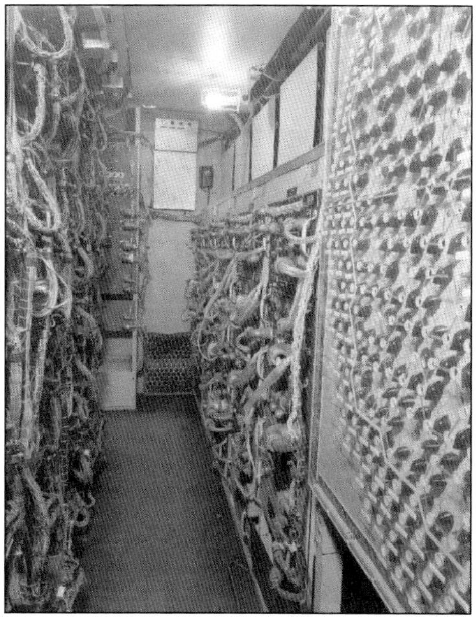

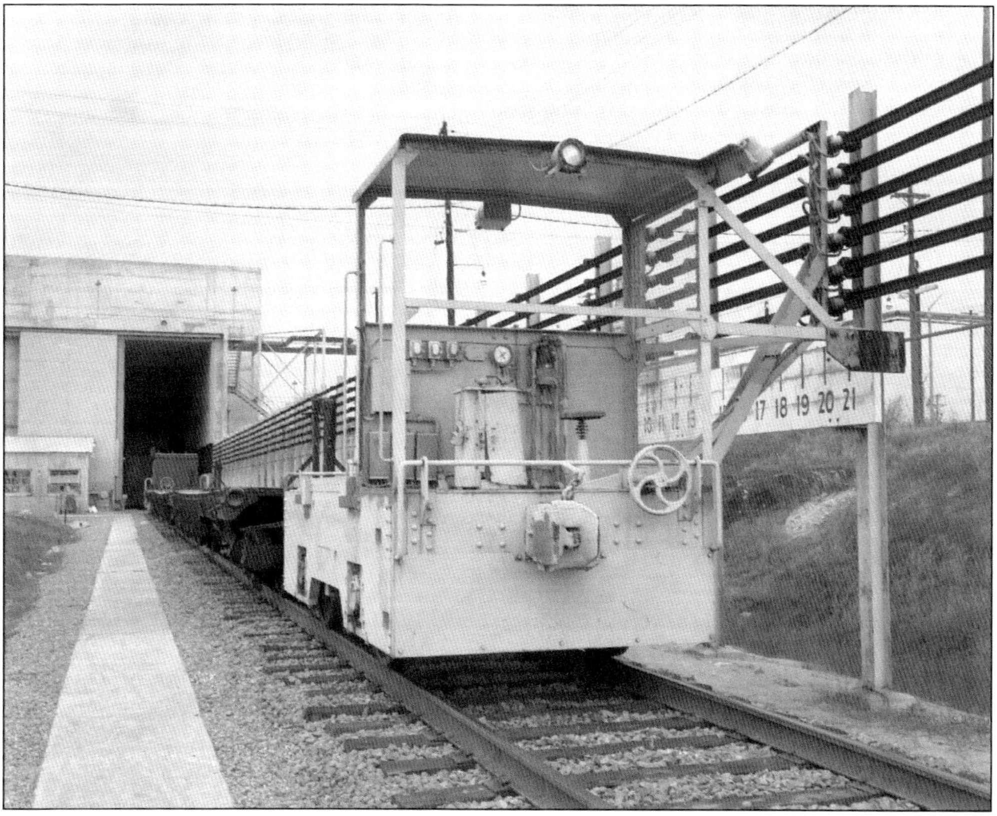

An electric engine known as a "dinky" was used to carry irradiated materials from the reactor area to the separations canyon in either F or H Area. The cars carried shielded casks containing material to be unloaded by an overhead crane. The material was then either moved to storage or taken for processing beginning on the hot side of the canyon.

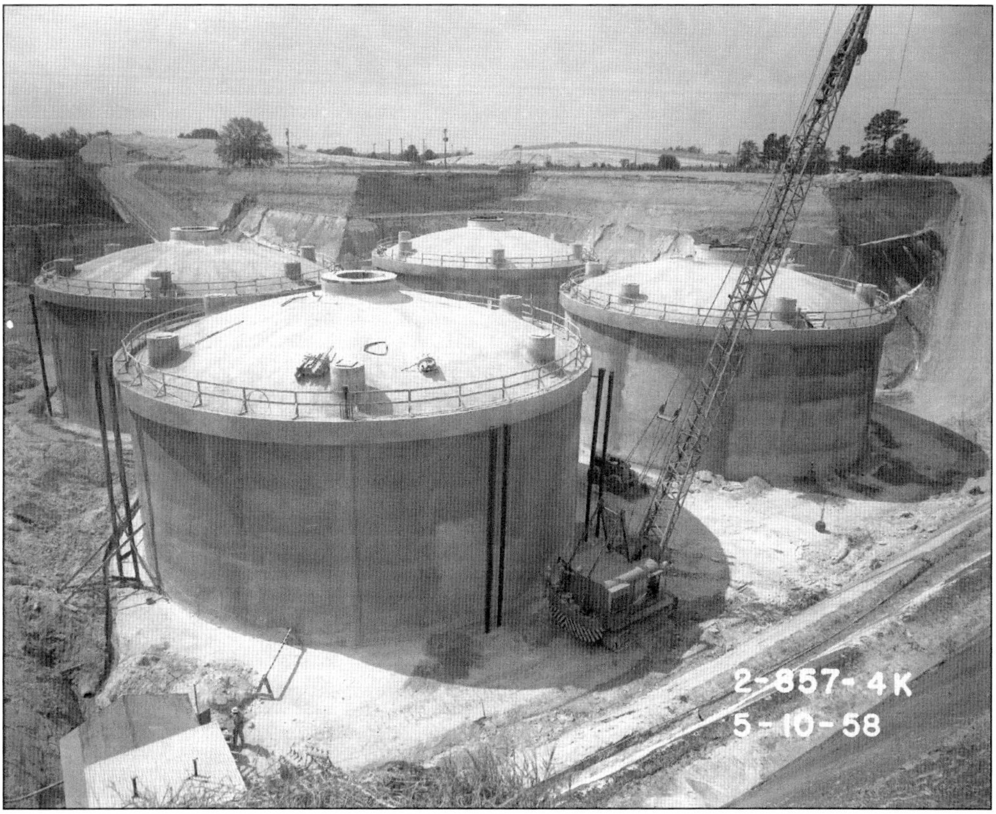

The separations process produced a lot of radioactive waste, and the solution was to temporarily store it all in massive waste tanks. Heavier, solid waste (called sludge) sinks to the bottom of the tanks, while liquid waste (called salt waste) rises to the top. SRP pursued different methods for processing each kind of waste. By the end of operations, these waste tank farms stored millions of gallons of radioactive waste.

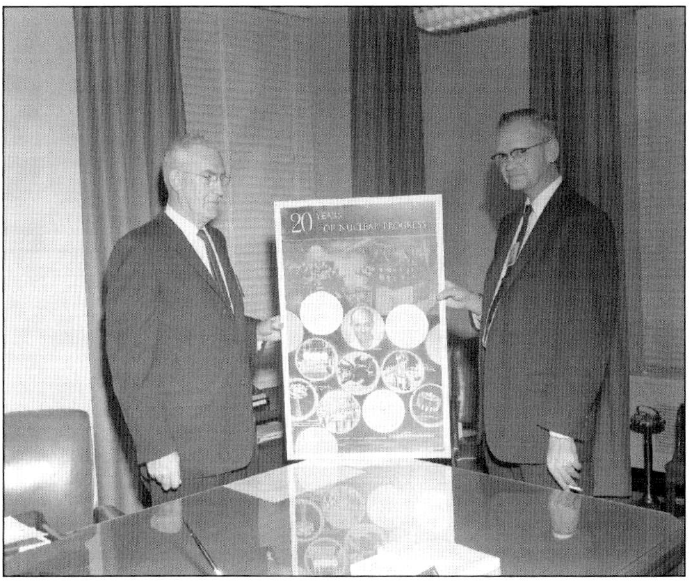

Savannah River Operations Office manager Robert Blair and Savannah River Laboratory director William Overbeck hold a poster celebrating 20 years of nuclear progress since the first sustained nuclear fission chain reaction. From the first experiments during the Manhattan Project to the large-scale mission at SRP, the power of the atom has changed the possibilities of nuclear science and the history of the world.

Four

Connecting the Workplace

Working at the Savannah River Plant was different from everyday businesses. Employees worked across a large site area and needed to be able to communicate about sensitive subjects. Administrative work, such as ensuring paychecks went out on time, was no small feat with thousands of employees to get paid. Still, tasks like providing food among multiple site cafeterias, creating photographic documentation of the new plant, and ensuring the production of a biweekly newspaper were unique to the Savannah River Plant.

The plant was gated and isolated, and so work relationships were important among employees, even more so due to geographic and scope of work restrictions. Lunch was eaten in the shared cafeteria with coworkers, and this provided a time for employees to connect on a more personal level. However, discussion of workplace matters was discouraged among those who did not have a need to know.

Whether it was direct connections of phone and mail correspondence or building relationships at lunchtime, workplace culture and keeping connected happened on a large scale among the thousands of employees at the Savannah River Plant.

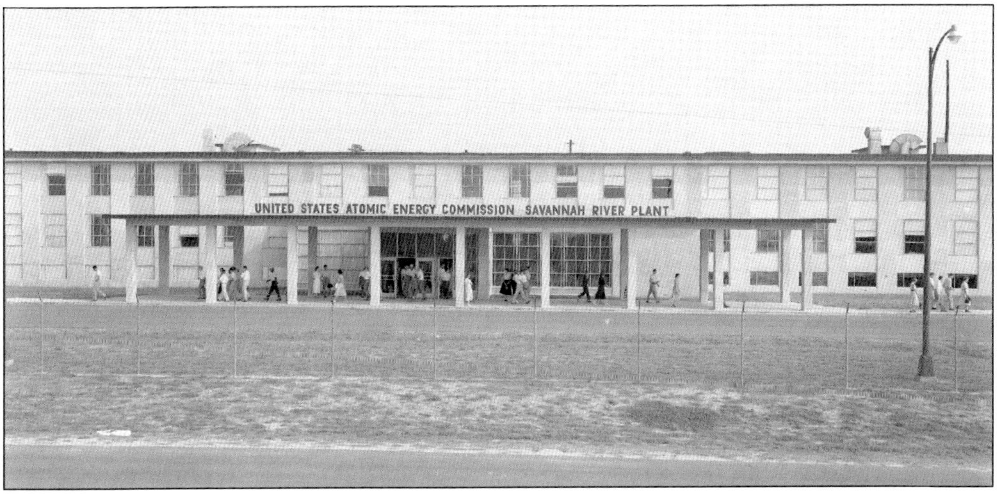

The SRP main administration building, 703-A, housed over 1,000 employees, including Atomic Energy Commission and DuPont management and later Department of Energy personnel as well. This building served as the face of the site for many years and, with its 1.5-foot-tall aluminum letters spelling out "United States Atomic Energy Commission—Savannah River Plant," hosted many photograph opportunities for departmental groups, management, and visitors.

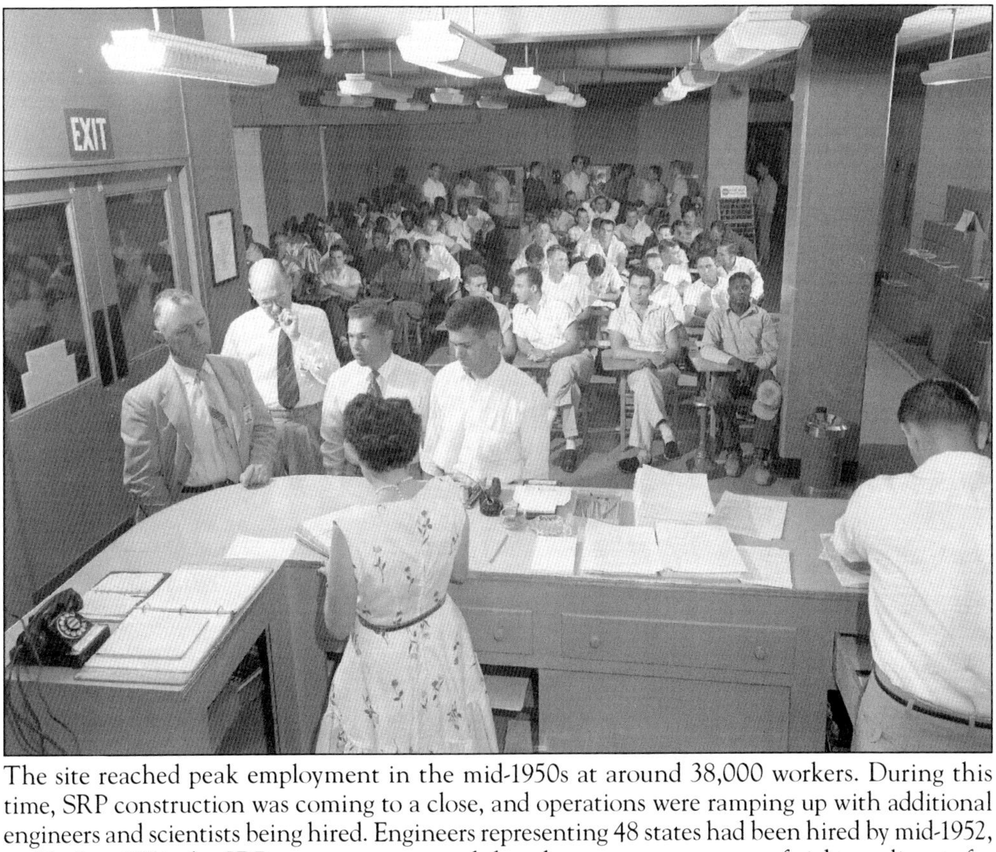

The site reached peak employment in the mid-1950s at around 38,000 workers. During this time, SRP construction was coming to a close, and operations were ramping up with additional engineers and scientists being hired. Engineers representing 48 states had been hired by mid-1952, and by late 1954, the SRP newspaper reported that there were an average of eight applicants for every job posted.

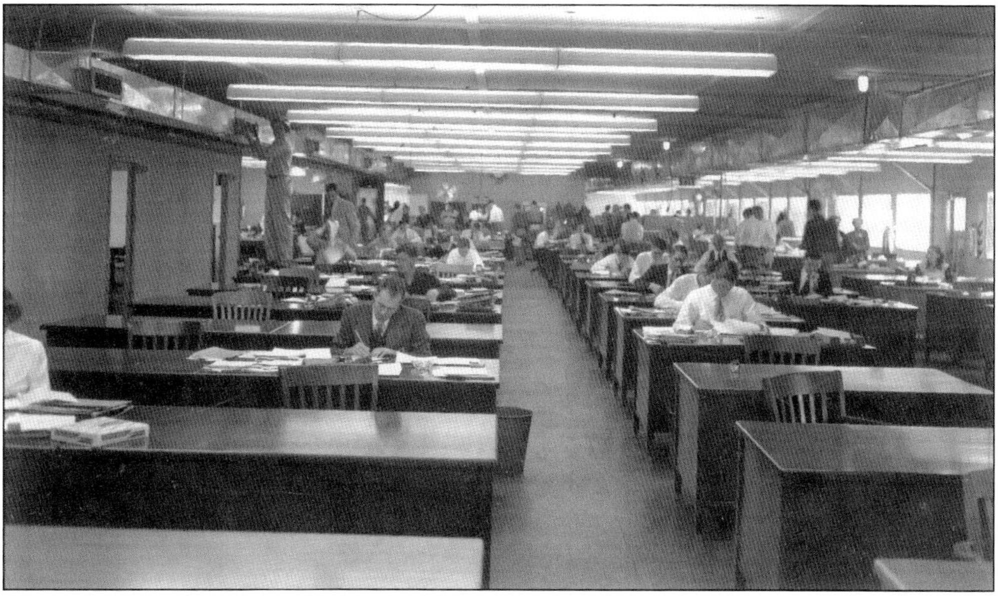

The accounting department had several locations during the early years of SRP. In December 1950, accounting, along with receiving, purchasing, transportation, and payroll, was located at Daniel Field in Augusta, Georgia. DuPont's personnel moved to temporary construction offices, TC-1 and TC-2, in May 1951 (above). The main administration building, 703-A, was completed in October 1953. Around 1,000 workers, administration and management, were housed in 703-A, and the majority of them walked through this lobby each day (below). Before the modern SRS badge office was built in 1989, the front facade of SRP was 703-A, and all visitors checked in at visitor control, located in the 703-A lobby for a temporary badge.

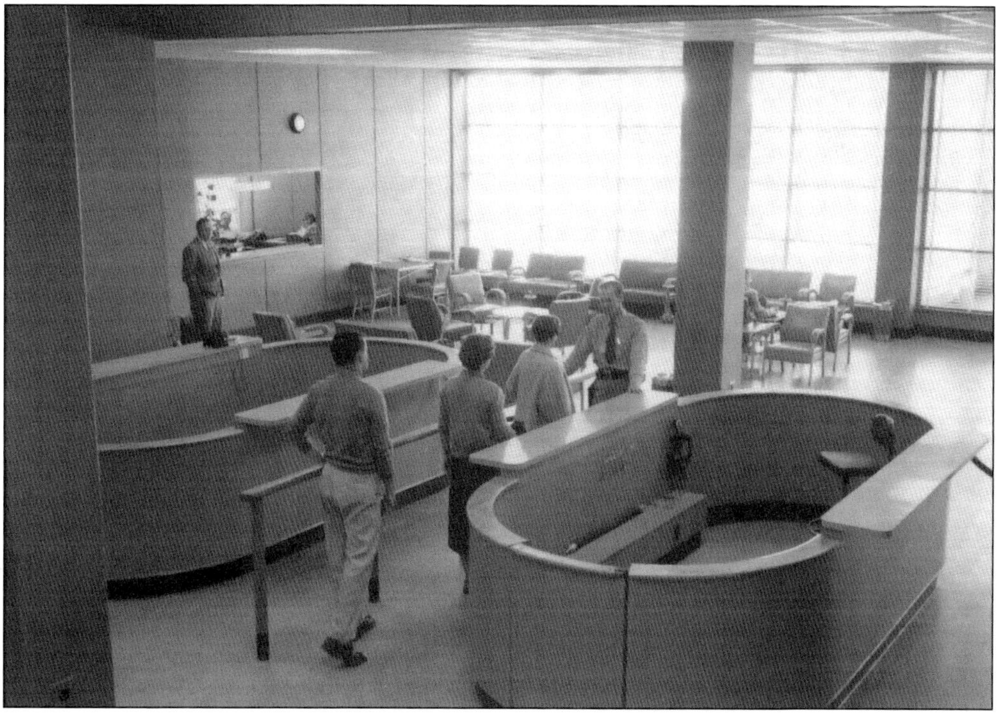

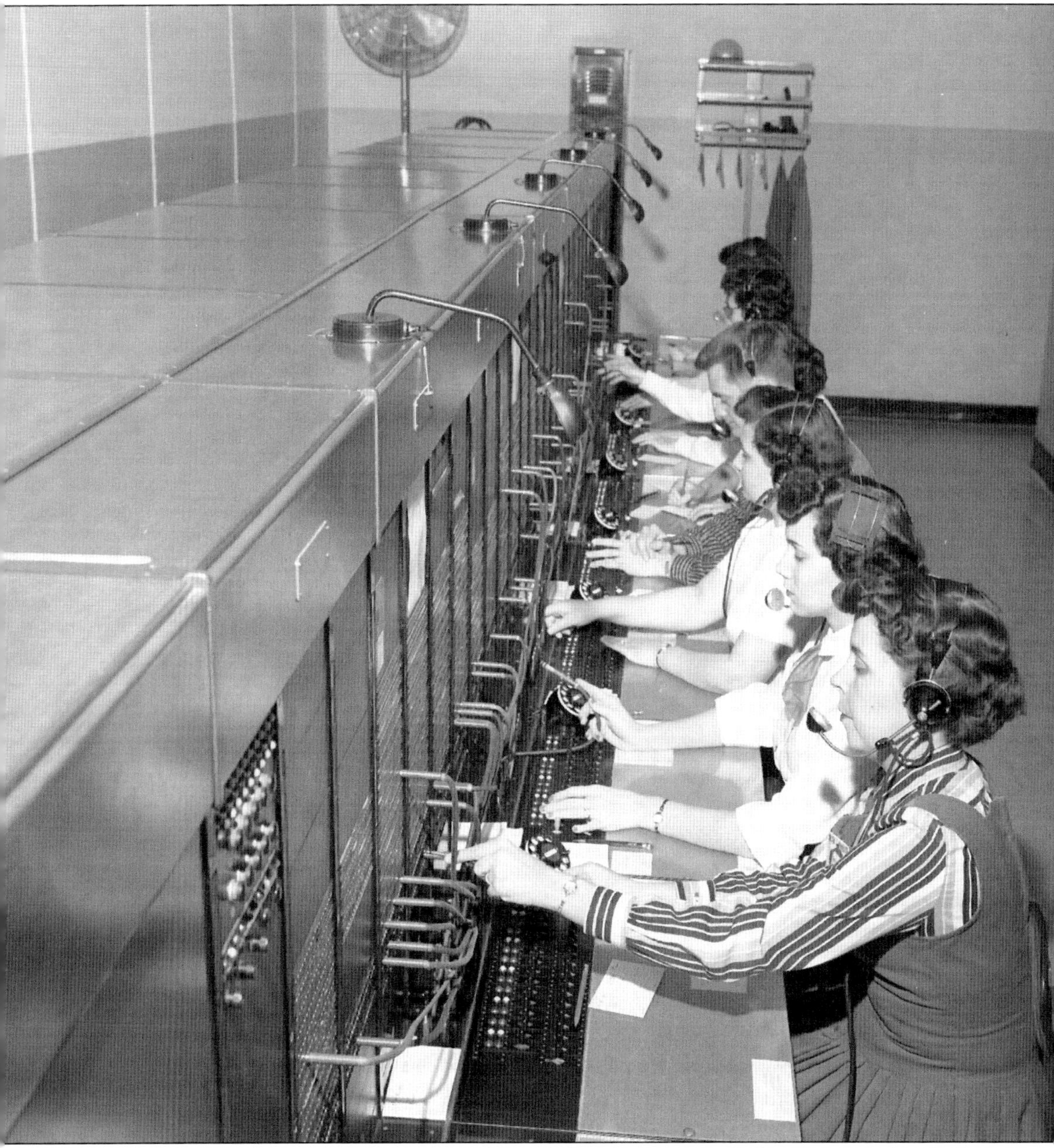

SRP's communication needs quickly grew beyond the early support of Ellenton's Cassels Telephone Company. Telephone lines were first set up in the temporary construction area followed by the 300/700 area by the Southern Bell Telephone and Telegraph Company. Between the calls made from the administration area, production area, and off-plant, SRP's telephone exchange connected an estimated 37,000 daily calls during the late 1950s.

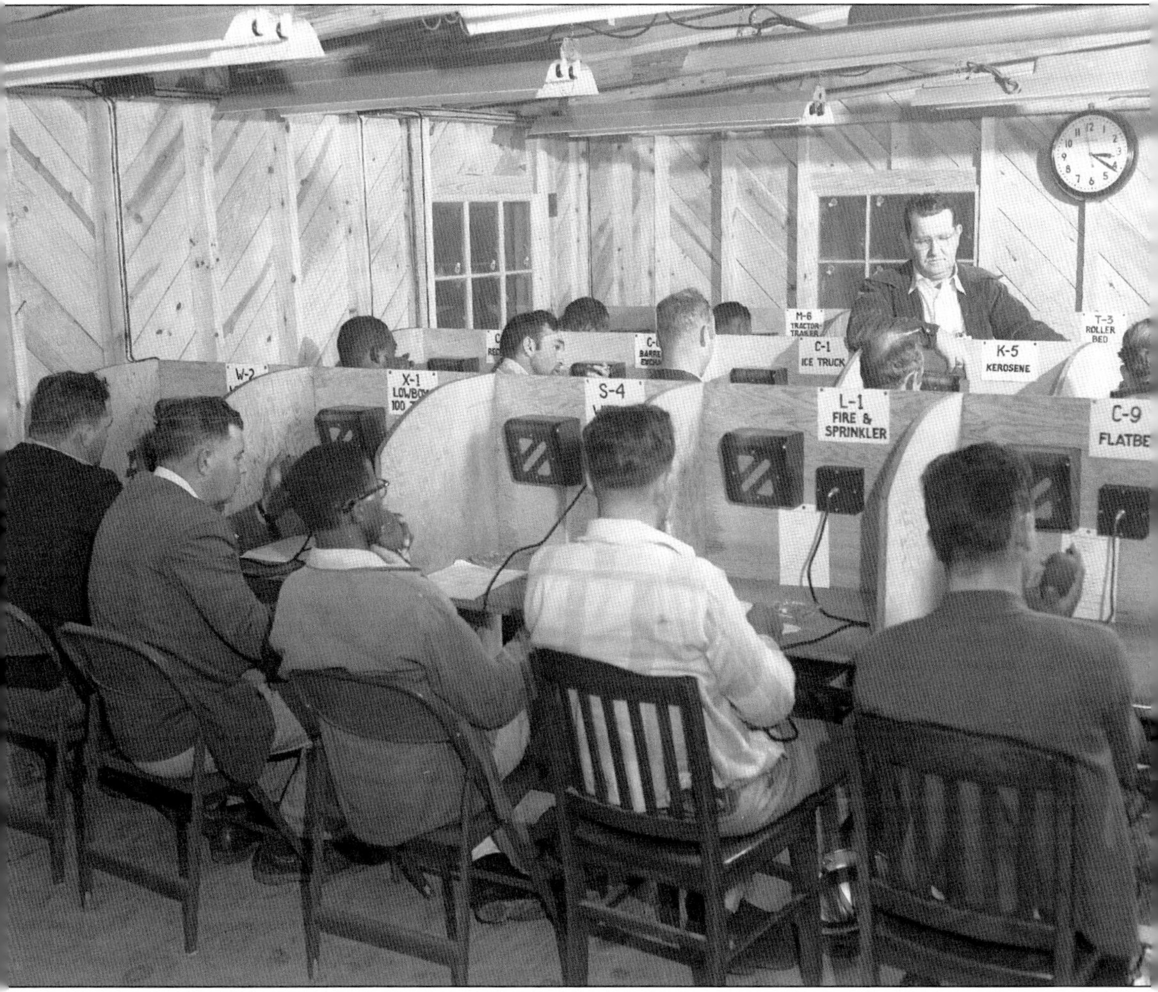

Around 500 radio transmitters were used for communicating across the vast expanse of SRP, particularly during construction. Transportation installed two-way radios in vehicles to cut down on trips back to headquarters for assignments and to communicate with railcars. Dupont Patrol used radios to exchange information between the patrol headquarters and its vehicle fleet. The US Forest Service used units in the fire towers for quick relay of messages.

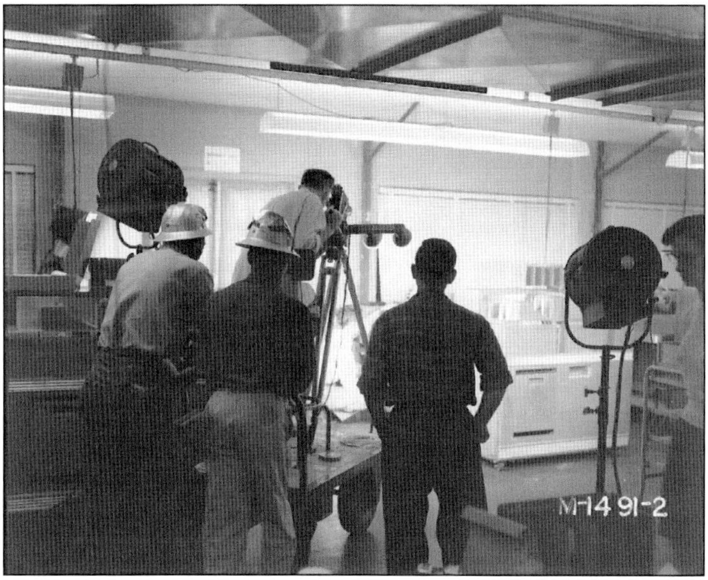

Dupont's photography and video department at SRP began documenting as early as March 1951. The group was kept busy detailing construction, procedures, experiments, site culture, events, and special visitors. Here is a behind-the-scenes look at a recording of the International Business Machines (IBM) group in August 1952. The video services department is still central to recording events at SRS today.

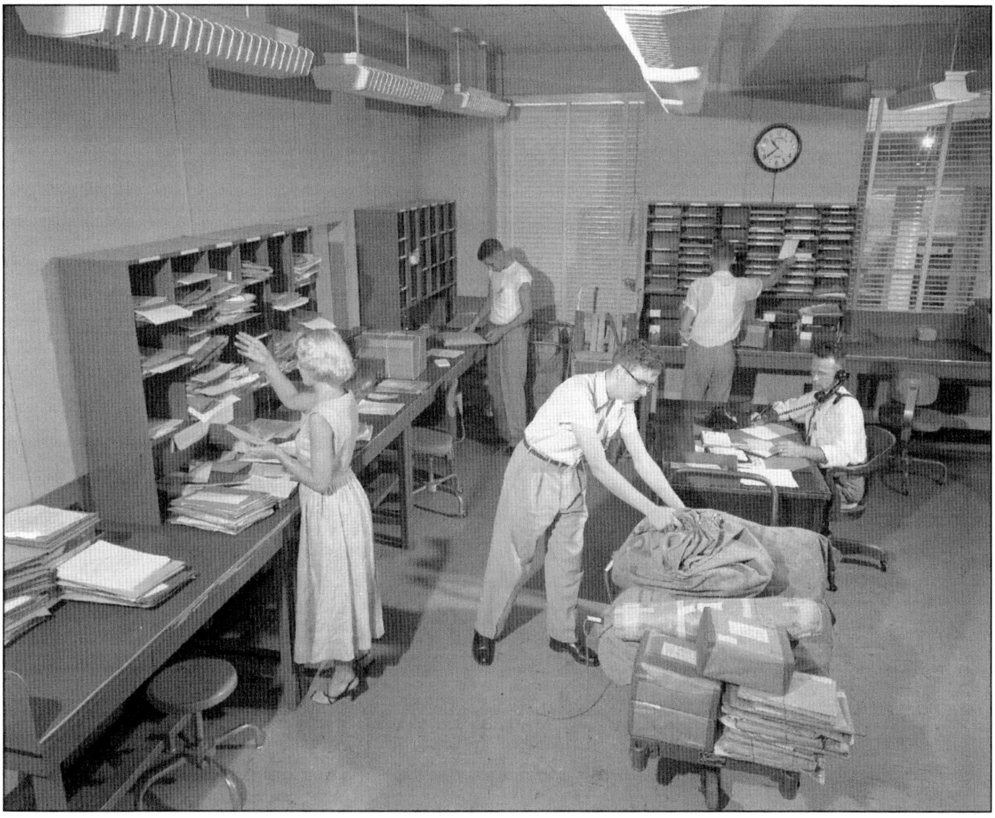

Mail was essential to efficient communication, and the SRP's mail room handled all intraplant and off-site mail (including classified mail). Construction and operations overlapped during the early 1950s, which inflated the mail volume. According to the SRP newspaper, the mail room handled 257,243 pieces of mail in July 1954. For perspective, the Aiken Post Office processed only 224,000 in the same month.

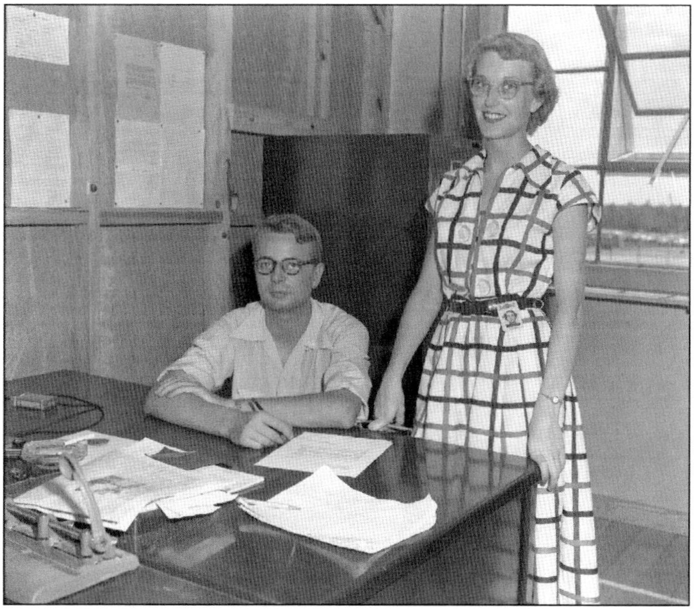

The *SRP News and Views*, the plant's first newspaper, was published every other Friday throughout the initial construction. The operations newspaper, the *Savannah River Plant News*, began in February 1953 and was published every other Wednesday. Publication for both ended in 1989, followed by an era of primarily online communication. The *SRP News and Views* and the *Savannah River Plant News* covered safety topics, general site happenings, and employee community involvement.

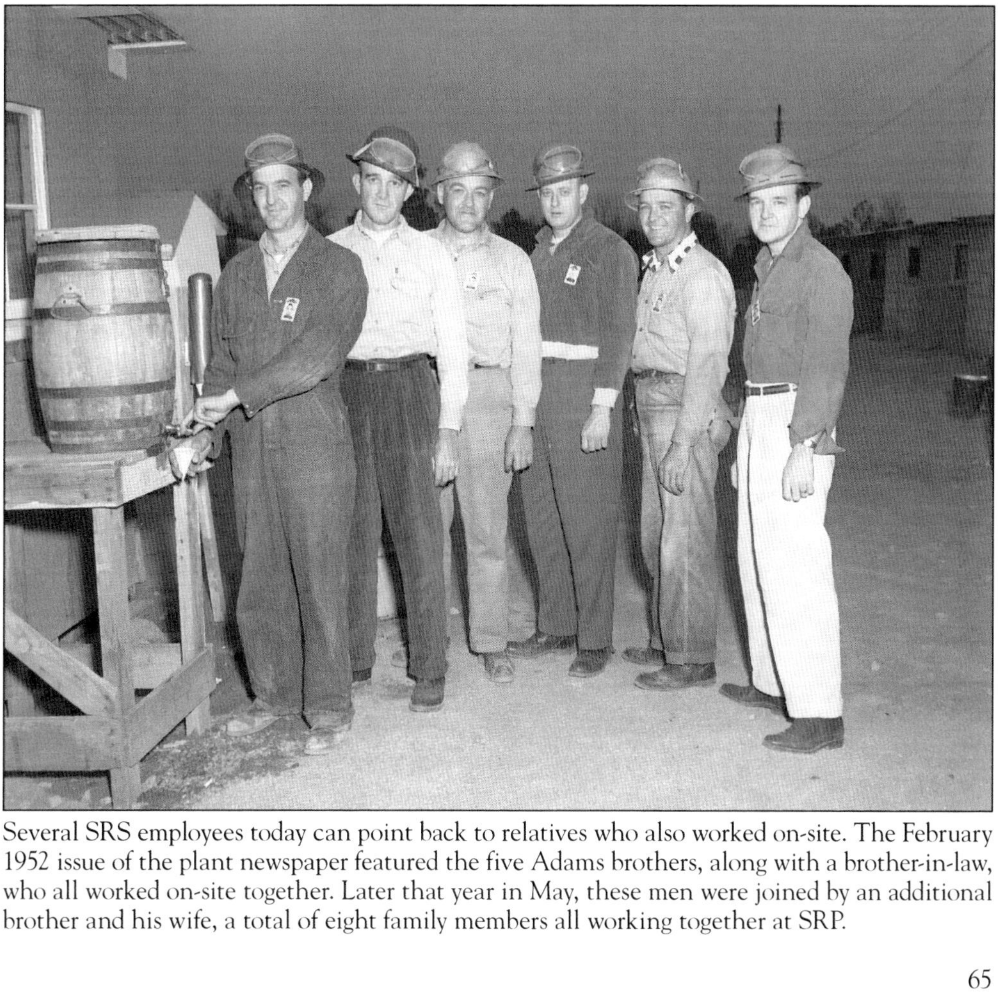

Several SRS employees today can point back to relatives who also worked on-site. The February 1952 issue of the plant newspaper featured the five Adams brothers, along with a brother-in-law, who all worked on-site together. Later that year in May, these men were joined by an additional brother and his wife, a total of eight family members all working together at SRP.

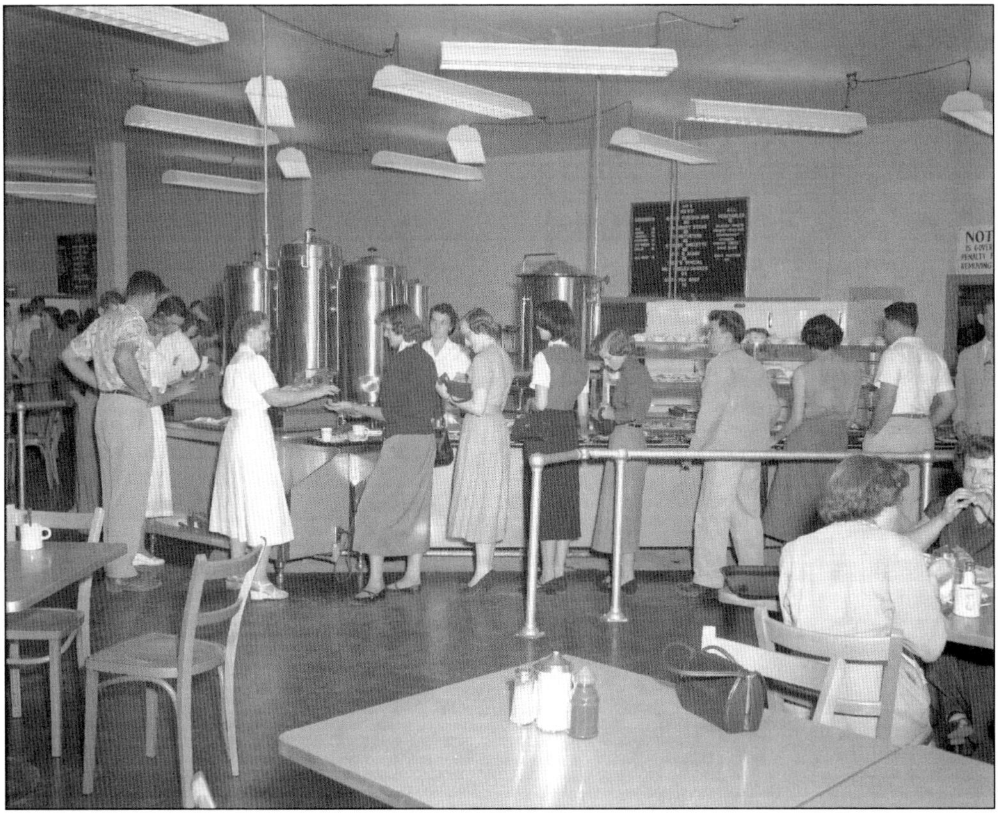

The designed isolation of SRP's location created a unique challenge for the typical workday lunch. During peak employment, the cafeterias were busy enough that they remained open for all shifts in each of the main work areas. Dine-in and carryout options were offered by Nilon Brothers catering, and bringing a homemade lunch was also a popular option. The cafeteria in building 708-A was used for all food preparation and seated about 650 employees. On an average day, up to 5,000 people between two peak shifts were served. Common lunch items included Salisbury steak, a sirloin sandwich, or fried chicken.

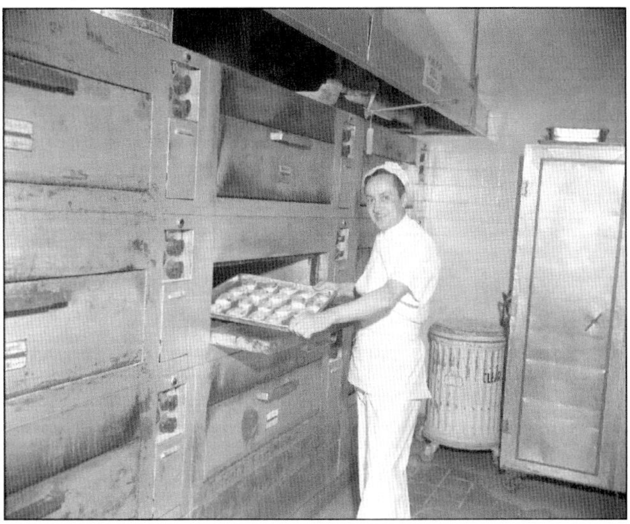

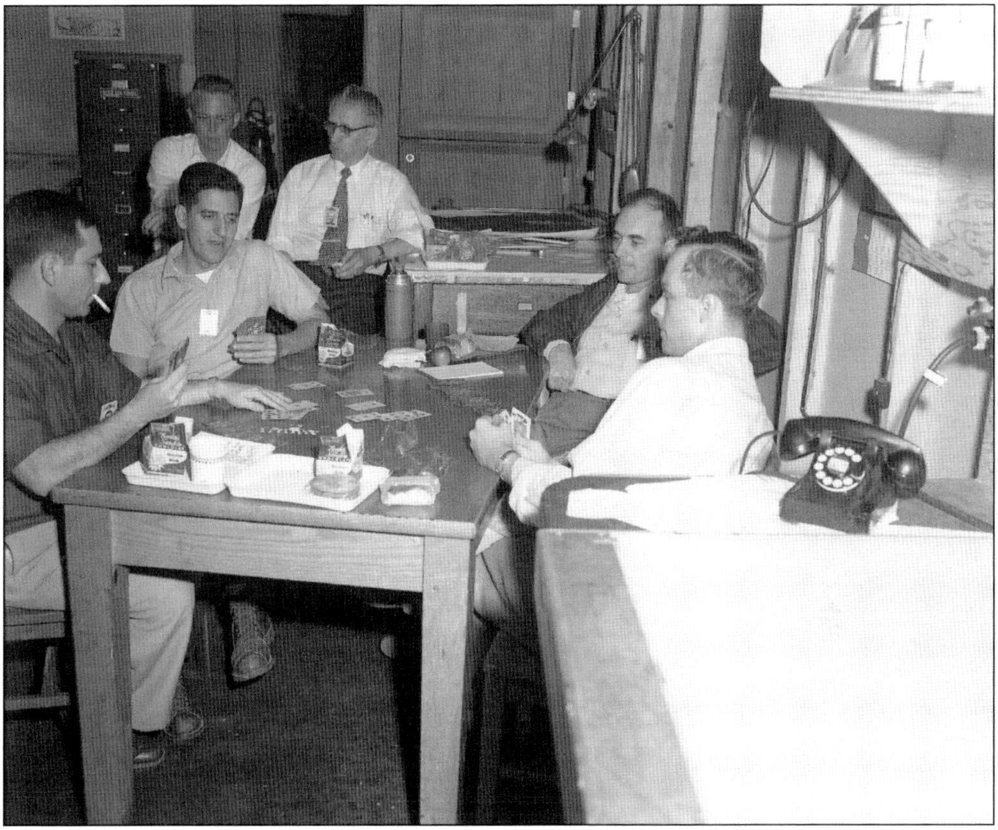

During lunch on-site, a group of men plays a quick round of bridge (a trick-taking card game) to pass the time and have a little fun. It was not unusual to turn the mind from work during breaks, and it was encouraged for employees to engage in games and activities that built comradery yet also distracted them from speaking of the projects they were working on.

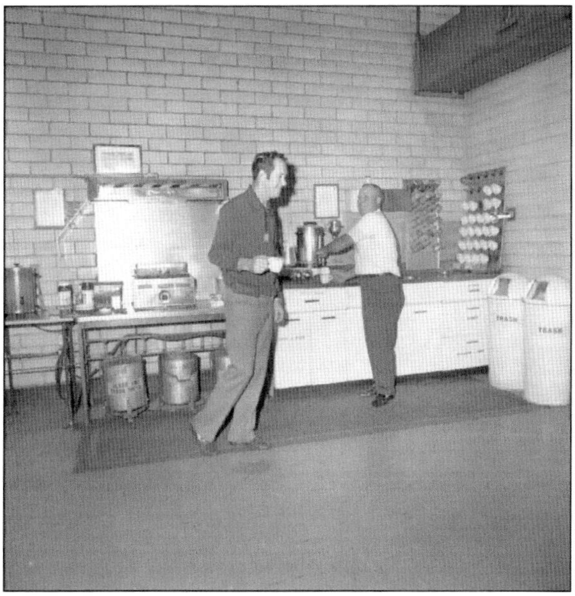

Having an organized break room with plenty of coffee cups was a must. At SRP, some employees worked through the night and did not get off the "graveyard" shift until nearly 8:00 a.m. Coffee could fuel an early morning shift and get the day started, but to those working through the night, it made all the difference.

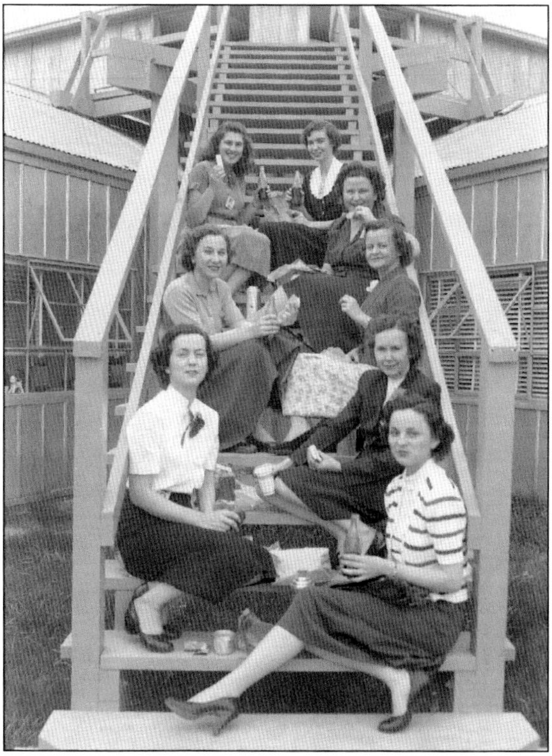

While each Savannah River Plant area had its own cafeteria during peak employment, employees often enjoyed gathering with friends to eat outside. These women are gathered for lunch on the steps of the temporary construction building. SRP employees became very familiar with each other in the setting of working together for a common, significant goal of establishing national security.

Proper work attire was expected at SRP. Safety regulations often dictated the uniform that most workers wore while at the plant, however, in the case of many women, there was a separate set of expectations. Attire often included curled hair, jewelry, a dress or skirt that fell to mid-calf, and high heels.

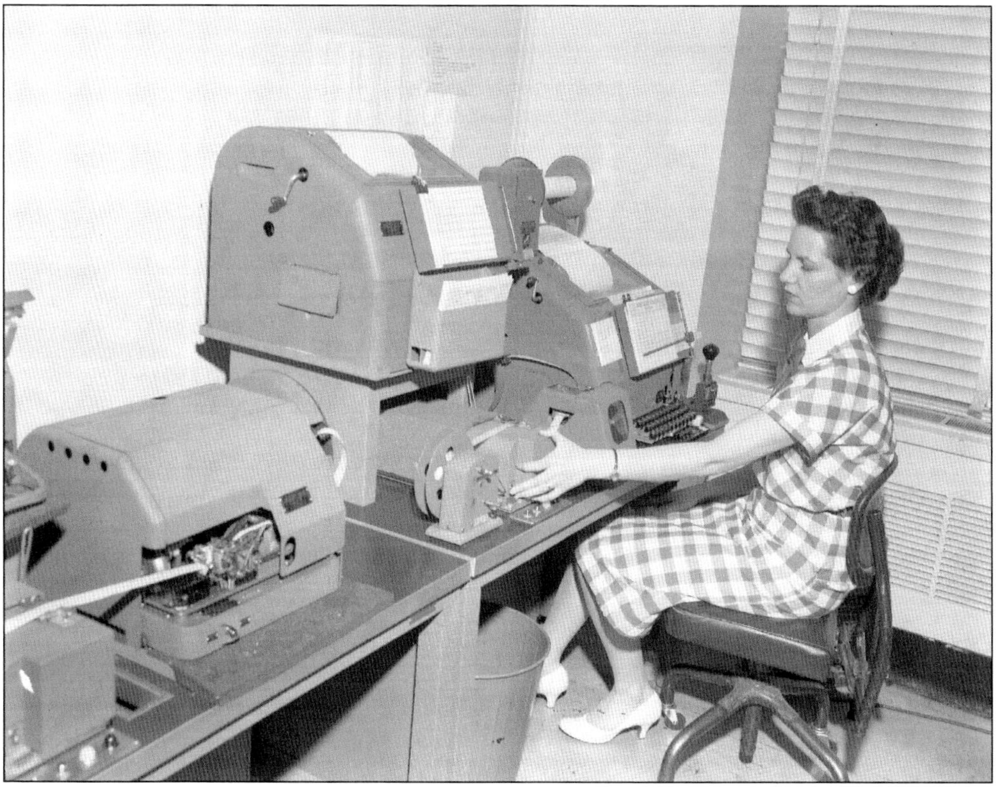

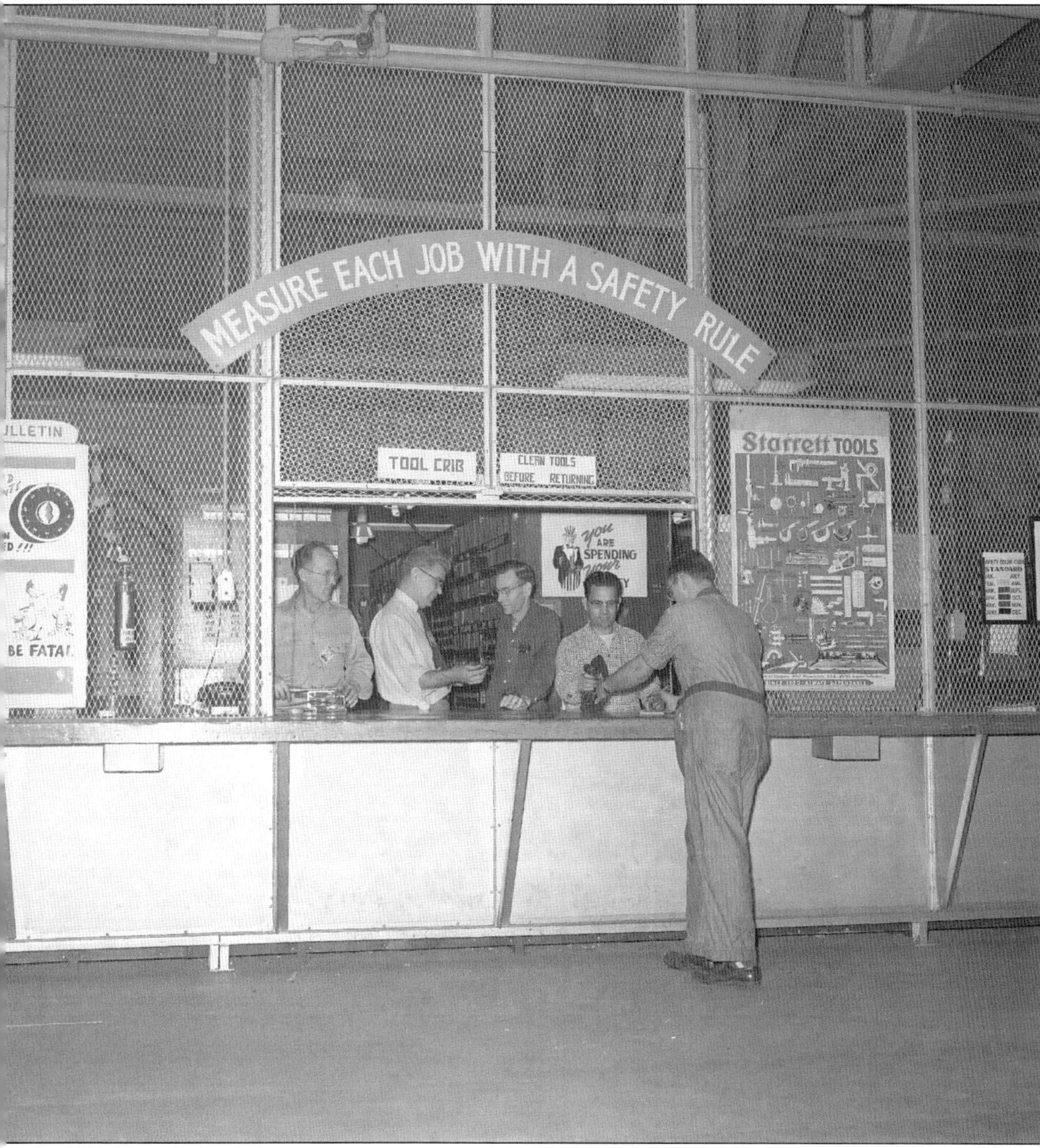

"Measure each job with a safety rule," read the sign above the tool crib in stores. Safety awareness united site workers, who collaborated to identify hazards and create a safe working plan before each project began. There also existed a standardized procedure for operating each machine or tool, typed plainly for workers to read and review. This ensured consistent quality and safety.

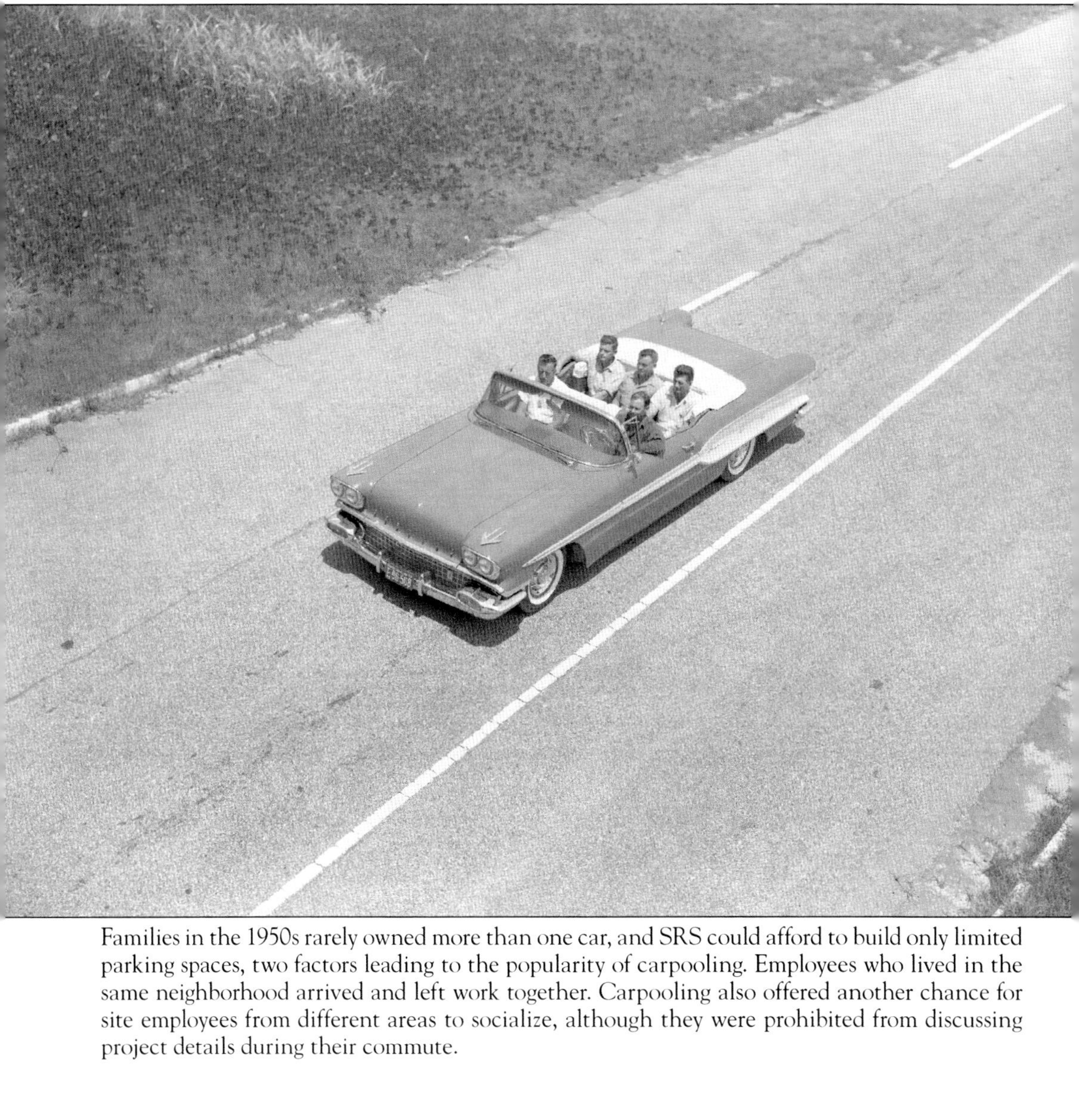

Families in the 1950s rarely owned more than one car, and SRS could afford to build only limited parking spaces, two factors leading to the popularity of carpooling. Employees who lived in the same neighborhood arrived and left work together. Carpooling also offered another chance for site employees from different areas to socialize, although they were prohibited from discussing project details during their commute.

Five

Lab and Innovation

Many of the improvements to the primary mission of Savannah River in making material for the nation's nuclear stockpile were made in the laboratories at SRP. The main laboratory, known as Savannah River Laboratory (SRL), and its associated research facilities had an indelible influence on the operational and technological history of the plant.

The history of science and innovation at SRL largely follows the mission history of the plant through time. These can be broken down into general periods of development. The first, from construction to the mid-1960s, concentrated on the production of plutonium and tritium, which includes both initiating and refining the production of these nuclear materials. During this time, the AEC asked scientists at SRP to begin research outside of the primary mission of the site. This includes the use of SRP reactors and laboratory facilities to produce plutonium-238 to power satellites and spacecraft for the US space program and test the feasibility of heavy water moderated and cooled power reactors resulting in the Heavy Water Components Test Reactor (HWCTR) in the early 1960s.

From 1964 until the late 1970s, SRL was primarily focused on the further streamlining of the main mission through new equipment, processes, and the use of computers. Other research not focused on the primary mission expanded in the 1960s and 1970s with the transplutonium program that produced many radioisotopes for scientific, industrial, and medical use. Finally, new missions introduced in the 1970s and 1980s slowly began to supplant the primary mission focus of SRL. These missions include environmental remediation and waste processing. The change in focus of the lab can be seen in a name change from Savannah River Laboratory to the Savannah River Technology Center in 1989. The laboratory became the Savannah River National Laboratory (SRNL) in 2004.

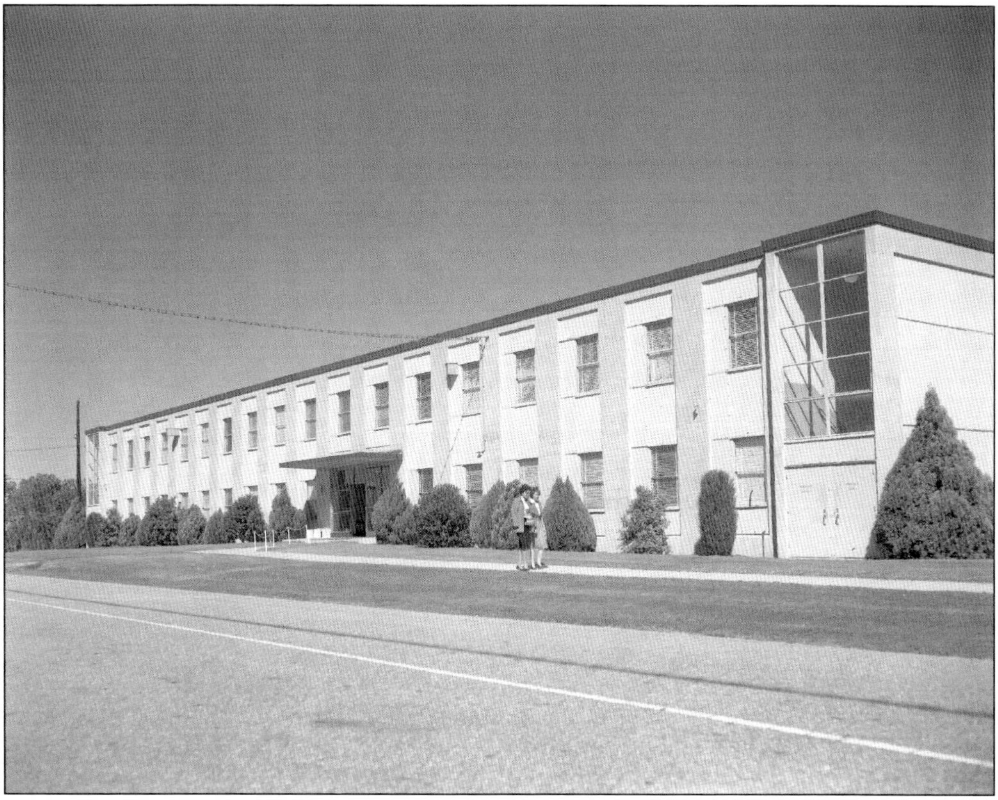

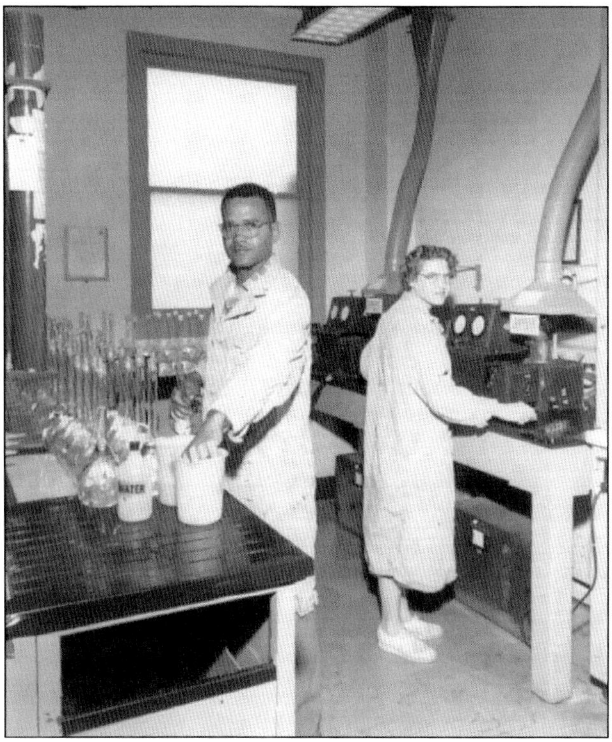

Scientists and researchers at SRL worked to improve the design and process of SRP operations beginning in the 1950s. This included the development of new technology, the improvement of facility processes, and the invention of better tools and equipment. The main laboratory building at SRP in A Area was the Cold War home of the SRL and housed many research laboratories and facilities to meet these goals.

The Savannah River National Lab's beginnings date back to the early 1950s. Along with the main lab, the laboratories section operated around 12 analytical control laboratories in production areas and had 12 research and development laboratories with SRL personnel working with the technical division.

In 1952, DuPont spent $52 million on innovative research at 40 laboratories in 26 locations across the country, including SRP. In this image from August 1, 1953, Virgil Birch uses a conductivity bridge to perform research and take measurements of the resistance and electrolytic conductivity of a solution.

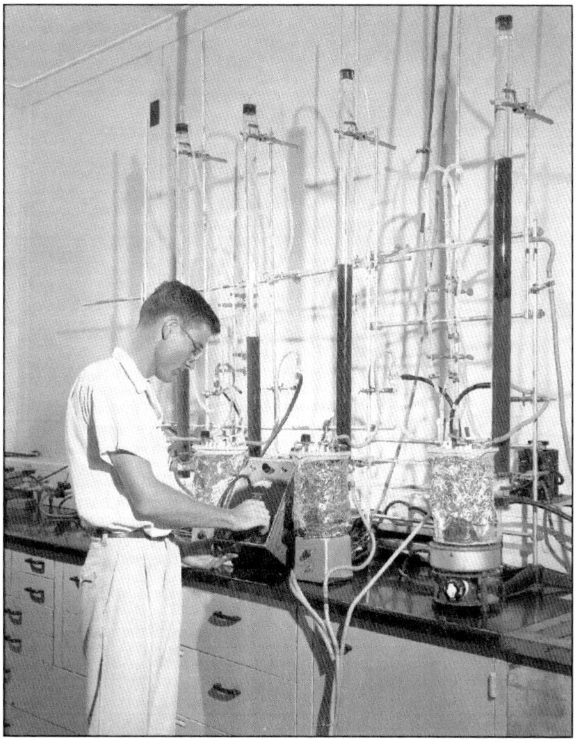

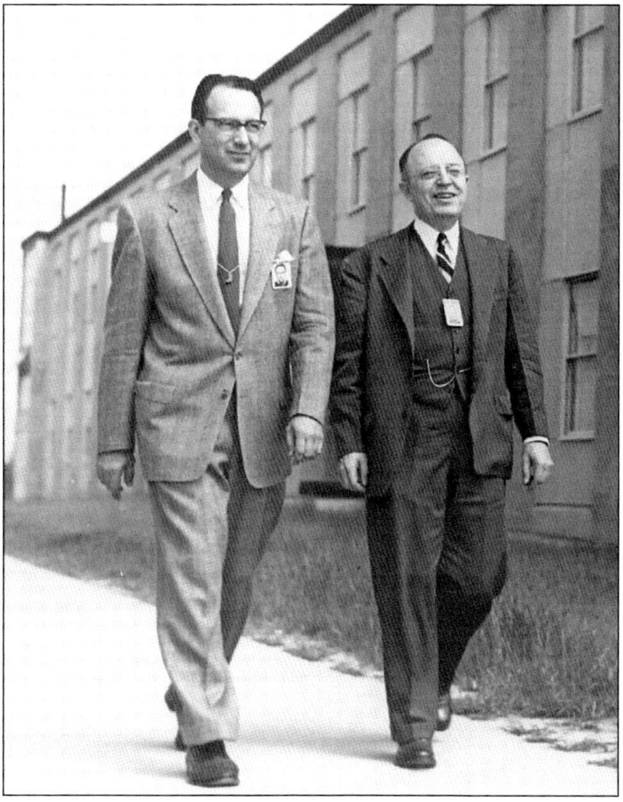

Dr. Milton Wahl (left) was the first director of the SRL, a position he held from 1952 to 1960. He was responsible for directing much of the early research that contributed to the successful and timely startup of radioactive operation at SRP. Here he is pictured outside of the main laboratory building with Dr. Hood Worthington (right), director of DuPont's technical division.

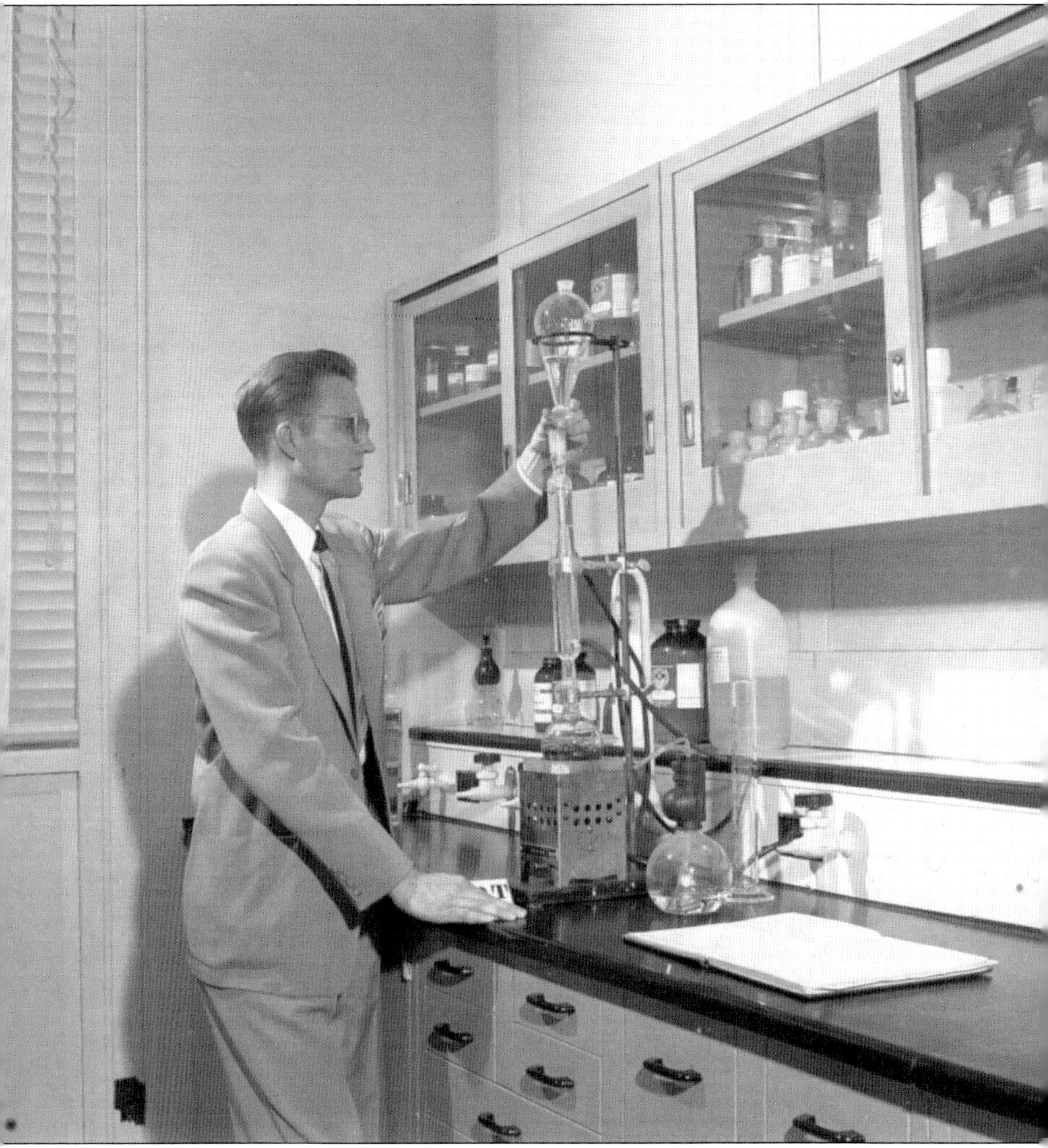

According to the April 1955 issue of the site newspaper, this works technical researcher is testing the carbon content of octyl alcohol to find methods by which to improve SRP's chemical processes. Each lab researcher was given a lab notebook to carefully document every step of his findings.

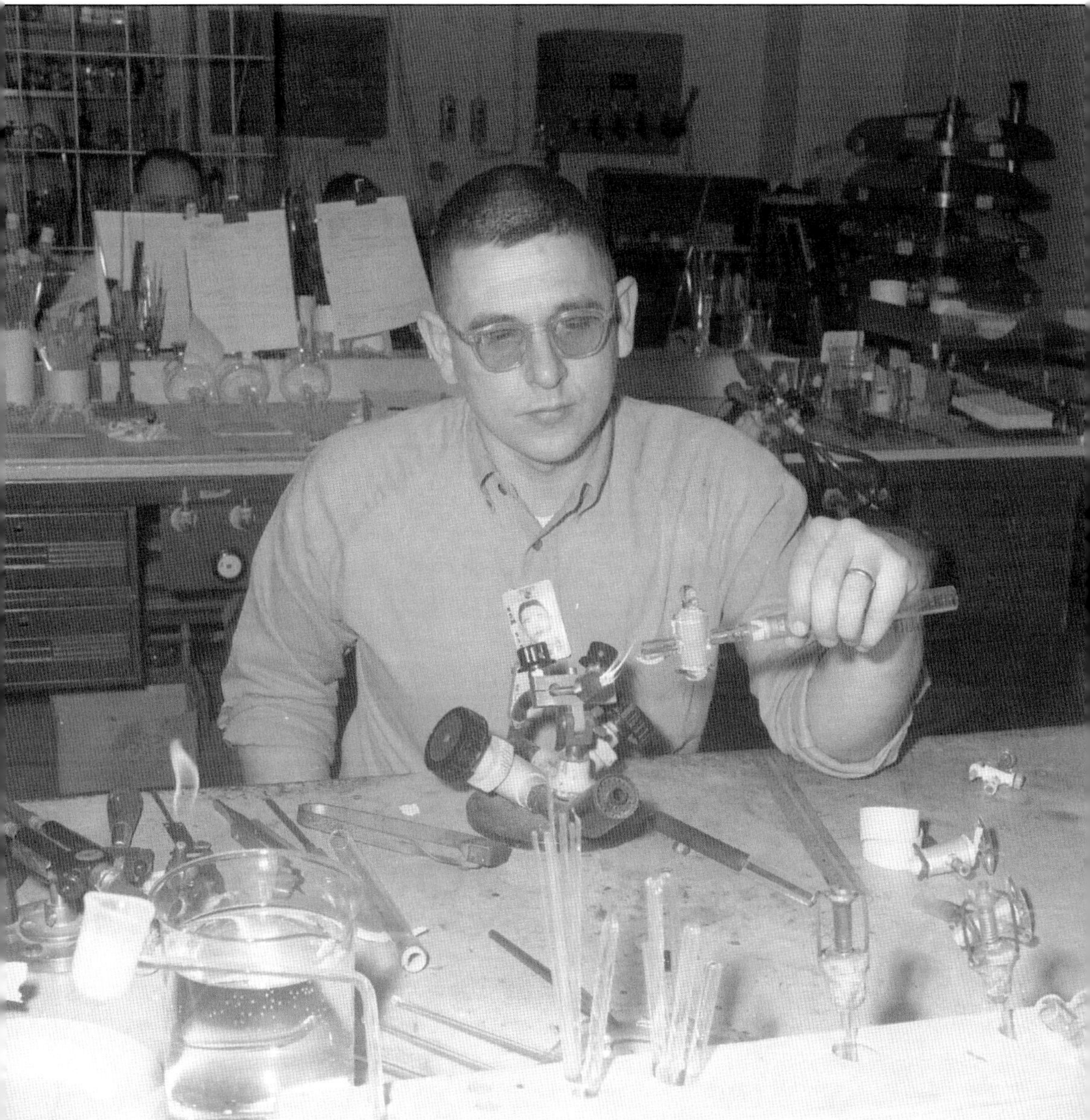

The glass shop, located in the basement of the main laboratory building, began manufacturing custom apparatuses for the plant and the Savannah River Lab's scientists in August 1953. These innovative pieces allowed SRP to quickly improve chemical processes and move forward. Today, scientific glassblowers still use their unique skills to design, fabricate, and repair glass models and mock-ups for the lab.

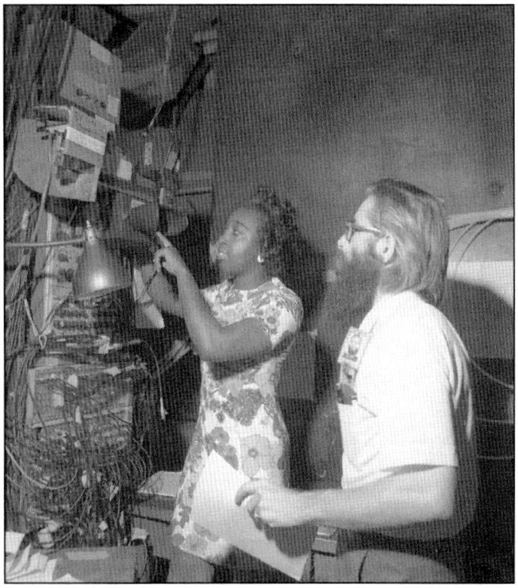

Dr. Henry Gurr, a neutrino physicist, and his assistant, Thomasina D. Godbee, worked on neutrino experiments at P Reactor. The neutrino, a subatomic particle, was discovered at P Reactor in 1956 by Doctors Reines and Cowan, a feat that later earned a 1995 Nobel Prize. Experiments on the elusive neutrino continued at the site in 1966 and lasted until the reactor's shutdown in 1988.

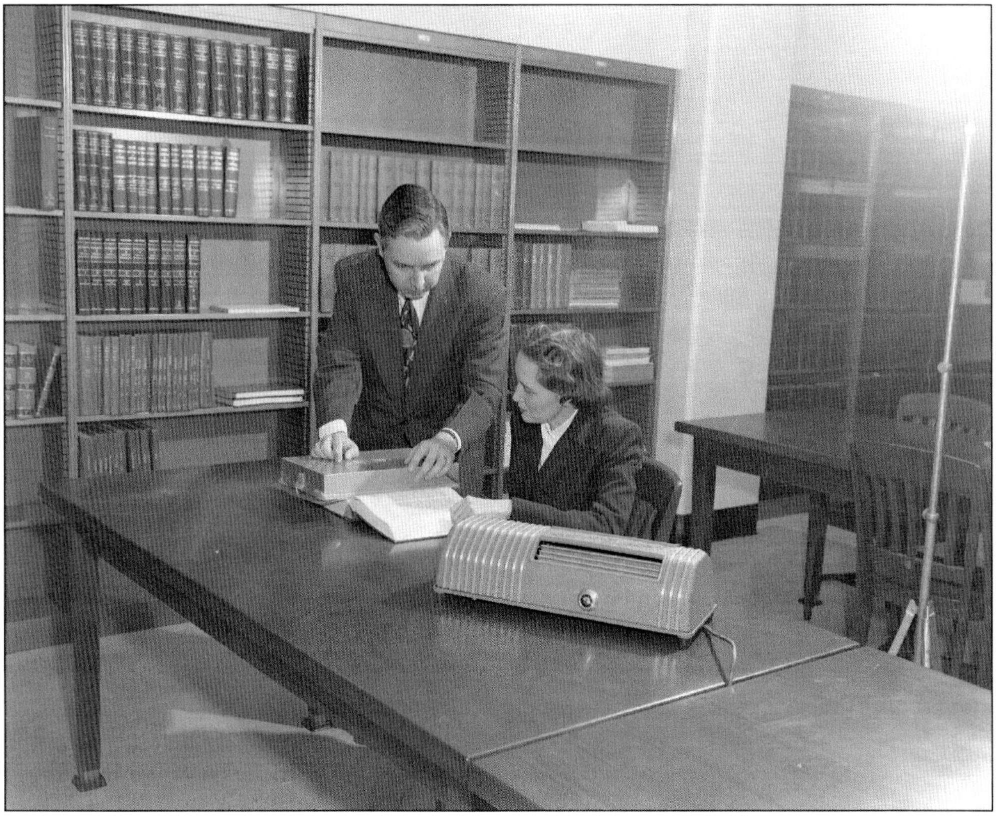

The Technical Information Service Library moved from its original location at the former Ellenton Baptist Church into the lab area, where the library is still located for SRS personnel today. In the early 1950s, the collection included about 18,000 volumes and 500 periodical subscriptions to assist engineers and scientists in staying connected to the most accurate scientific and technical information of the time.

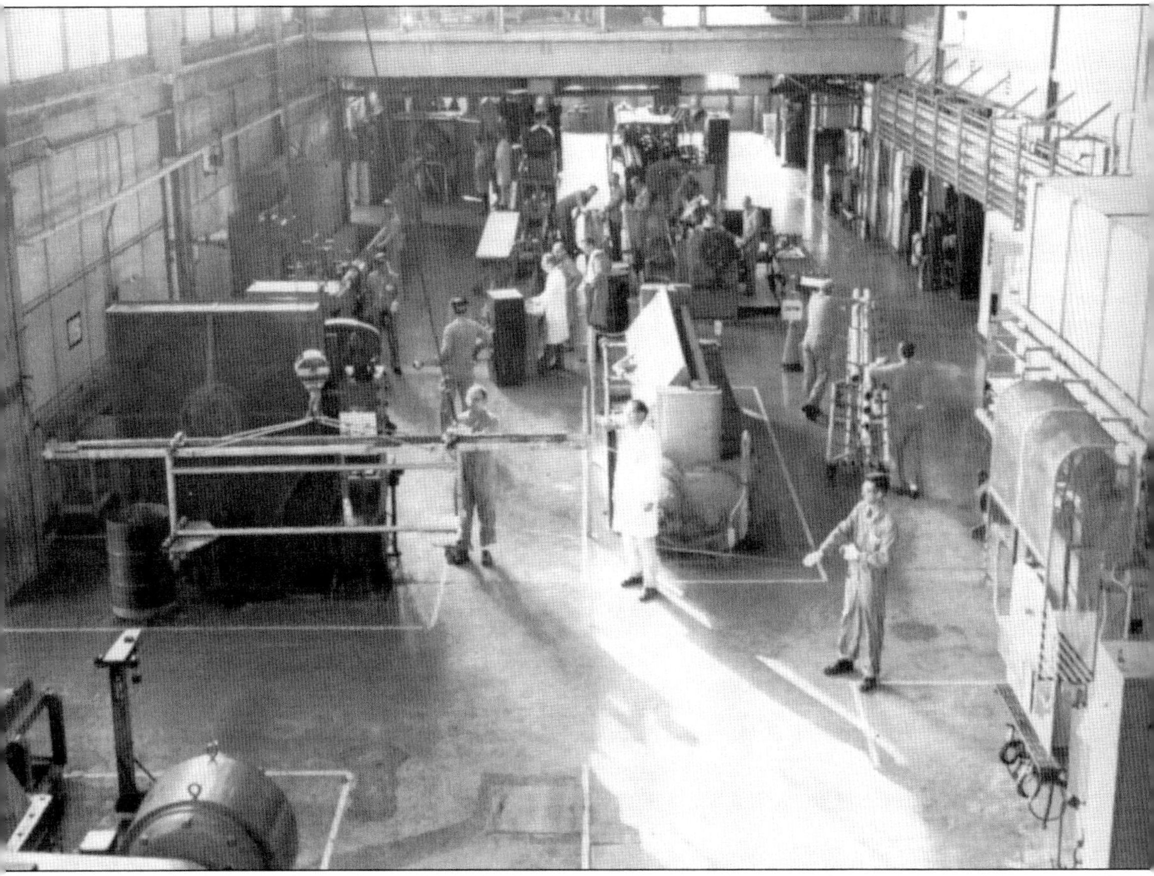

SRL scientists and engineers were constantly improving the shape and arrangement of the rods that fueled the heavy water moderated reactors at SRP. Known as fuel and target rods, the fabrication laboratory, or "Fab Lab," in the main laboratory building helped develop many different designs throughout the Cold War to increase efficiency and produce different nuclear materials. In the early 1950s, rods were solid pieces of metal known as slugs, which were limited in their product and performance. The Fab Lab developed some of the first variations of these slugs and over the years came up with many innovative design improvements. Each new design was given a number designation known as a mark to distinguish between the designs. Working in tandem with the manufacturing area, also known as M Area, by the early 1970s fuel and target assemblies had been standardized to produce a variety of nuclear material.

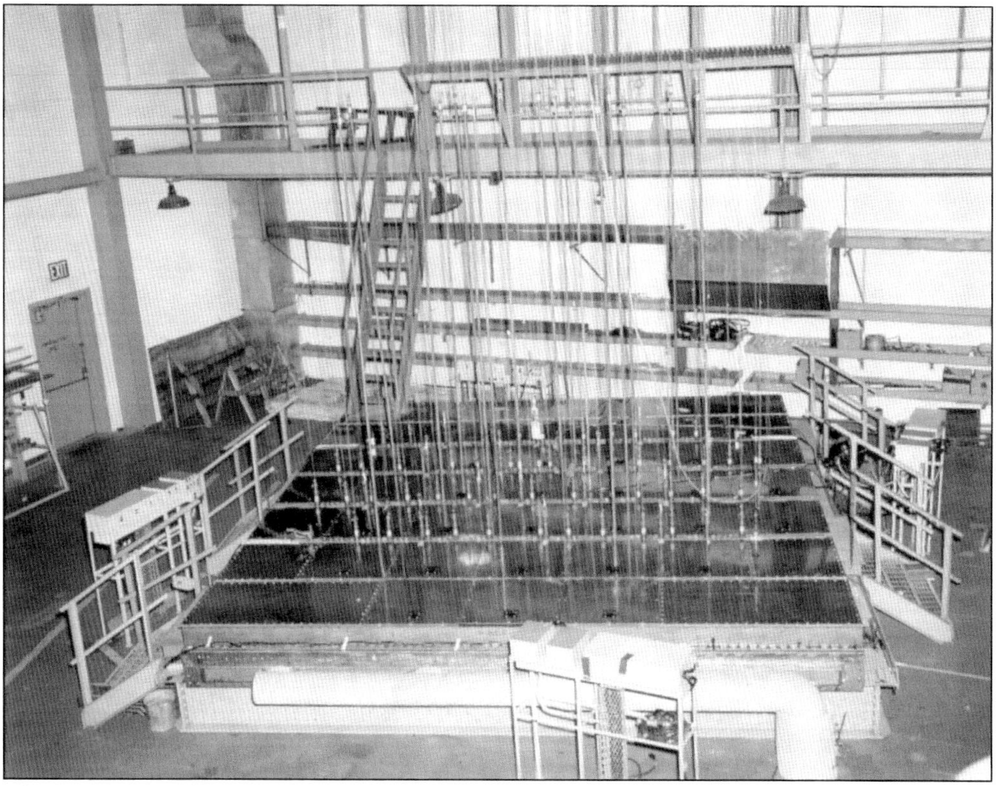

The Process Development Pile (PDP) was the centerpiece of reactor research during much of the Cold War. Located in building 777-M, this very low-power reactor was a full-scale mock-up of the production reactors. In the early years of reactor operations at SRP, it was instrumental in understanding the physics of large heavy water moderated reactors, something not well understood at the time. The PDP allowed researchers to set safe operational limits and test reactor setups before they went to the production reactors. The PDP was also instrumental in the development of the Heavy Water Components Test Reactor. The PDP was largely obsolete by the 1980s, replaced by advances in computer modeling technology developed by SRP scientists and engineers as well as the establishment of optimal reactor charges.

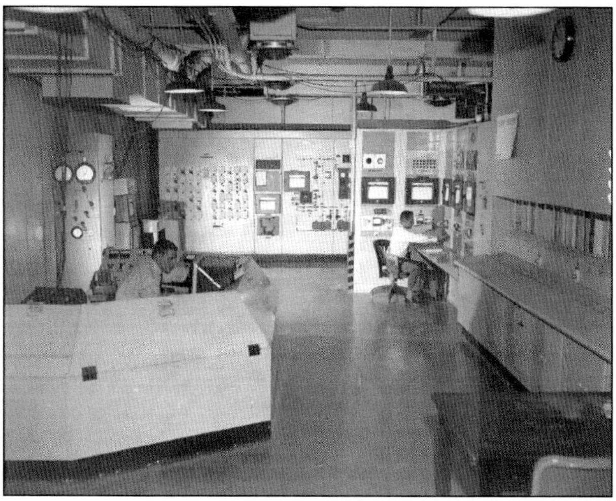

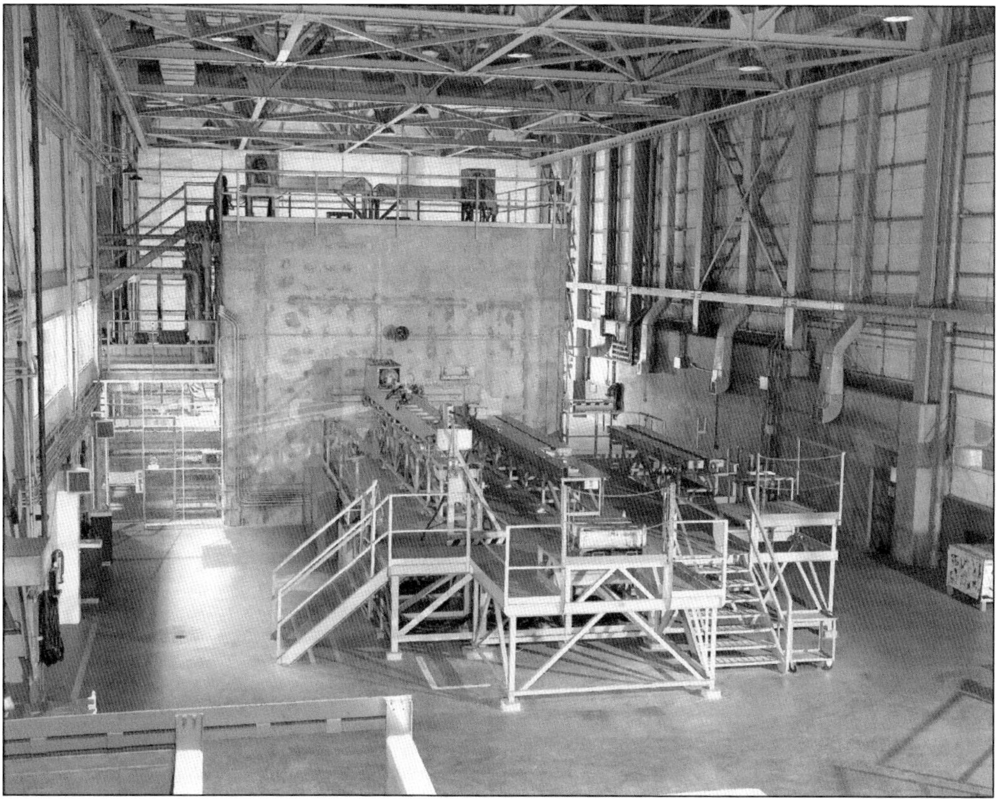

Although SRP's production reactors were heavy water moderated, a graphite test pile was built early during the construction project to test the slugs and control rods produced in M Area. Modeled after Hanford's test pile and made from graphite blocks machined at Hanford, 305-M was built in June 1951, and the test pile reached criticality in September 1952.

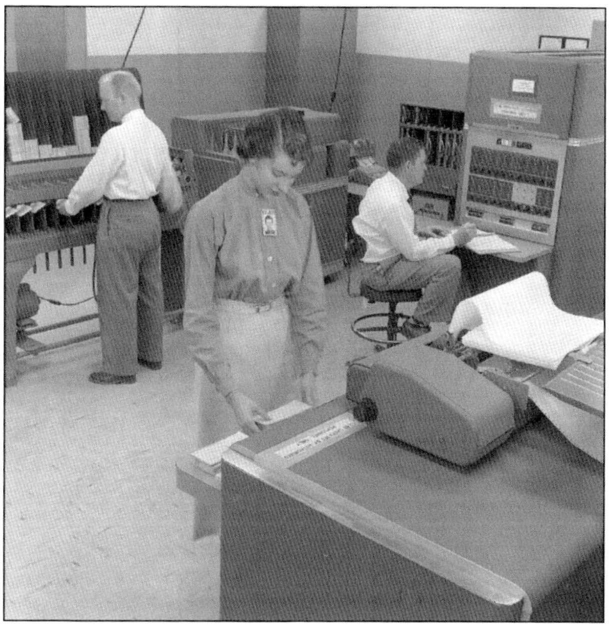

The IBM CPC, or Card Programmed Calculator (forefront), was the first in a long line of computers at SRP. It was used in some of the earliest scientific calculations for plant startup. Also shown here in 1956 was SRL's IBM 650 (back), the second of this model computer installed in the United States, which further expanded the speed and complexity capabilities of computing at SRL.

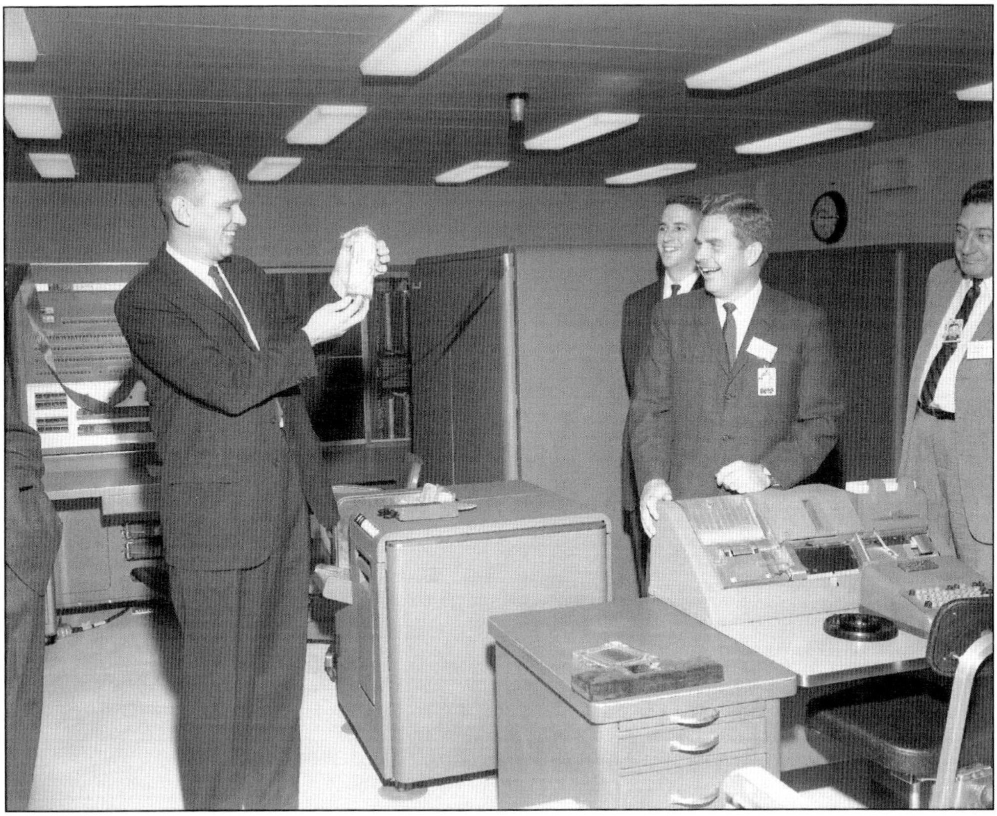

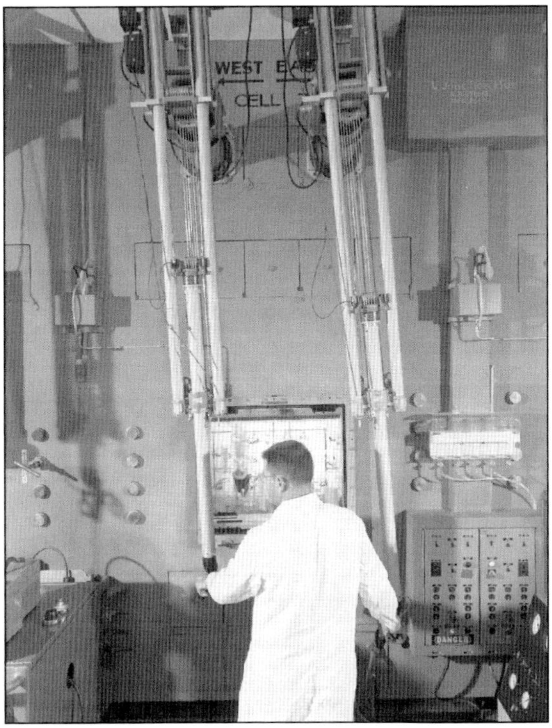

The installation of an IBM 704 computer in early 1962 was cause for celebration. It was 80 times more powerful than previous models at SRL. Computers like this and the IBM 360 installed in the late 1960s allowed the SRL to accurately model reactor behavior using the JOSHUA computer program. These advances in computer science led to the retirement of the PDP test reactor in the 1980s.

Savannah River Laboratory was the focus of separations sciences, metallurgical research and development, heat transfer studies, and radiation monitoring. Its "high-level caves" allowed chemical and metallurgical equipment studies on highly radioactive materials behind heavy shielding windows. The first high-level caves went into operation in December 1953. They have since been updated and expanded several times and continue to be used today.

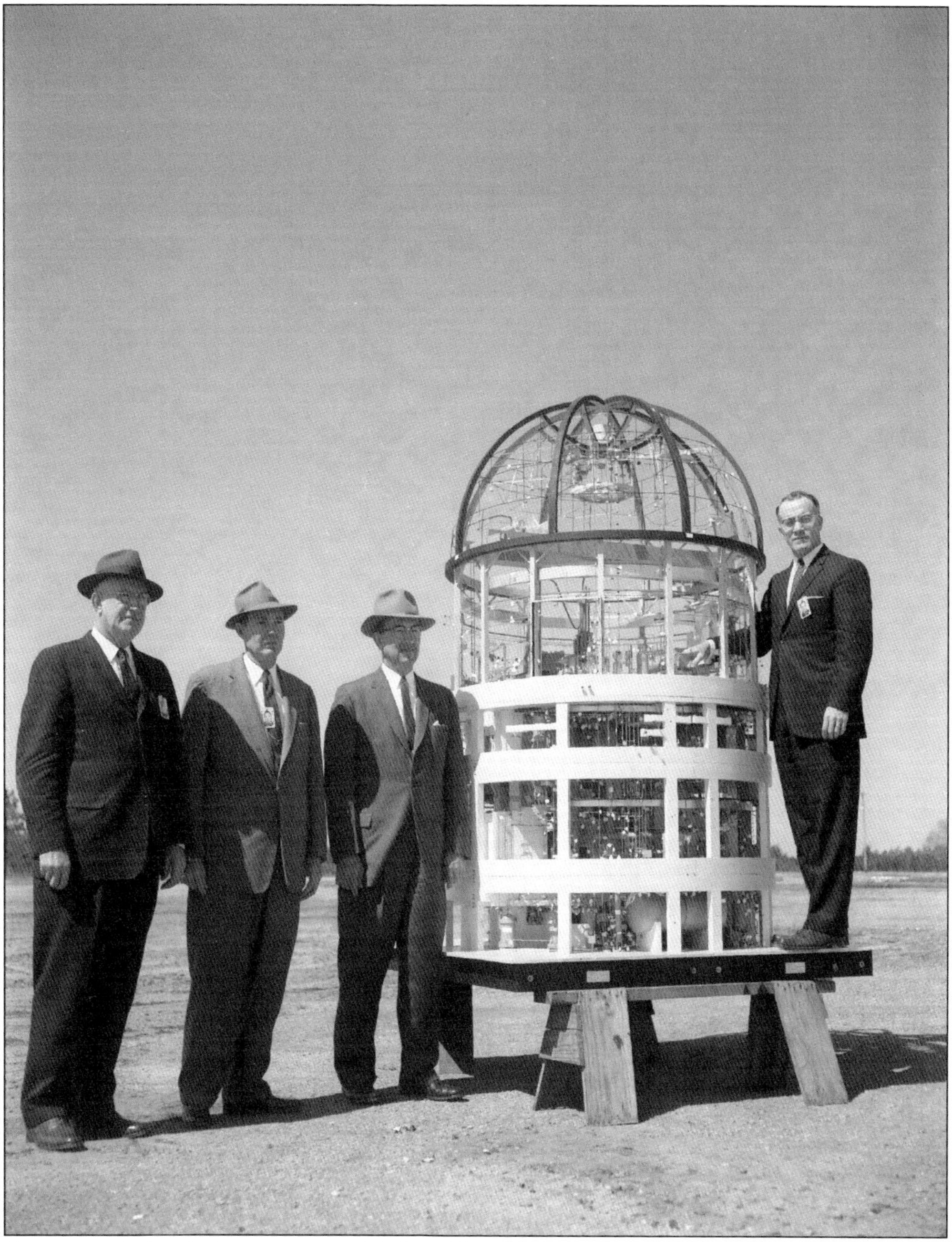

An extremely detailed miniature model of the Heavy Water Components Test Reactor is presented by a team of men. The model was created as a showpiece for the peaceful uses of atomic energy. The HWCTR was built on-site in the early 1960s when the Atomic Energy Commission was researching civilian power reactors. The model now resides in SRS Cold War Preservation Program's artifact collection on-site.

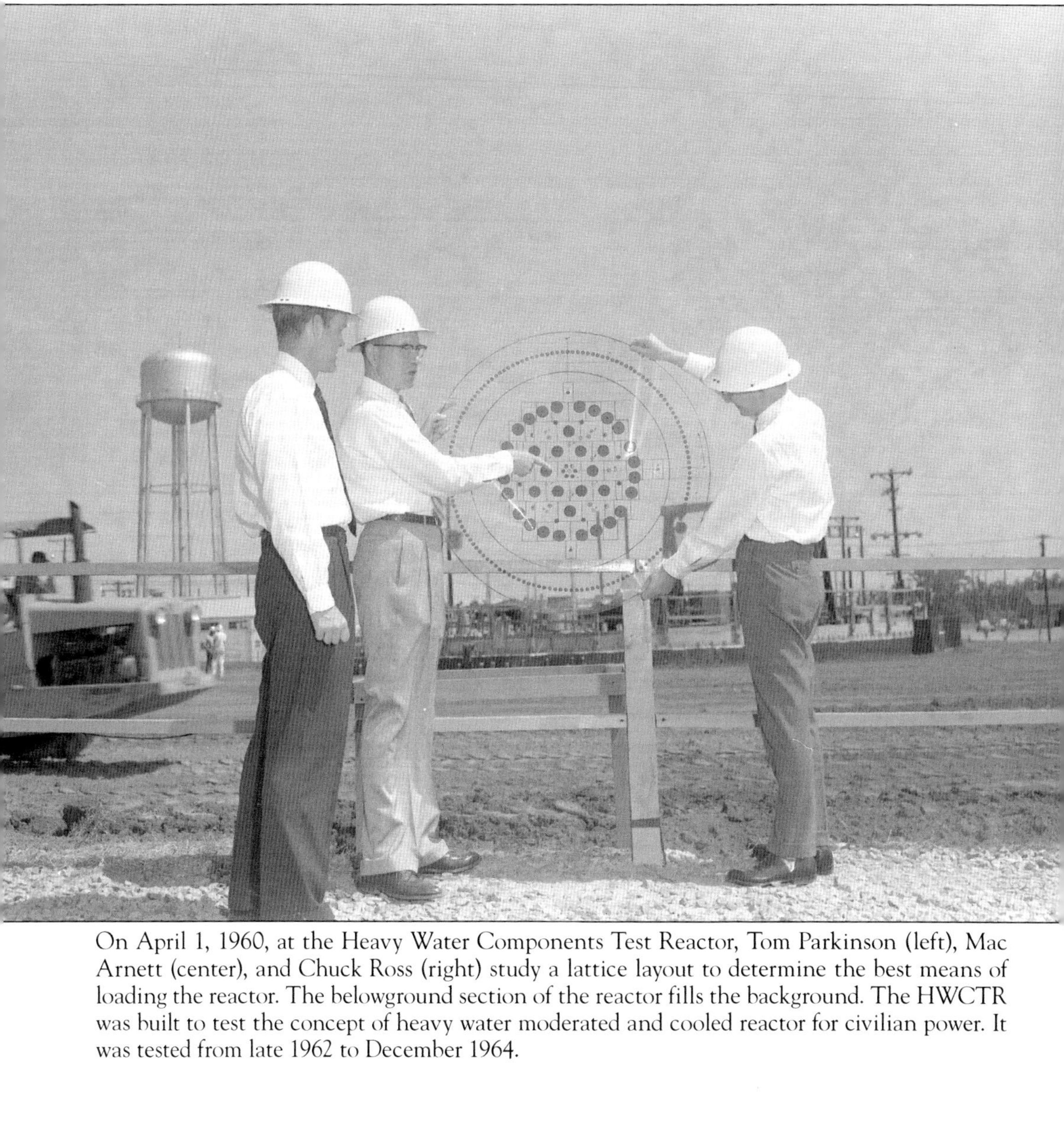

On April 1, 1960, at the Heavy Water Components Test Reactor, Tom Parkinson (left), Mac Arnett (center), and Chuck Ross (right) study a lattice layout to determine the best means of loading the reactor. The belowground section of the reactor fills the background. The HWCTR was built to test the concept of heavy water moderated and cooled reactor for civilian power. It was tested from late 1962 to December 1964.

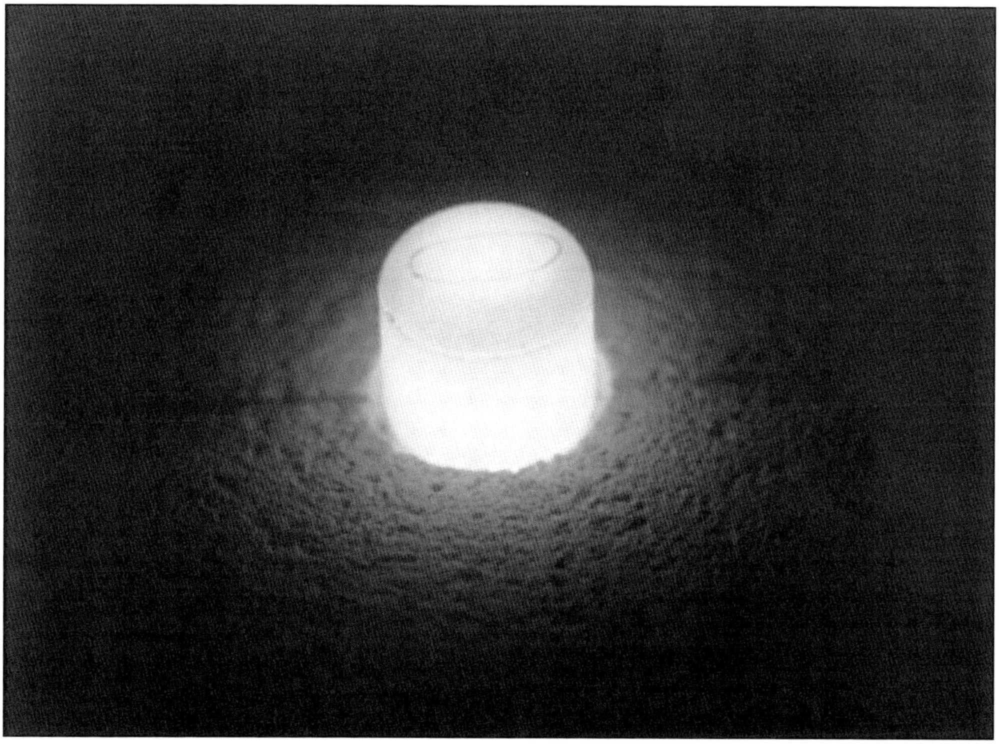

Plutonium-238, seen here glowing due to heat from radioactive decay, is used to power some spacecraft. First made at SRP in the late 1950s, production continued until 1986. Many NASA missions used SRP–made plutonium, including the Apollo missions to the moon and the deep space probes *Voyager I* and *II*, which are the first human-made objects to explore interstellar space beyond this solar system.

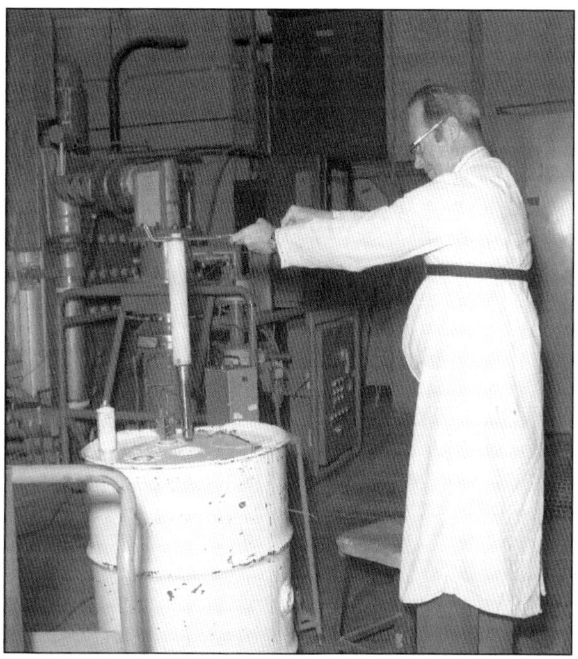

Californium-252 was one of many isotopes produced in SRP's trans-plutonium programs. It was processed through the Medical Source Facility in SRL's isotope process development laboratory to be used as a cancer treatment. Although never commercially available, plans were made for a small plastic tube containing thin seeds of Californium-252 that would be implanted directly into a patient's tumor.

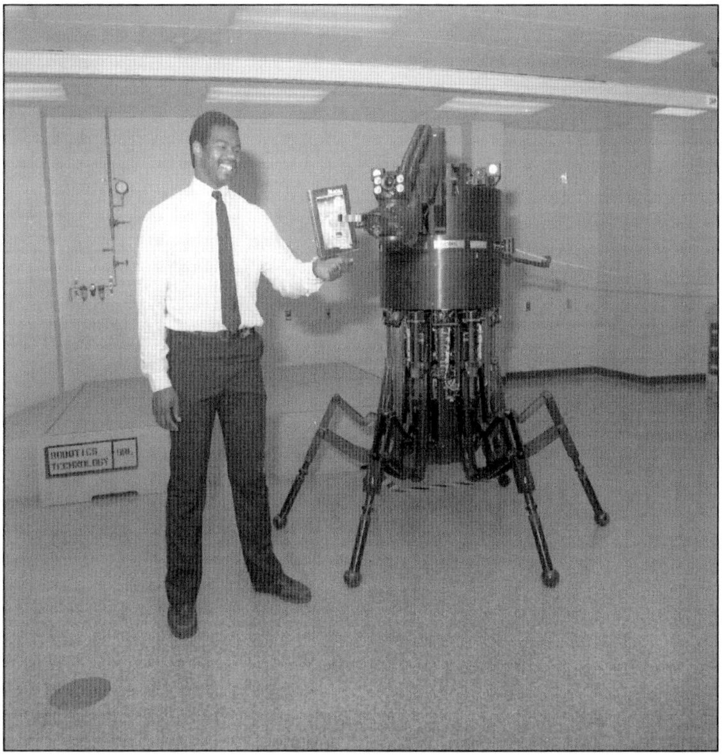

This robot, originally named ROBIN (robotic insect), walked on six robotic legs and used a manipulator arm to perform simple tasks. Scientists controlled ROBIN remotely with an ODEX control panel with three camera displays. In the 1990s, NASA borrowed ROBIN to aid in its own robotics research, and when it returned the robot to SRS, it had renamed it CHARLOTTE after the famed spider.

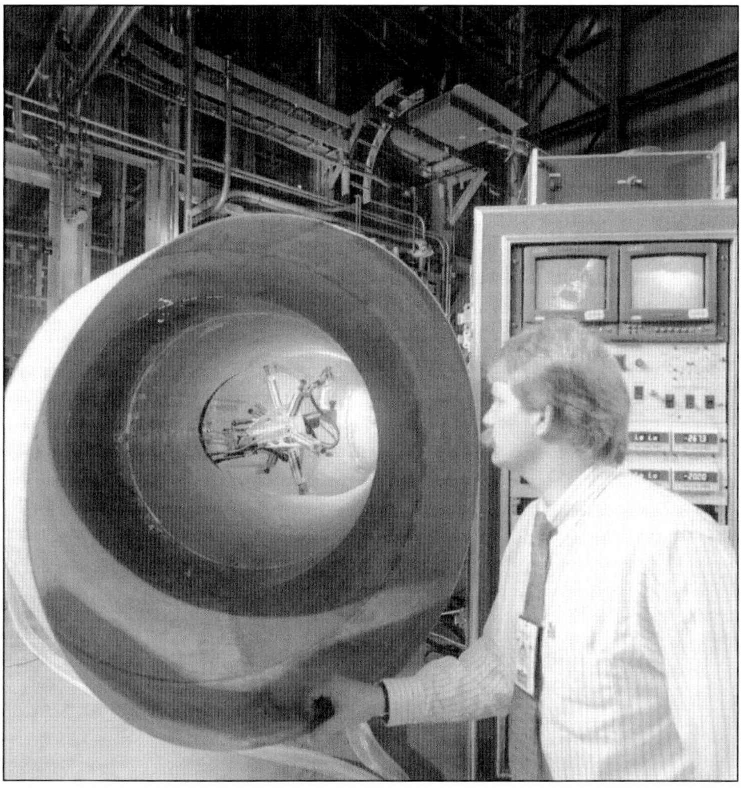

A scientist demonstrates a robotic pipe crawler in action, developed by the laboratory to traverse hard-to-reach areas inside pipes. Different versions of the pipe crawler have been developed and allow scientists to perform inspections and maintenance in underground or inaccessible pipes.

During a tour of the Savannah River Technology Center in 1992, students learned about the Robotics Laboratory, where robots are designed and evaluated to determine how best to withstand radiation. The advent of robotics allows radiation workers to spend less time in irradiated work areas because robots, with special shielding from radiation, could perform the work instead.

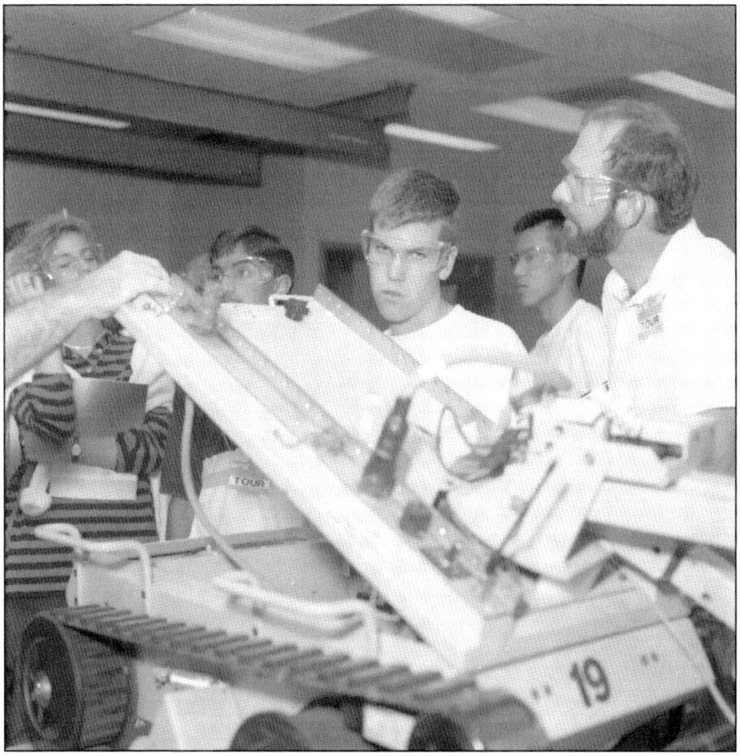

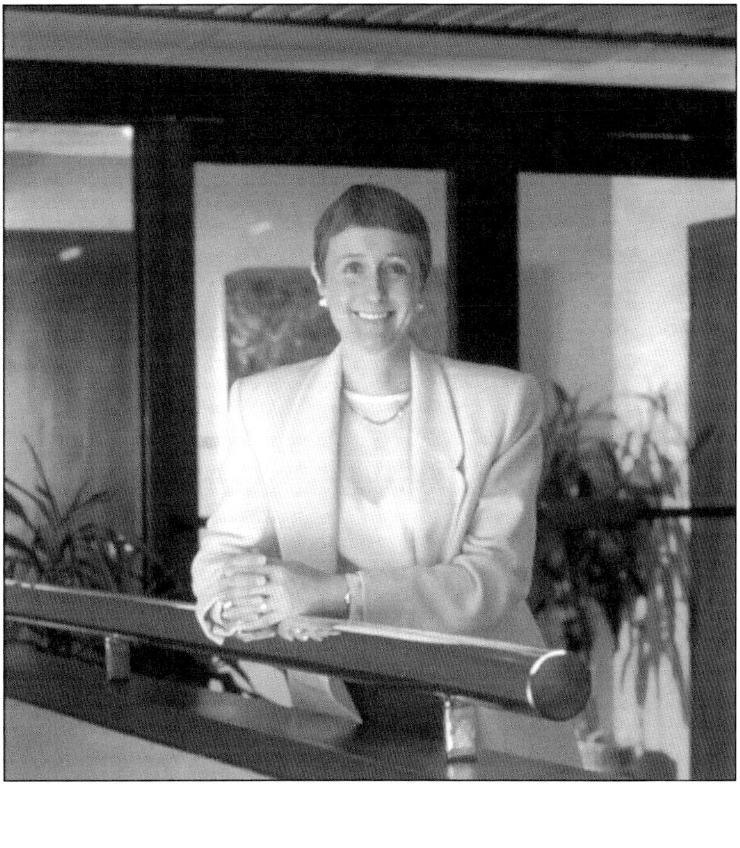

In 1994, Dr. Susan Wood became the first female director of the Savannah River National Laboratory, known as Savannah River Technology Center before receiving the national distinction. Dr. Wood earned her doctorate in materials engineering from the University of Pittsburgh, holds patents in materials engineering, and performed extensive work in advanced analytical techniques.

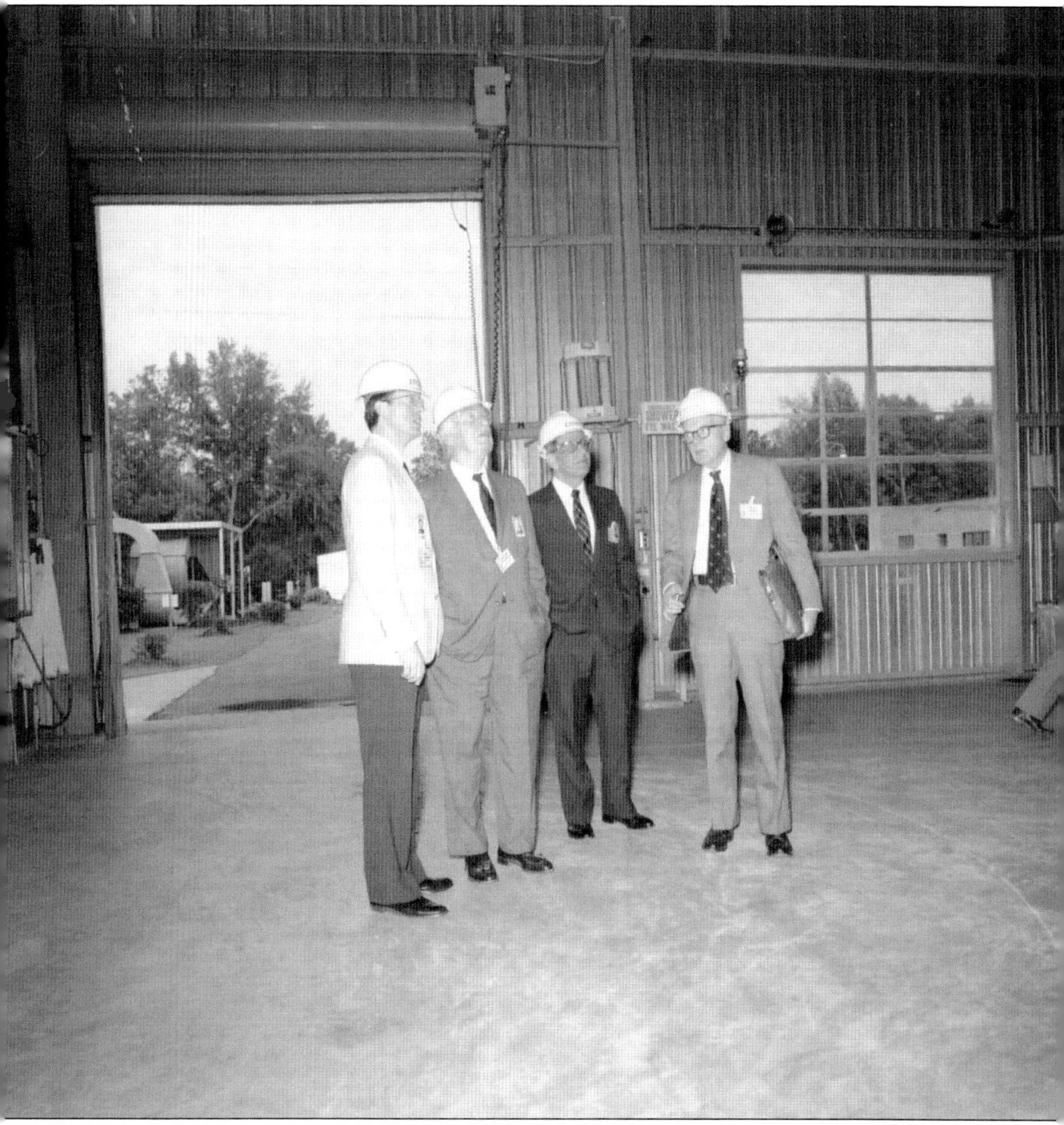

During the groundbreaking event for the Defense Waste Processing Facility (DWPF) on November 8, 1983, more than 500 guests gathered to celebrate the achievement. The culmination of years of research, the event included a ceremony and, for some, including Crawford Greenwalt (second from left) and Frank Kreusi (far right) and two others, a private tour of the pilot facility. DWPF was SRP's answer to the problem of high-level radioactive waste that was a byproduct of the production of plutonium-238 and tritium for military use. Before DWPF, this waste was stored in several large underground carbon steel tanks, which had the potential to leak. SRL developed an innovative process that involved the immobilization of this waste in borosilicate glass. Known as vitrification, this process involves heating both the glass and waste to high temperatures and then solidifying them in large stainless steel canisters. The radioactive startup of the DWPF was in March 1996.

Six

Stewardship

Stewardship of the site began at its inception. Massive amounts of construction materials were used to create the Savannah River Plant. The statistics are staggering, attesting to the large-scale nature of the undertaking. The construction activity, however, was confined to an industrial core area, leaving a large buffer zone of land untouched. In this zone, an equally grand undertaking mostly orchestrated by nature occurred. The retirement of thousands of acres from cultivation, the impact of grading from construction, and human neglect factored into the making of a new landscape.

The US Forest Service (USFS), under contract with the AEC for land management services for areas outside of operations, set out about 10 million pine seedlings along the plant perimeter for screening and erosion control in 1952–1953 and then launched a plant forest management program that continues successfully today.

The AEC invited scientists from the Universities of Georgia and South Carolina to collect baseline data on plant and animal communities that would provide a "before" picture with which to measure the impact of the plant's processes on the environment. The University of Georgia went on to develop a program that operates today as the Savannah River Ecology Laboratory. UGA's Dr. Eugene Odum's large-scale study of ecological succession charting change as centuries of agricultural cultivation disappeared and natural succession occurred was groundbreaking in the developing world of modern ecology. DuPont was responsible for bringing a team from the Academy of Natural Sciences in Philadelphia under the leadership of Dr. Ruth Patrick to perform a biological study of the Savannah River. A third landmark initiative was the study of natural local radioactivity conducted by the plant's incipient health physics group conducted in 1951.

The 1980s would bring the South Carolina Institute for Archaeology and Anthropology's Savannah River Archaeological Research Program to the site to manage its rich cultural heritage. The same decade would bring environmental cleanup to the fore as the plant's missions changed.

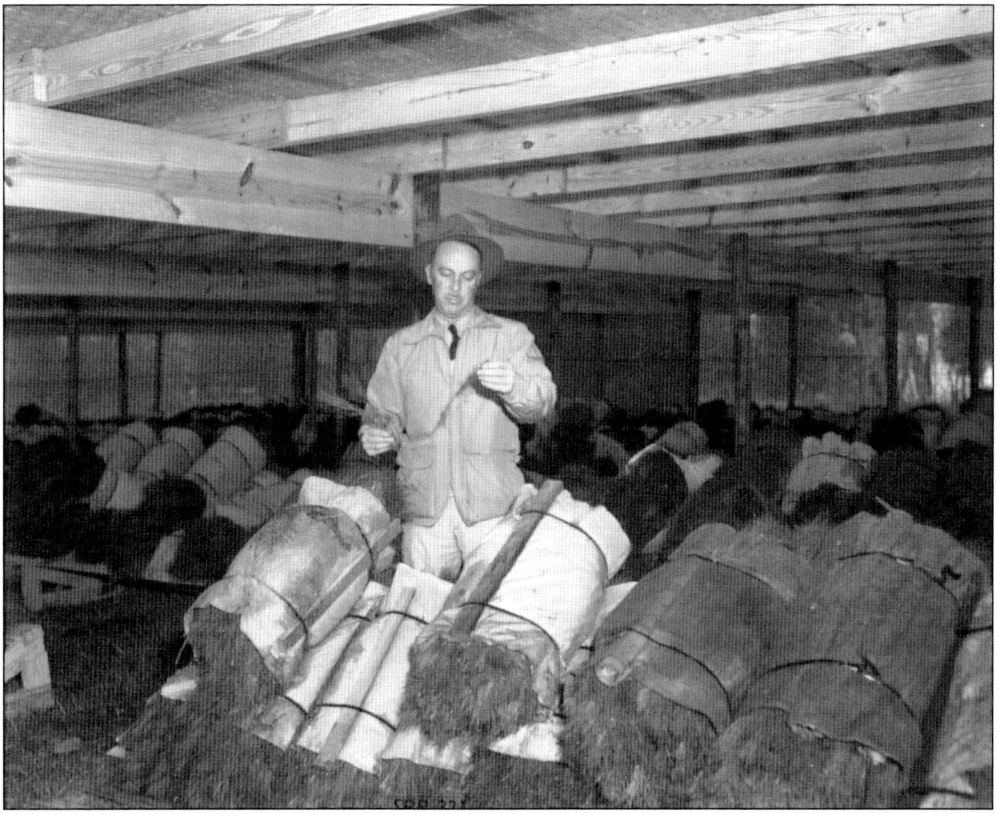

As early as August 1951, the US Forest Service provided land management for the land not being used for operations, initially nearly 67 percent of the site. Their first contract required planning about 10 million one-foot longleaf pine seedlings on 30,000 acres to provide a visual buffer. In this photograph, SRP forester John Hatcher checks out the quality of the seedlings to be planted.

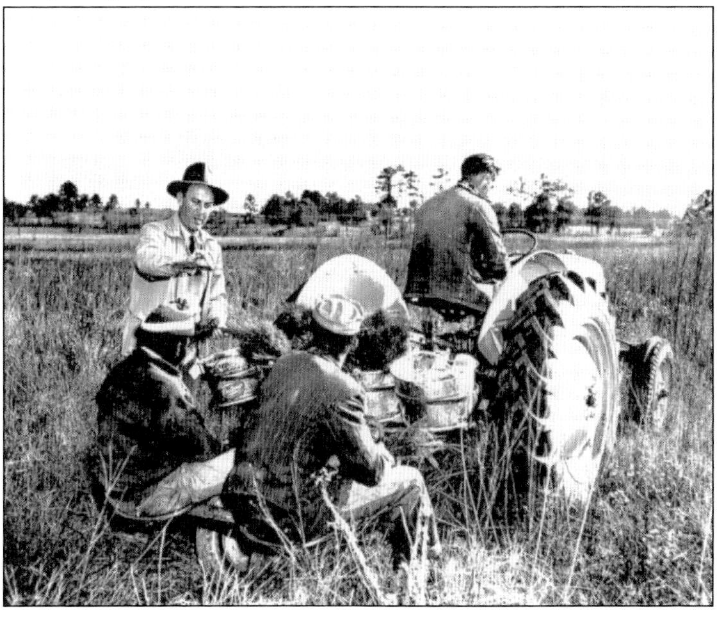

In 1953, the US Forest Service specially outfitted a tractor with a two-seated attachment and galvanized seedling bin. In this photograph, forester John Hatcher (left) trained men to ride on the attachment, working together to plant pine seedlings, while another group of men worked ahead of the tractor to dig holes—an efficient, mechanized system.

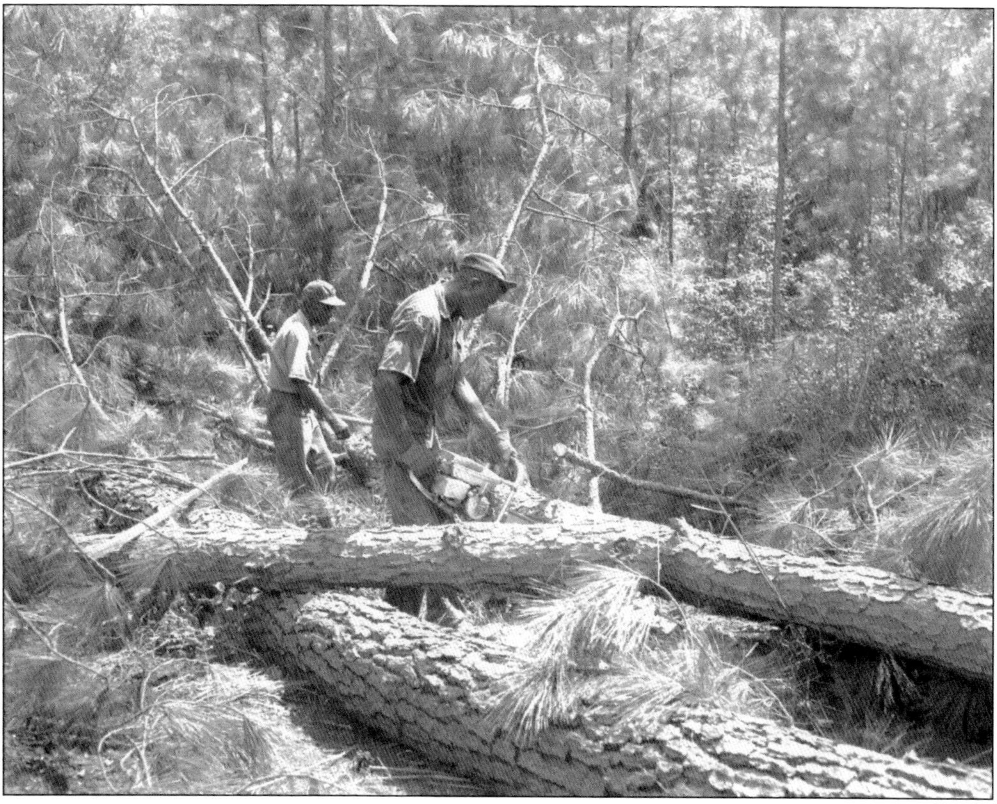

From 1951 to the present, the US Forest Service has worked at SRP to provide timber and pulpwood government sales. While pine trees have primarily produced revenue from tree products, the sale of pine straw has also been reinvested into the infrastructure development, restoration, and management of natural resources.

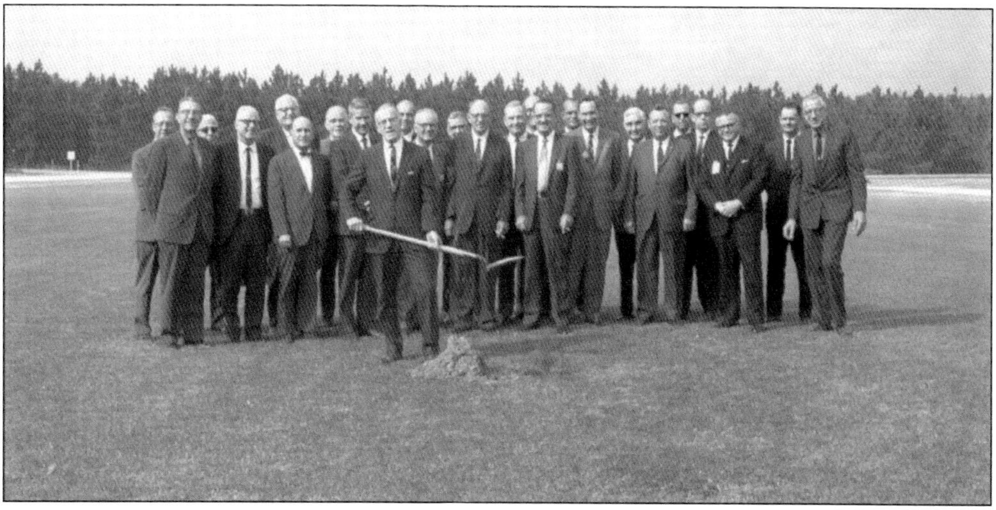

In November 1968, the US Forest Service Savannah River forestry program planted its 100 millionth pine tree. By 1968, the program had matured for 16 years and provided a $26 million asset to the government. Every year since this milestone celebration, nearly a million seedlings have been planted on-site.

Pictured is forester John Hatcher surveying the results of the 1953 planting 10 years later. This area was known as the "pine plantation." When Hatcher took over the direction of the program, he sought to plant pines on an additional 60,000 acres. In the first two years of his tenure, his team planted 26.5 million pines and then 10 million pines every year until 1960. These longleaf

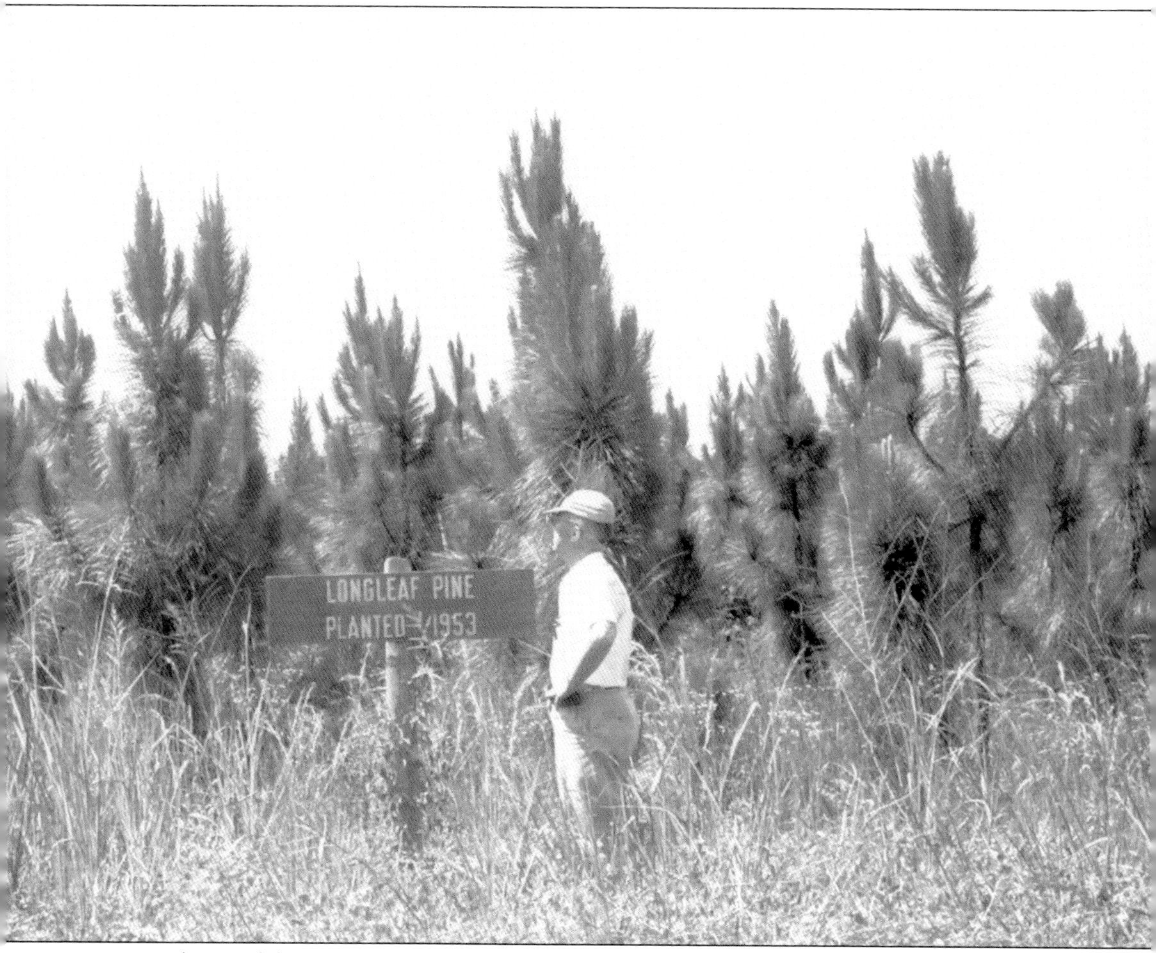

pines served several functions; in an era during which spies were more likely to operate on foot than fly over the area in a plane, these pines blocked the view from the boundaries of the site. The pines also helped prevent erosion, dust, and overgrowth of weeds.

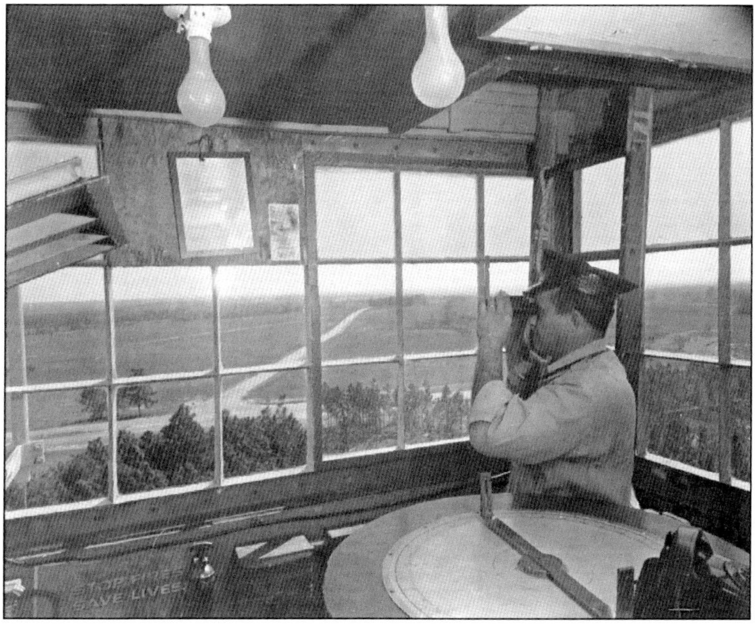

From a lookout tower 85 feet tall, Bill Jowers searches for warning wisps of smoke. Fire Protection employees were on guard day and night during the dangerous dry seasons to protect the 200,000 acres of SRP. In the bottom left of the image, the phrase "Stop Fires Save Lives" can be seen printed on the wooden inside of the tower.

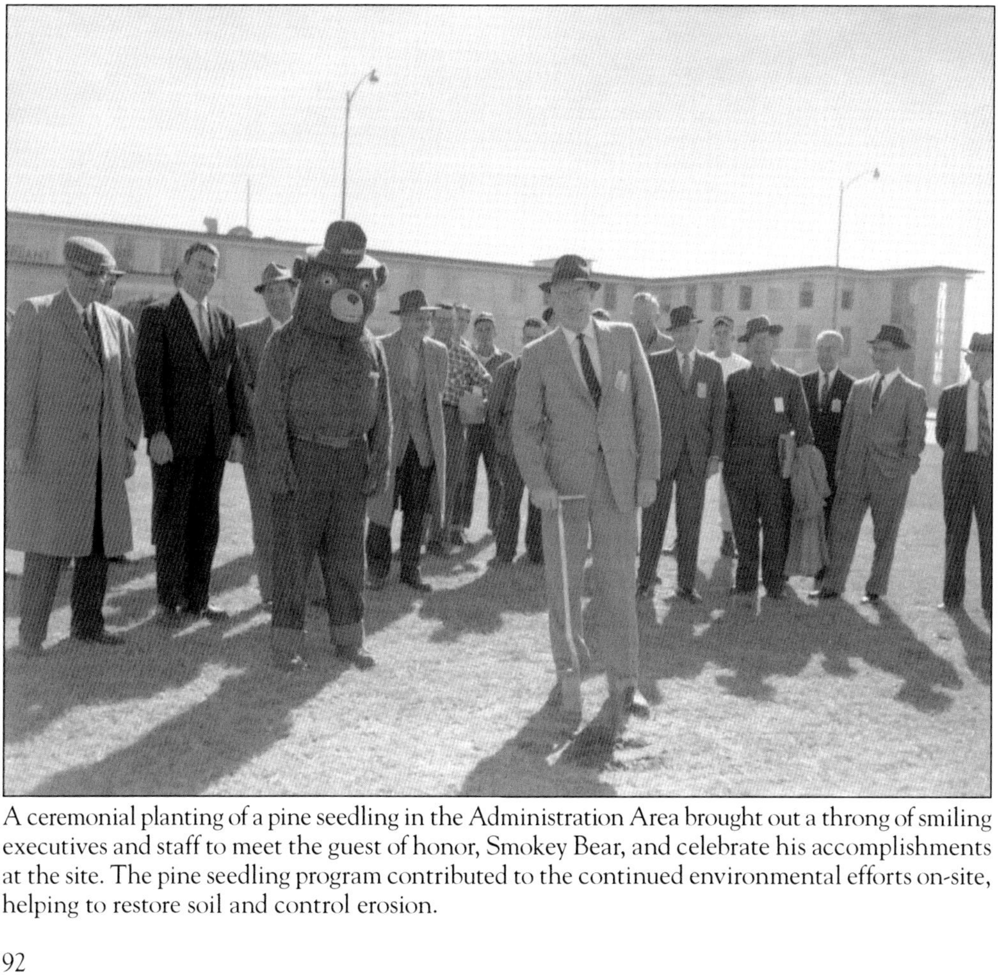

A ceremonial planting of a pine seedling in the Administration Area brought out a throng of smiling executives and staff to meet the guest of honor, Smokey Bear, and celebrate his accomplishments at the site. The pine seedling program contributed to the continued environmental efforts on-site, helping to restore soil and control erosion.

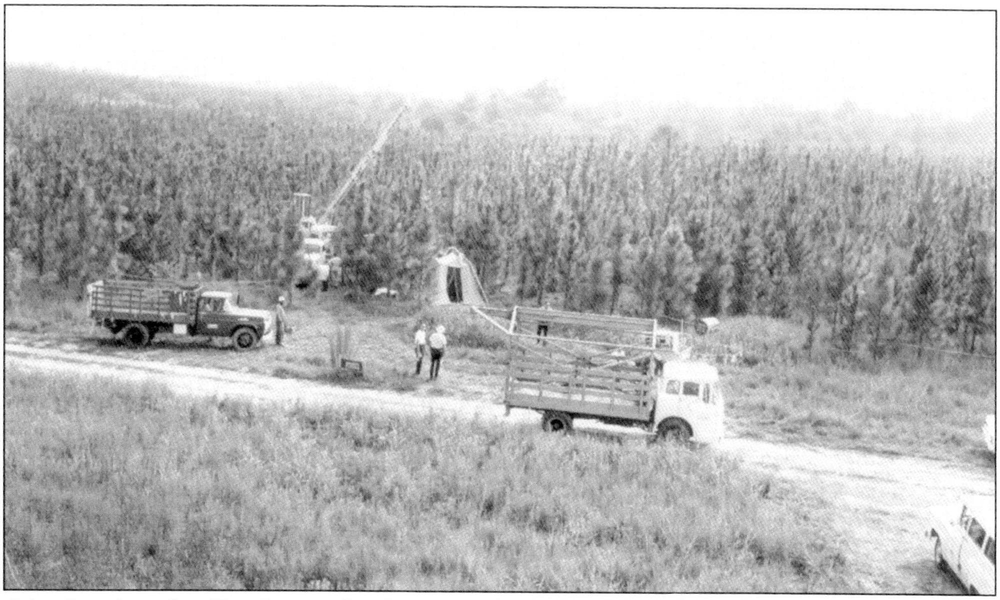

A landmark study of local natural radioactivity began in 1951 and ended in 1953. The site survey group, led by Bill Reining, established a series of monitoring stations over a 1,500-square-mile radius. Although these kinds of radioecological surveys are required now for nuclear facilities, such a survey was unprecedented in the 1950s. Pictured is the environmental monitoring station in the state park outside site boundaries in Jackson, South Carolina.

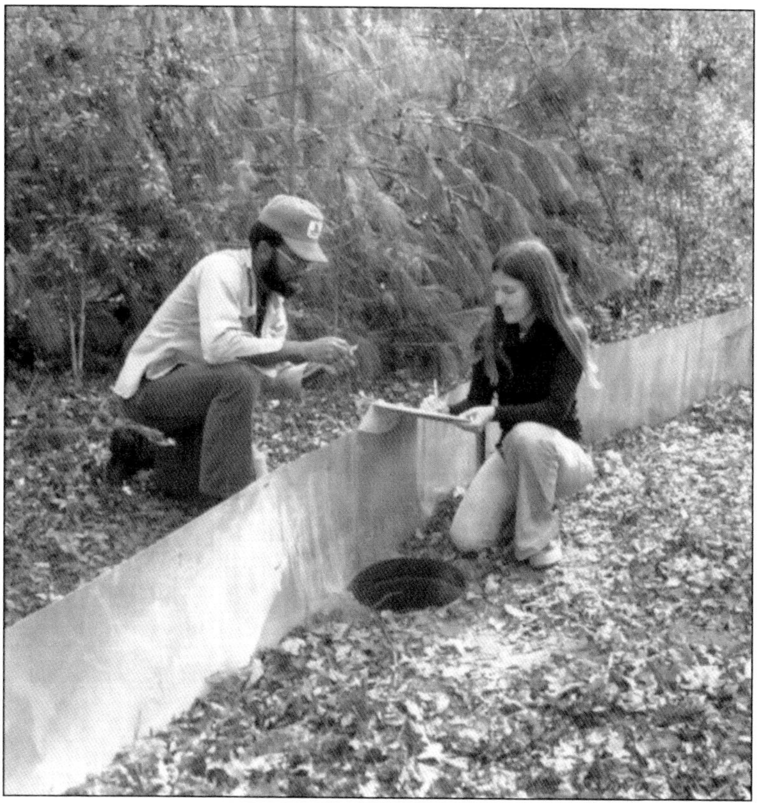

The site survey group, in addition to testing radioactivity in natural habitats, also tested the natural radiation of crops left behind by former residents. They even tested the open wells, pictured here, to determine a baseline for radiation in pre-site sources of water. While some of these wells were left open for future testing, others were filled in and disused.

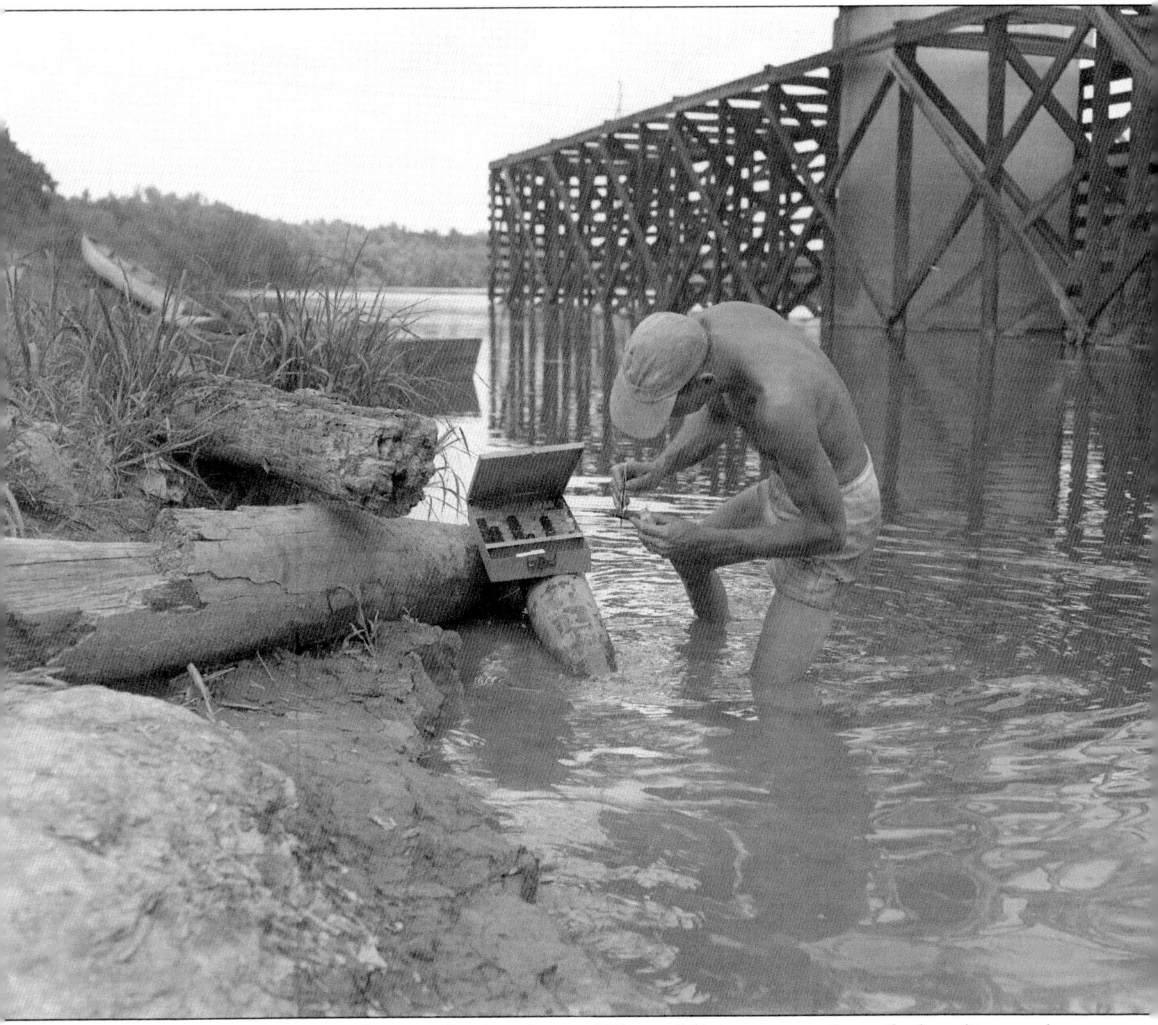

Before reactor operations began, the Academy of Natural Sciences conducted a baseline study on Savannah River's biological diversity as well as determining the quality of the natural environment and average river water temperatures. Researchers also studied pollution levels on a plant-by-plant basis. This established baseline would allow future researchers a point of reference as the environment changed due to plant operations.

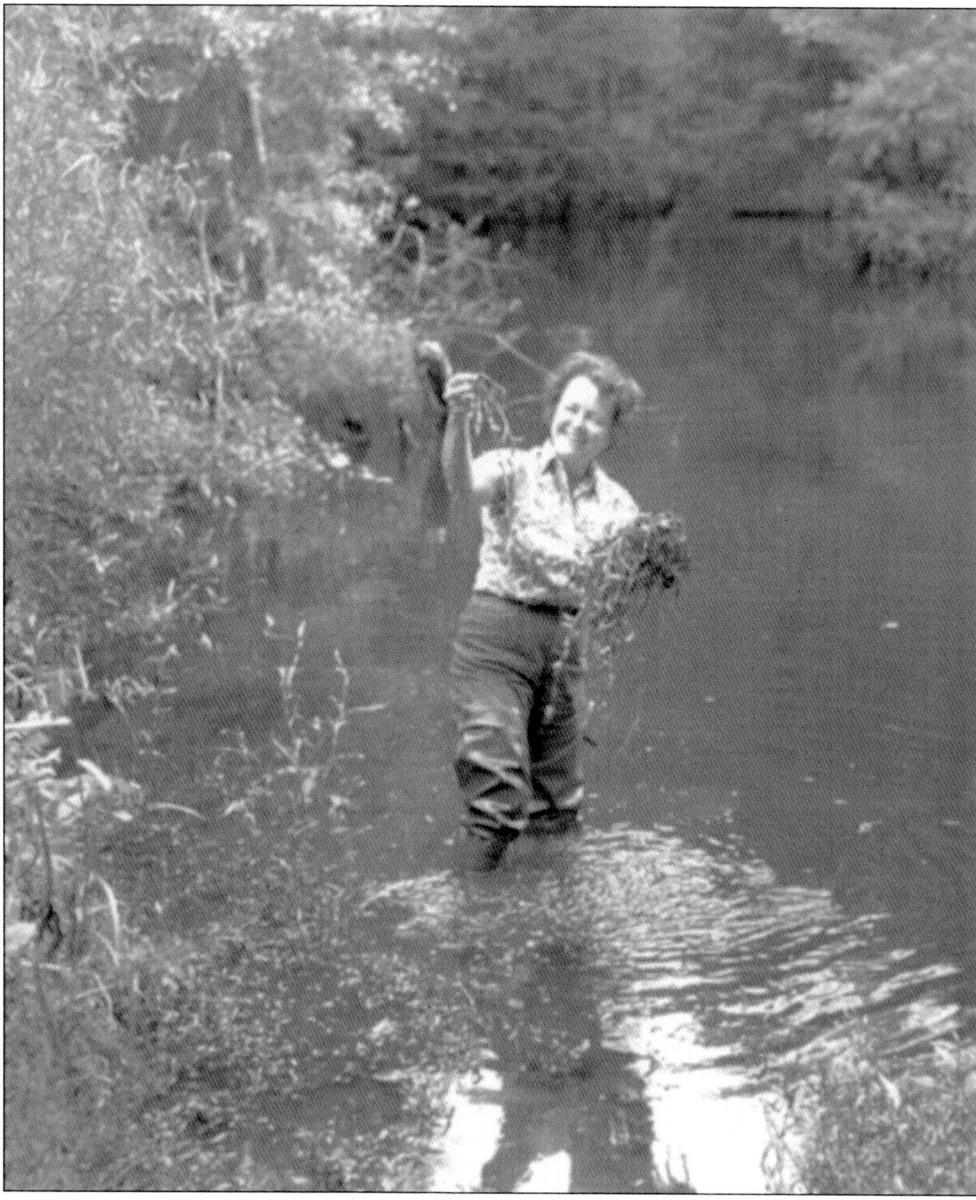

In 1951, Dr. Ruth Patrick brought her expertise to SRP to conduct the baseline survey. This c. 1965 photograph shows Dr. Patrick in her element in the Savannah River. She was one of three female ecologists in the nation in 1950. Her previous work showed that biological diversity matters in understanding problems that affect an ecosystem, and DuPont noted her pioneering research.

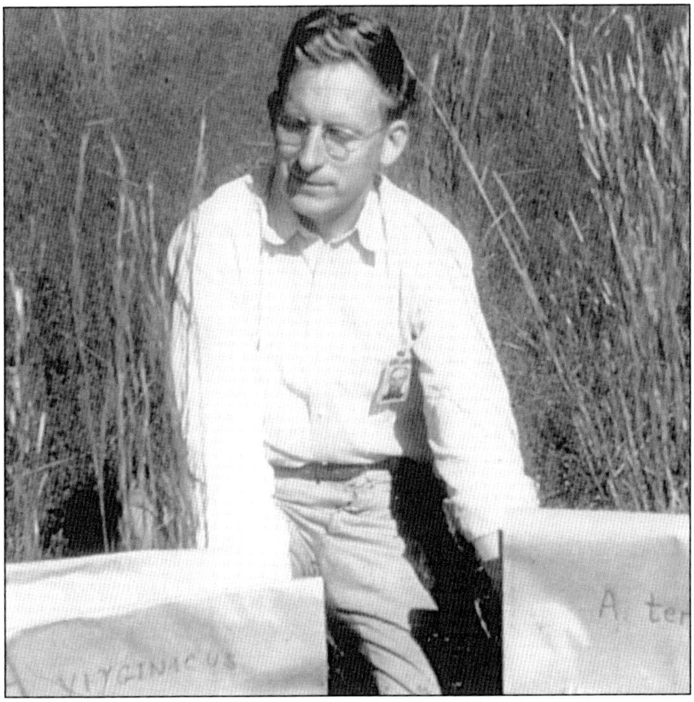

University of Georgia professor Dr. Eugene Odum responded to an AEC request asking for a university-led preinstallation environmental inventory early in 1951. His proposal established the need for a large-scale study of what he considered a vast field laboratory for the study of old field succession.

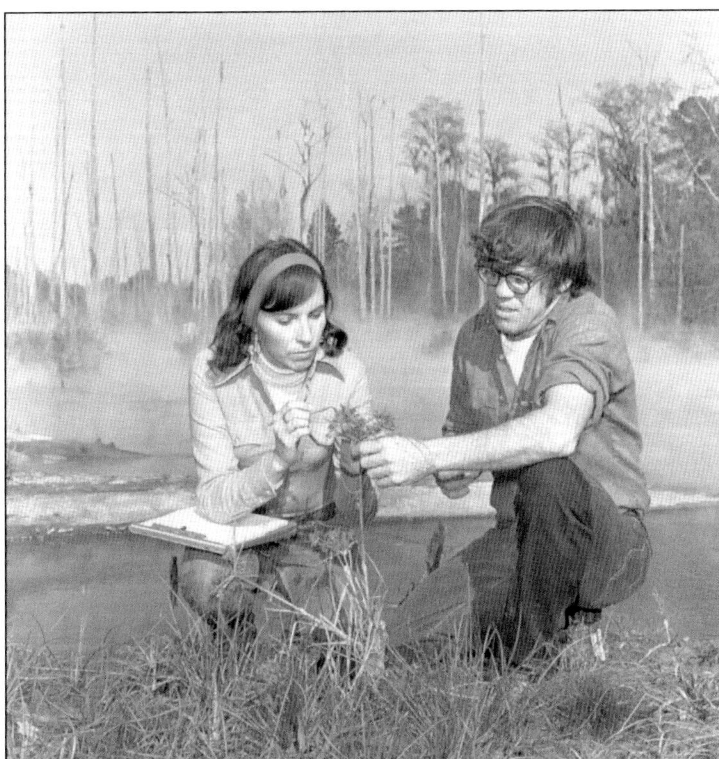

SREL researchers Dr. Rebecca Sharitz and Dr. J. Whitfield "Whit" Gibbons investigate the effects of thermal effluent from the reactors on the Savannah River Swamp in 1974. Dr. Sharitz, a SREL senior ecologist and professor at the University of Georgia, researched wetlands ecology, plant community ecology, and conservation of rare species. A herpetologist, Dr. Gibbons is a professor emeritus at the University of Georgia and senior research ecologist emeritus at SREL.

John Knox, a Savannah River Ecology Lab research technician, examines a smooth purple coneflower (*Echinacea laevigata*). Not to be confused with its commercially available relative, purple coneflower (*Echinacea purpurea*), the smooth purple coneflower is a perennial herb and was first found present at SRP in 1979; the flower is federally listed as an endangered species. Without fires, woody plant species create shade and limit the growth of smooth purple coneflower.

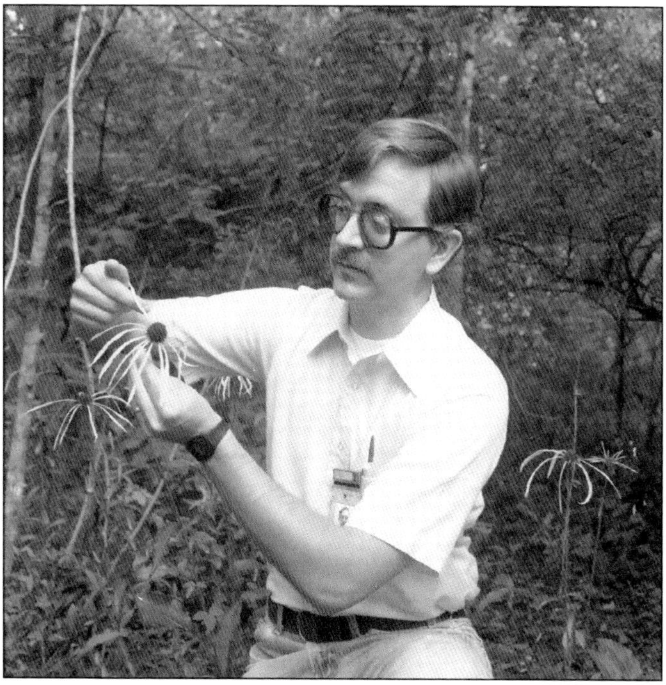

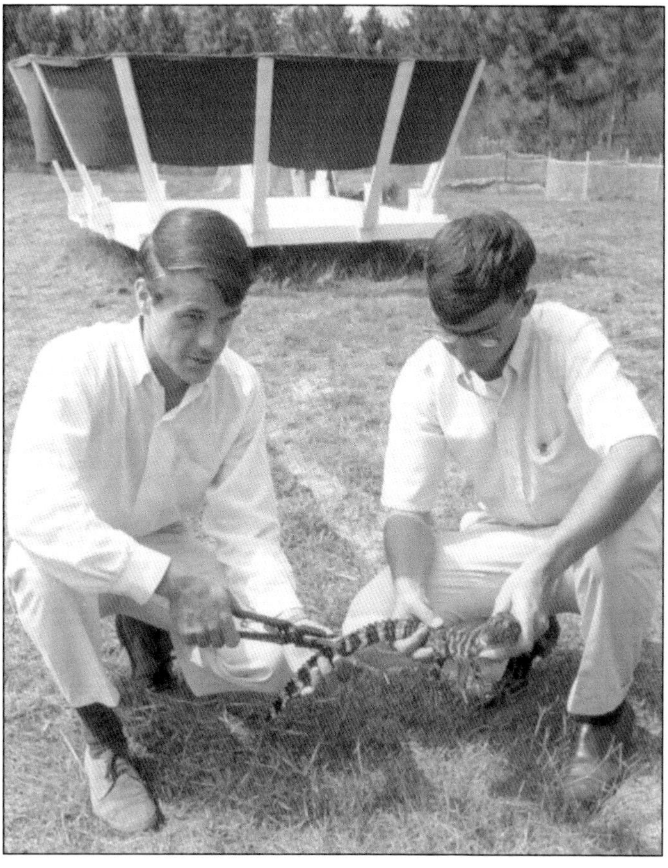

Dr. I. Lehr Brisbane (left) and Dr. C. Phillip Goodyear (right) place an identification tag on a young alligator prior to its release in thermally affected PAR Pond. SREL researchers studied seasonal movements and ecology of the alligator population on-site. Researchers commonly used tags and collars to understand what populations different species rely on and how industrial development might affect habitats.

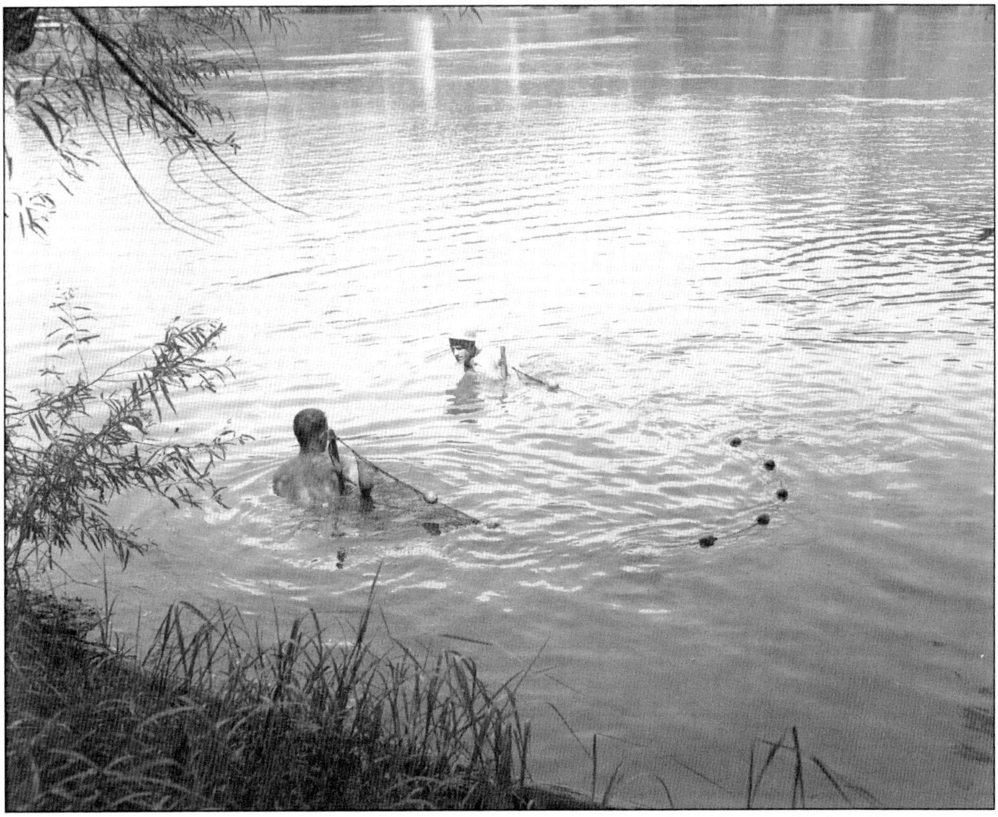

The Savannah River played a major role not just in operations but also in the local ecosystem. Dr. Patrick and her colleagues placed special emphasis on the relationship between species on land and species in the river. The research team from the Philadelphia Academy of Natural Sciences piloted small boats with five-horsepower engines. They used just a few tools for their work, including a weir used to trap fish, as pictured here.

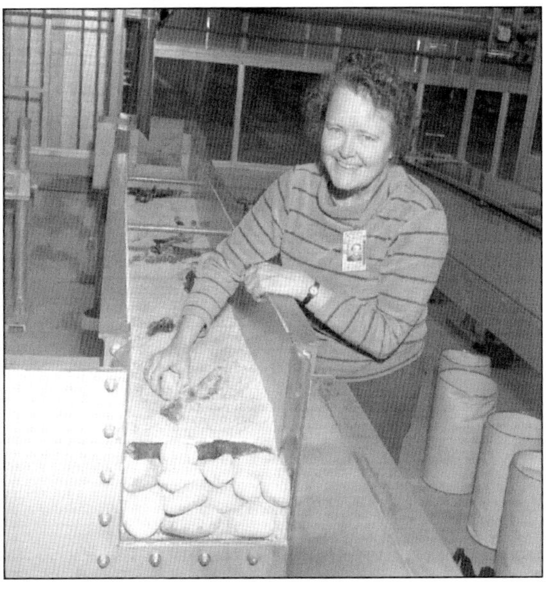

Dr. Ruth Patrick prepares an artificial stream in the Thermal Effects lab to study freshwater plants. This study focused on stream organisms found at Upper Three Runs Creek, a diverse 20-mile waterway that runs across the site; it contains more than 575 species of aquatic insects and as many as 700 invertebrate organisms.

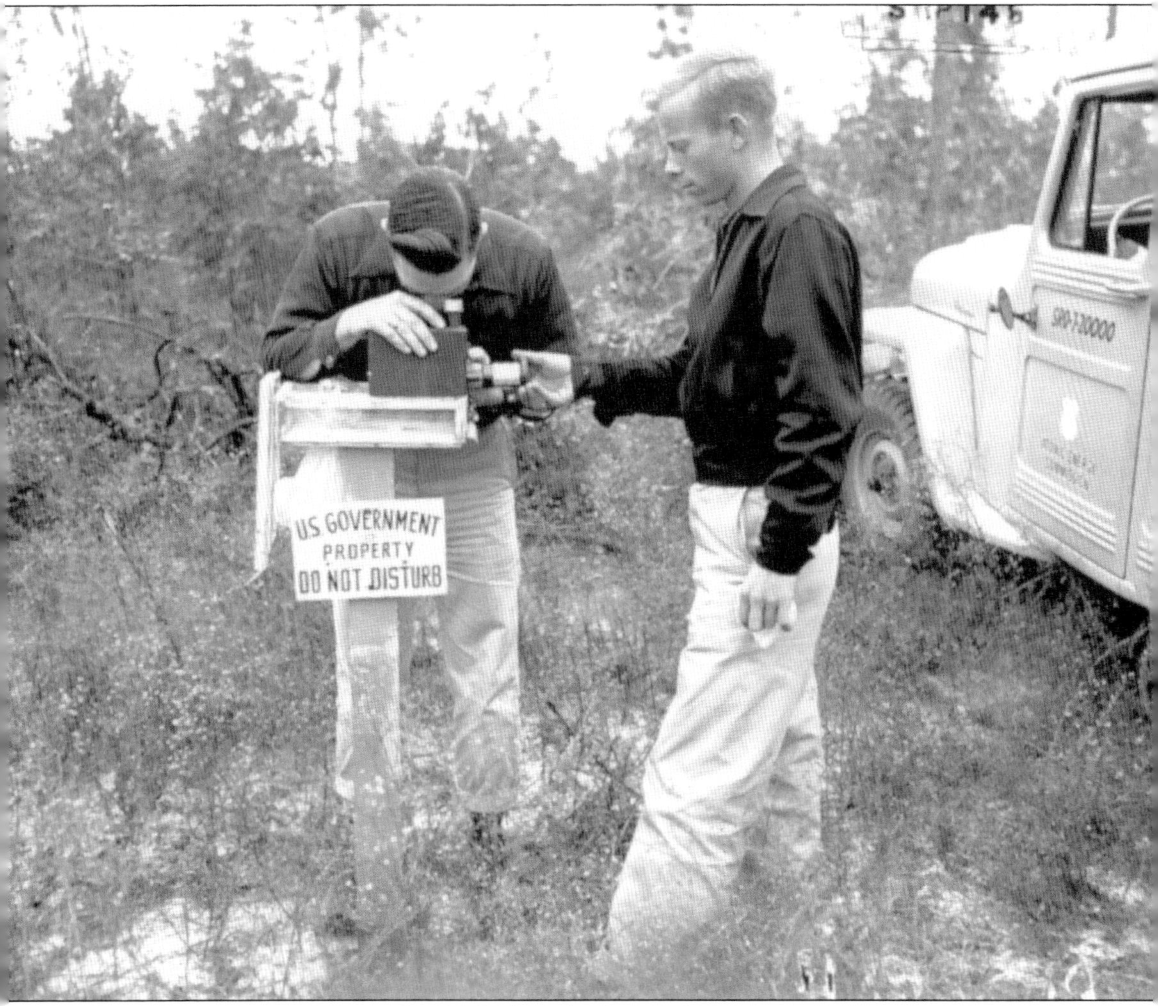

After the site survey was completed, the health physics department continued the work of monitoring radioactivity in the habitats of the Savannah River Site. Health physics personnel placed monitors on stakes throughout the site, including equipment to collect rainwater and air samples, and they regularly checked this equipment, as pictured here around 1955.

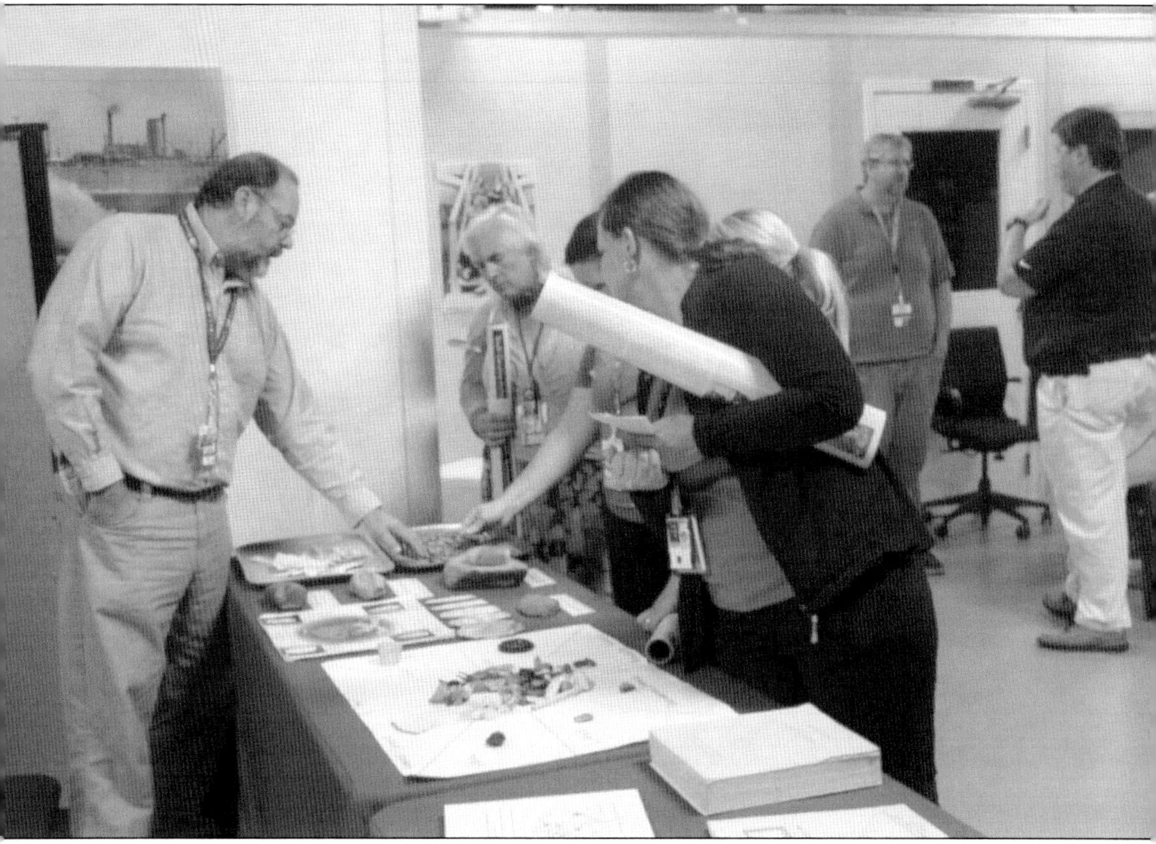

George Wingard, the program coordinator for the Savannah River Archaeological Research Program, points out the differences between prehistoric pottery designs during an outreach event for the program's 40th anniversary. The Savannah River Archaeological Research Program, operated by the University of South Carolina, collects archaeological artifacts that give context not only to the displaced historic towns but also to the early prehistoric sites, dating from 10,000 BCE to 1950 CE. (Courtesy of the Savannah River Site Archeological Research Program.)

Seven

Safety and Security

Safety and security have long been cornerstone values for SRS workers. Breaches in security or safety incidents carried the consequence of national security, to ensure that the United States remained ahead during the Cold War's nuclear arms race. SRS workers today continue to train to maintain secrecy around classified information and missions and must complete annual training to combat possible terrorist or insider threats. They also continue to follow safety protocols to reduce the number of incidents on-site.

Cold War workers never shared the details of their work with anyone, whether it be a barber or a taxi driver or even their own family. Even site workers who carpooled together, often from different areas of the site, were discouraged from discussing even the most minute details of work life with one another. The SRP workers operated on a strictly need-to-know basis.

Although site employees were working on a mission of national importance, they maintained a healthy sense of humor. Reminders of safety and security appeared as witty puns painted onto billboards, hung in office buildings, or even printed on cafeteria napkins. During safety training seminars, employees enacted silly skits to better communicate the tenets of a safe work environment.

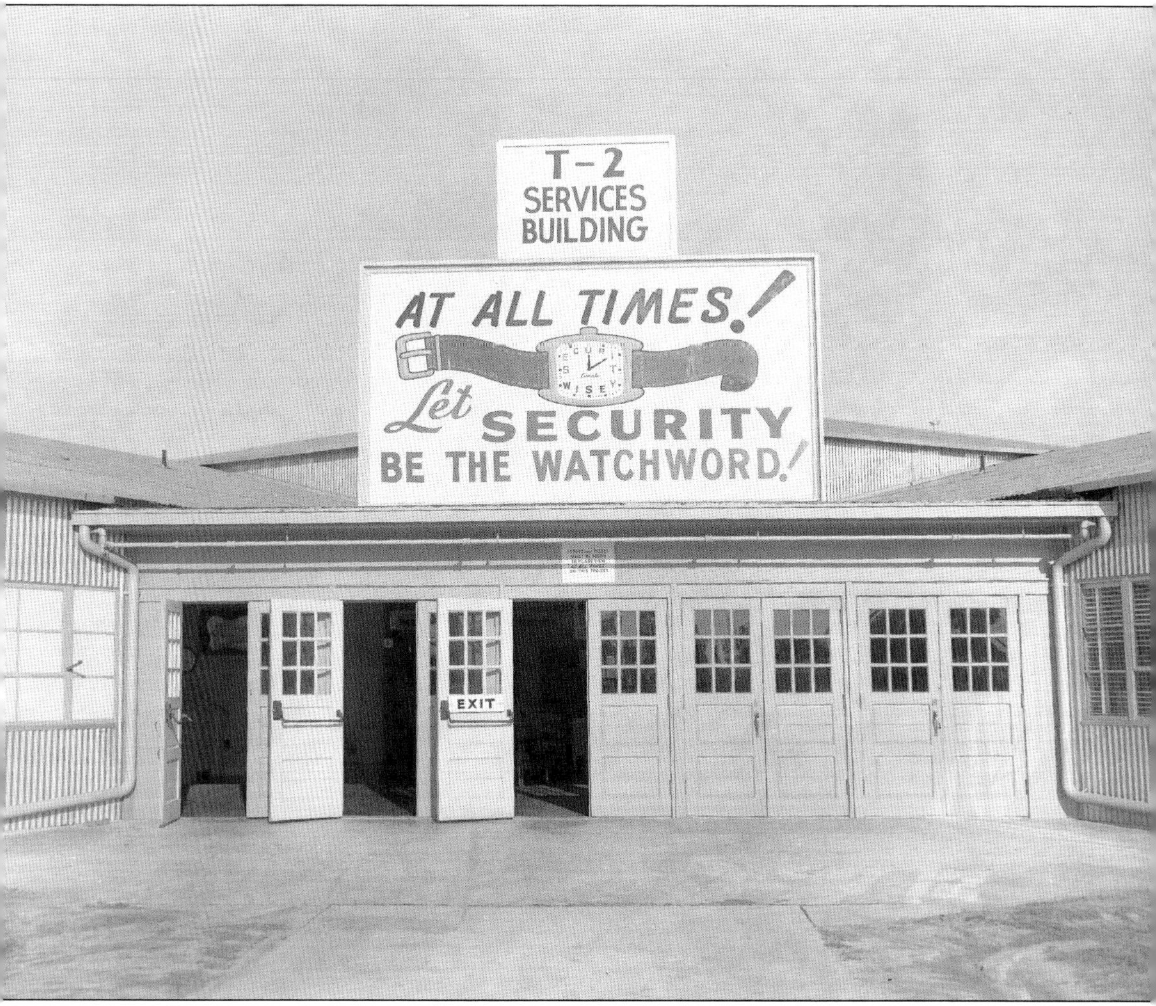

"At All Times! Let Security Be the Watchword!" Signs like this one, placed atop the T-2 building, were common throughout the site as persistent reminders of the importance of security. The SRP T-2 building housed administrative offices for the employment personnel and central medical employees. This was often the first stop for new employees to sign paperwork and perform preemployment physicals to ensure they were fit for duty.

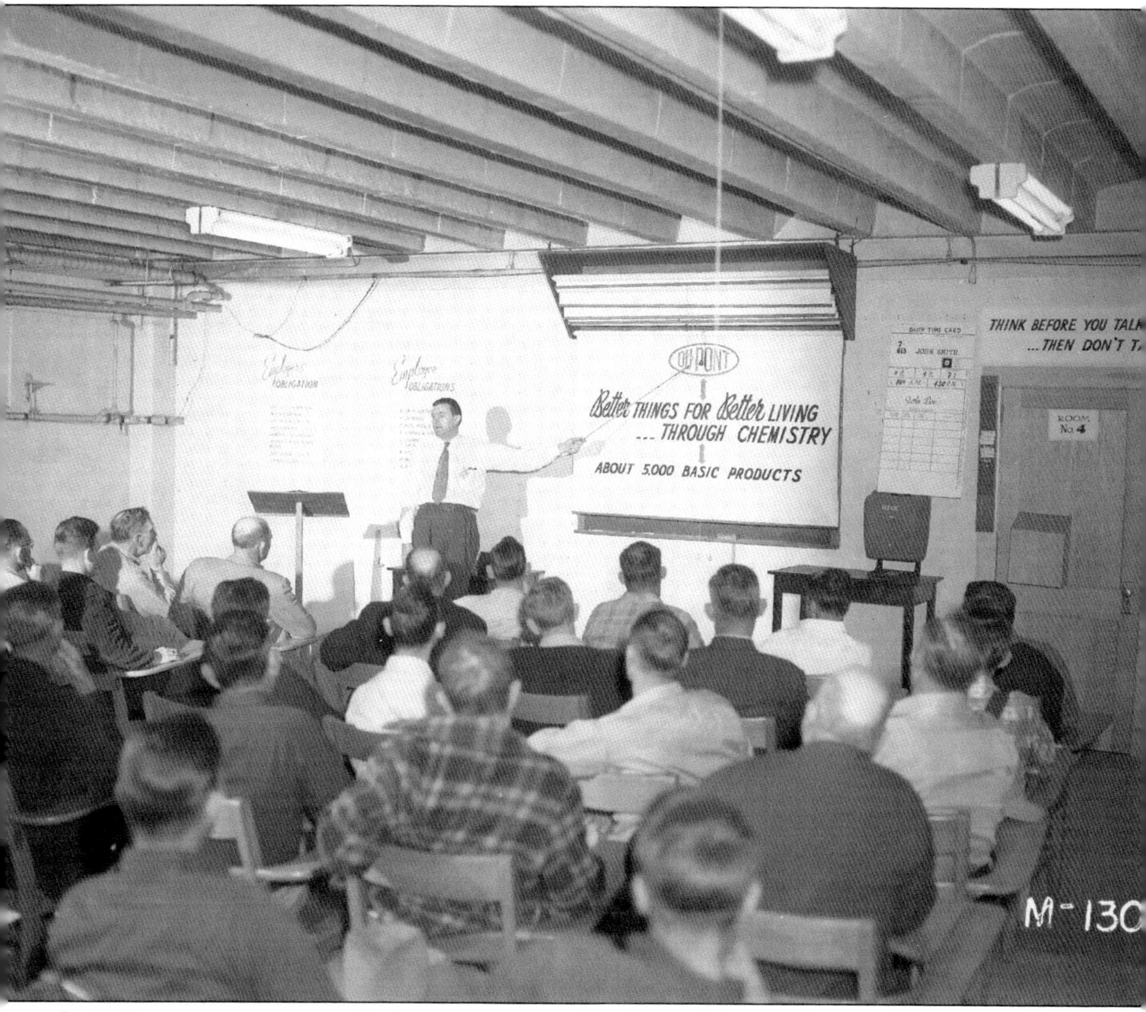

By 1953, every state, except Utah, was represented in the workforce at Savannah River Plant. Hiring procedures included being fingerprinted, photographed for a badge, and receiving a payroll number. A mandatory half-day orientation on safety and security was required for all employees, and additional training was provided for supervisors, office personnel, and skilled workers.

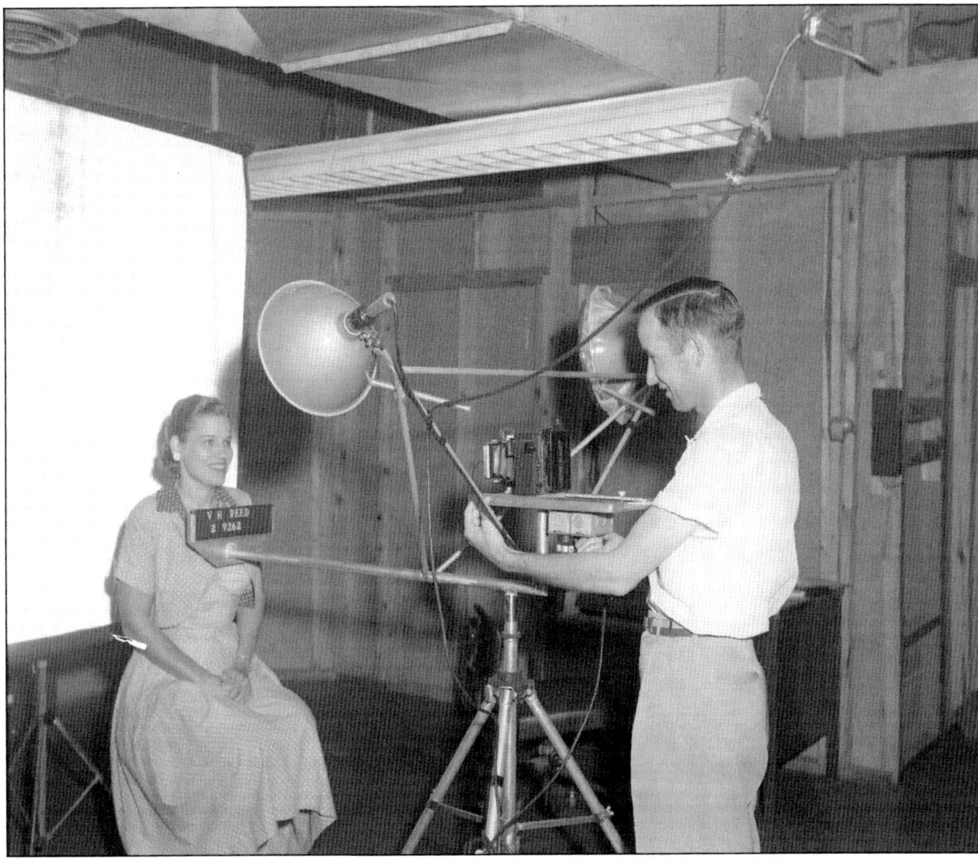

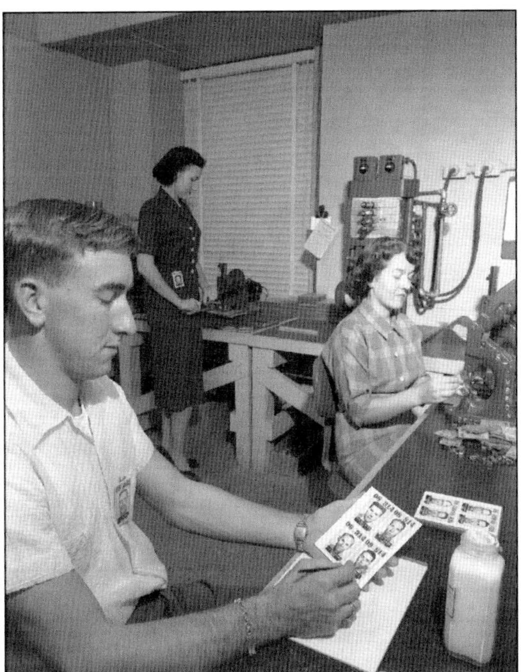

All Savannah River Plant employees on-site, past and present, receive a security badge complete with a photograph and identification number. The designs have changed over the years, and the technology to produce the badges has evolved too. A new employee in 1955 gets her badge picture taken.

Original badge designs required photographs to be glued and dried, a process that took several hours. Between mid-1953 and 1954, the Savannah River badge office produced approximately 40,000 badges. Though the design and creation process has changed, photograph badges are still used to identify personnel on-site. These badges ensure that only authorized individuals gain access past site boundaries and restricted areas.

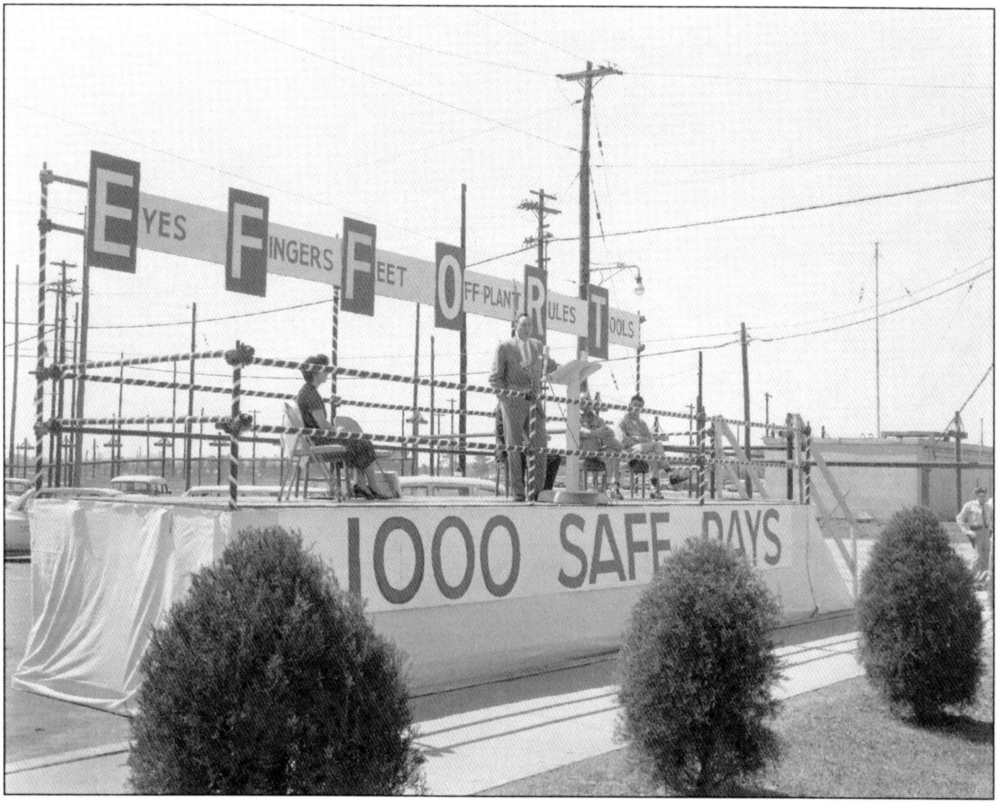

In April 1963, SRP manager Julian Ellet addressed employees during a special commemoration for 1,000 safe days worked. In a previous 1954 *SRP News* article on plant safety, construction field project manager Robert K. Mason explained the importance of this emphasis: "Without safety, we cannot be productive, and only by being productive can we be strong and preserve the freedom of America."

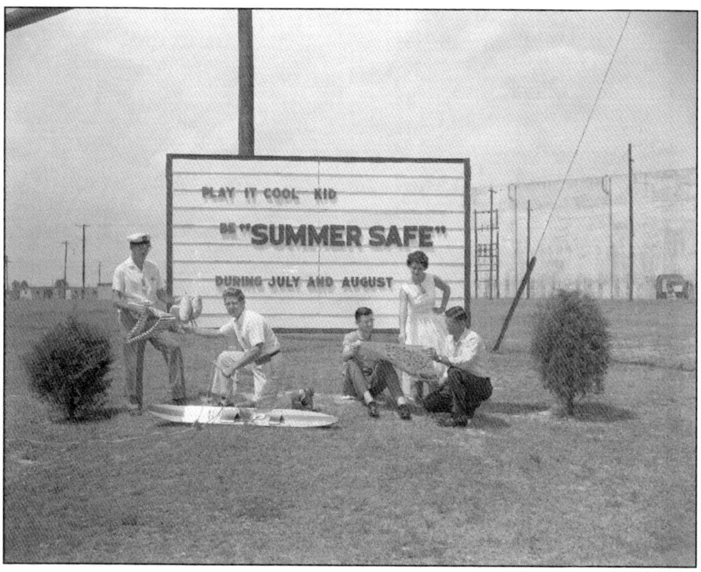

In keeping with July 1960's sitewide safety theme, H Area's safety sign urges everyone to be "Summer Safe." From left to right, "Skipper" Jim Rector reminds Gordon Chalfant to take life preservers when water skiing, while John Parker, Sue Greenway, and Bob Cansler map out vacation spots. Each SRP employee was given a family safety manual with detailed safety sections that included activities such as boating, biking, and safety in the sun.

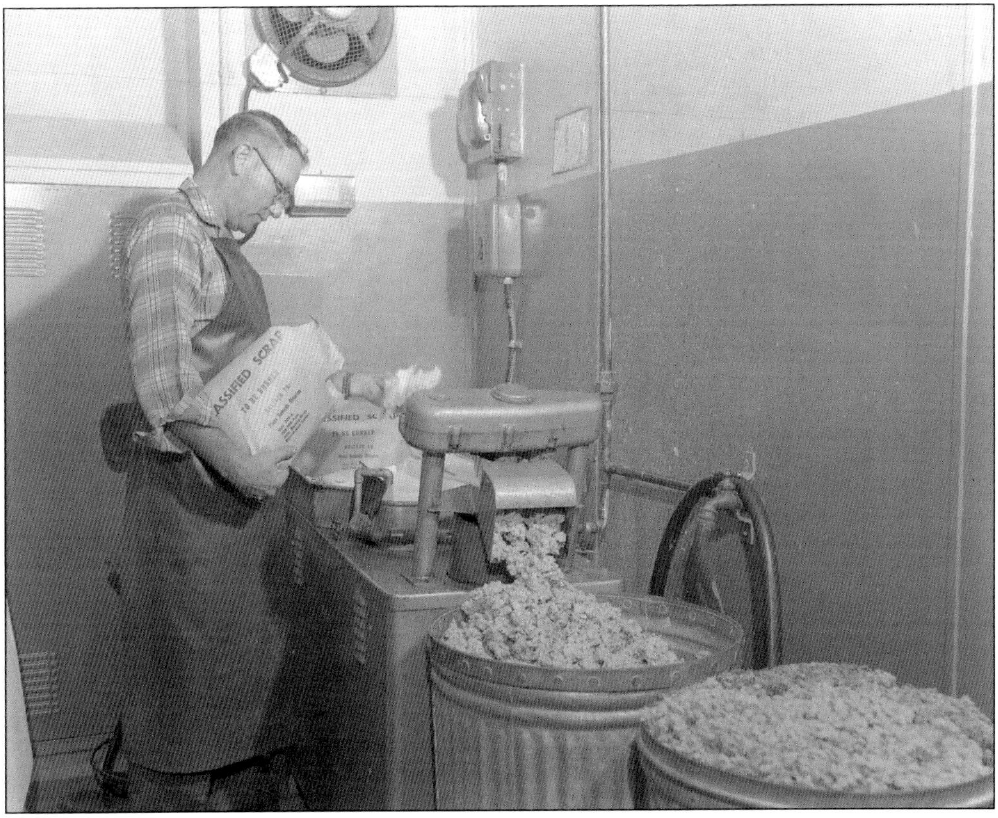

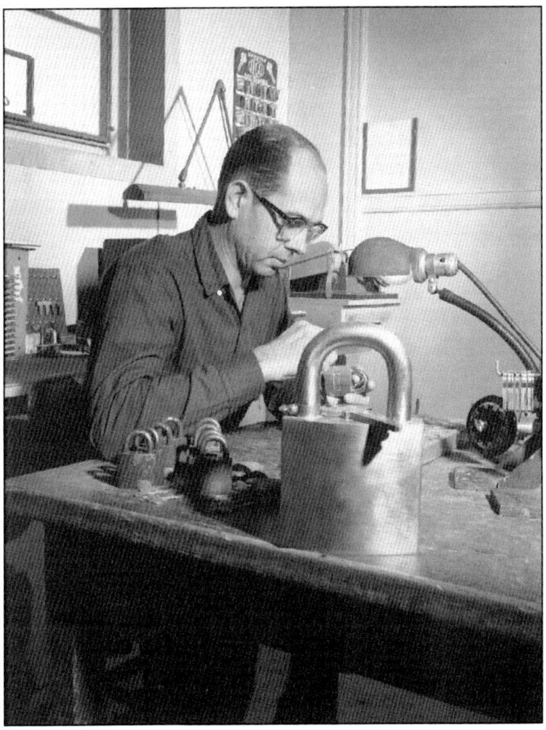

If sensitive information were to be leaked from SRP operations, it would place the United States and its allies in jeopardy. To prevent such a situation from happening, employees were trained on how to properly maintain, store, and destroy classified documents in the interest of information security. John Corley used this machine in 1954 to pulp classified documents and ensure that SRP secrets did not get into the wrong hands.

The Savannah River Plant locksmith maintained about 32,000 locks, including around 700 combinations and 11,000 master key padlocks of all different sizes. In this image, one giant lock and key are settled next to a row of smaller locks. Security was essential, regardless of how big or small the lock was.

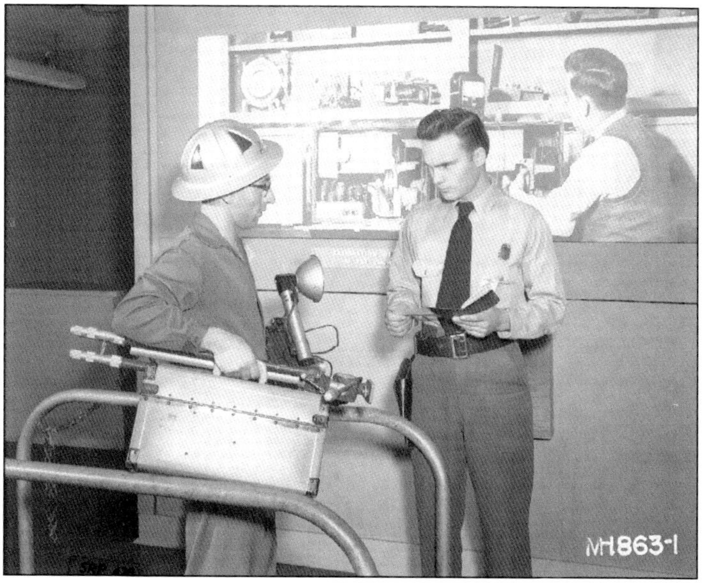

Joe Lista (left), a well-known photographer in Aiken, demonstrates entry through an SRP patrol checkpoint. The guard is looking for contraband and checking the equipment for the proper paperwork to enter the operations area. Prompted by work at the plant, Lista later opened a photography studio in 1953, which grew to serve the Aiken community. As of 2022, Joe's son Todd Lista still continues the family business.

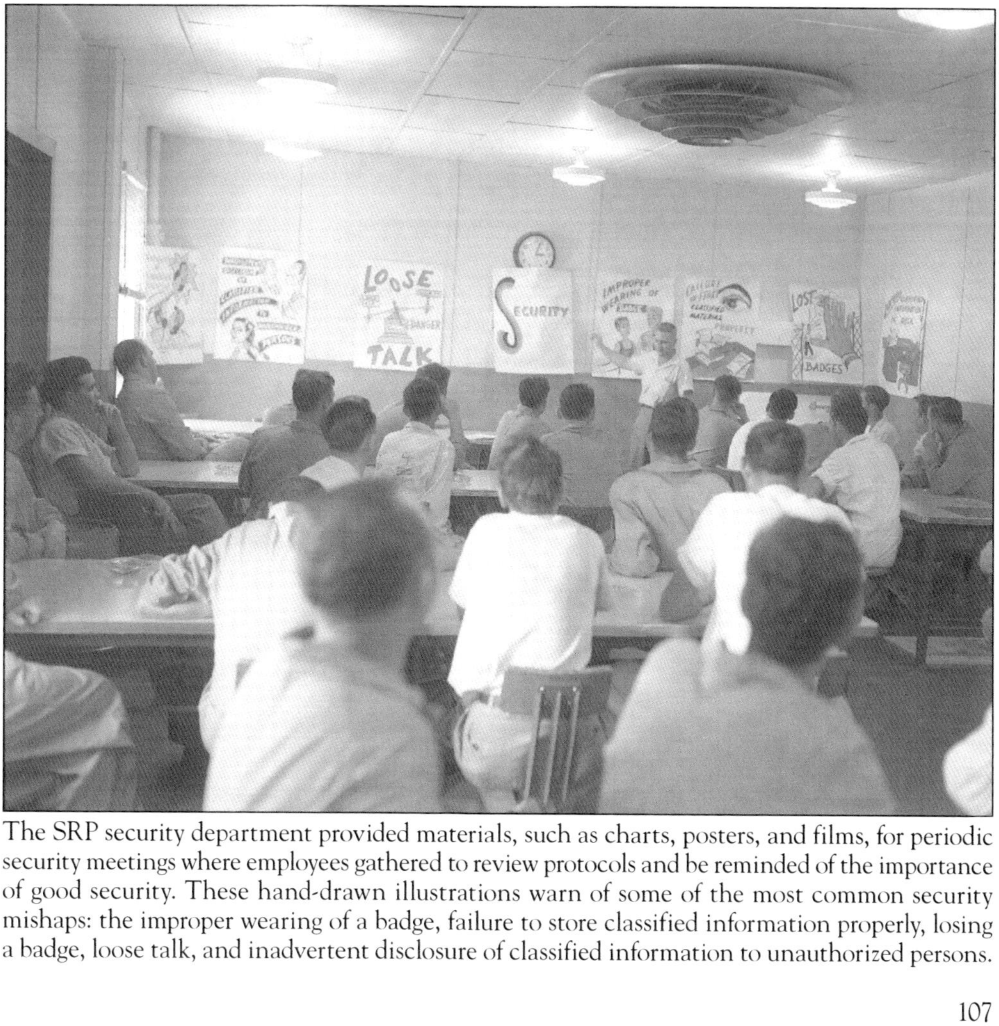

The SRP security department provided materials, such as charts, posters, and films, for periodic security meetings where employees gathered to review protocols and be reminded of the importance of good security. These hand-drawn illustrations warn of some of the most common security mishaps: the improper wearing of a badge, failure to store classified information properly, losing a badge, loose talk, and inadvertent disclosure of classified information to unauthorized persons.

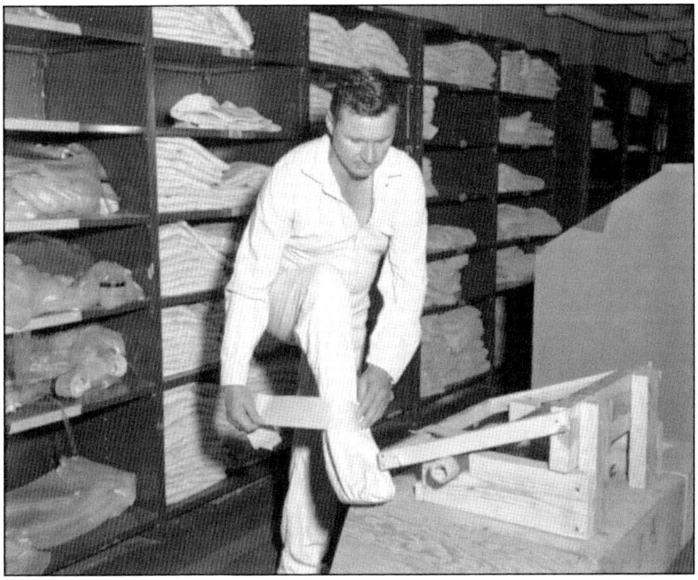

Safety at SRP included radiation and contamination protection. This worker at R Reactor is dressing out in white coveralls, white cotton gloves, and booties, with rubber gloves and shoe covers. Shoe covers were secured to pant legs using masking tape. The plastic suits seen on the far left shelf were used in tritiated environments (or environments containing tritium) after 1956.

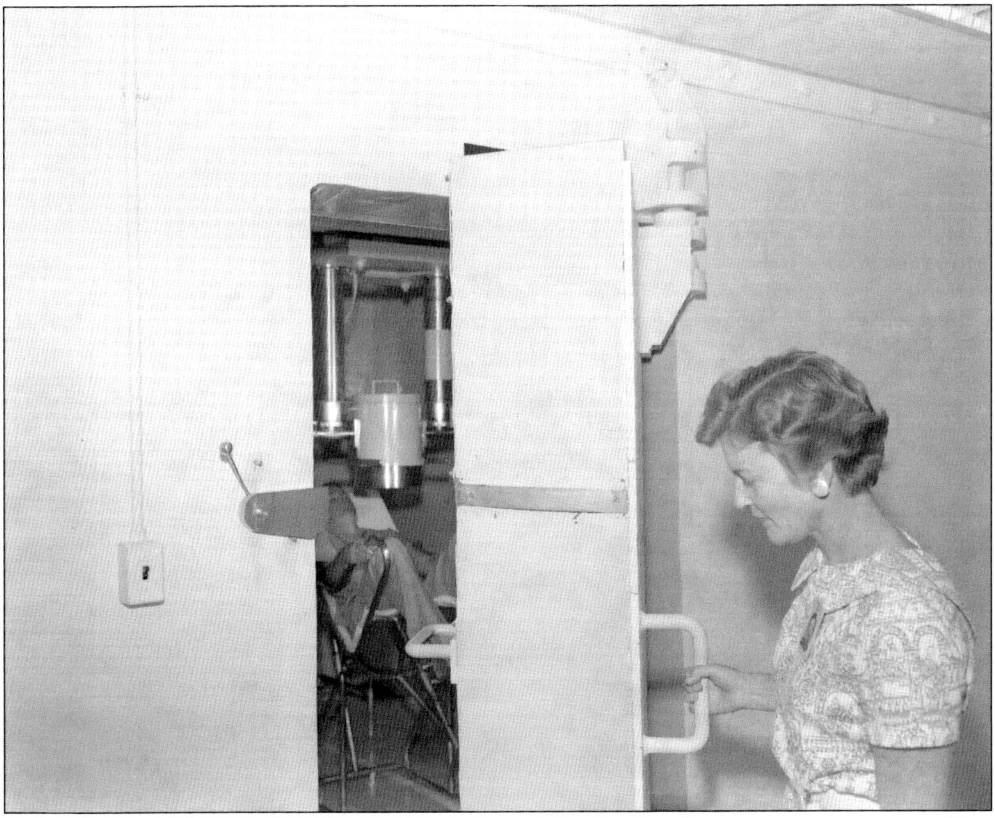

SRP radiation technicians used special procedures to monitor radiation exposure on-site. This whole body counter is designed to detect exposure on the surface and inside of the human body. Employees were placed on a tilted gurney inside of a room constructed of 12.5-inch-thick battleship armor. The door, although it weighed 10,700 pounds, was balanced and could be opened with the pressure of one finger.

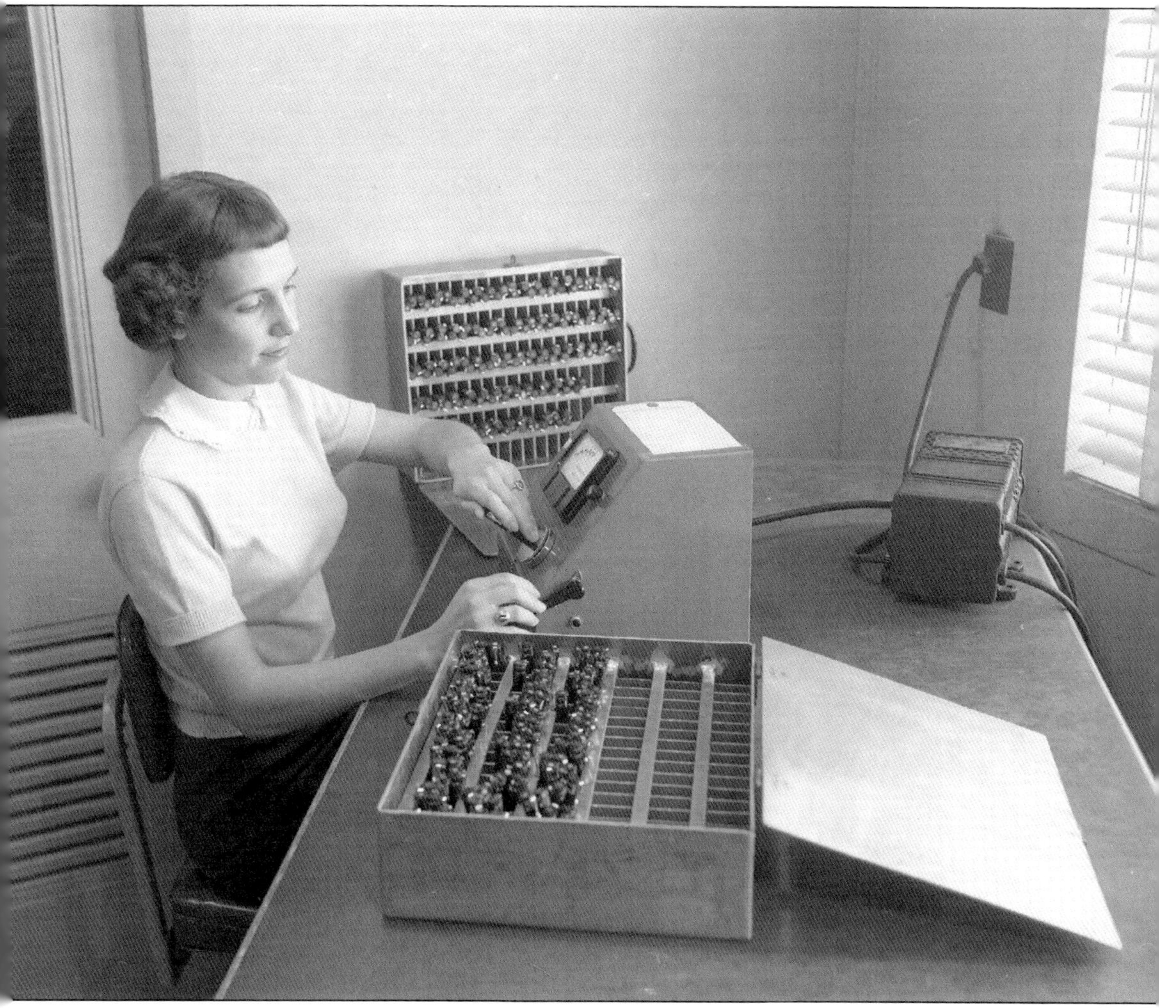

Health physics employee Beulah Whitaker assesses readings from a collection of dosimeters. SRP personnel wore pencil (or pocket) dosimeters to assess daily exposure to radiation, in addition to weekly measured film badges. The pencil meters, introduced in 1952, ensured that site workers were exposed to limited doses of radiation. Health physics employees read approximately 4,500 pencils daily. By January 1955, more than a million pencil dosimeters had been evaluated.

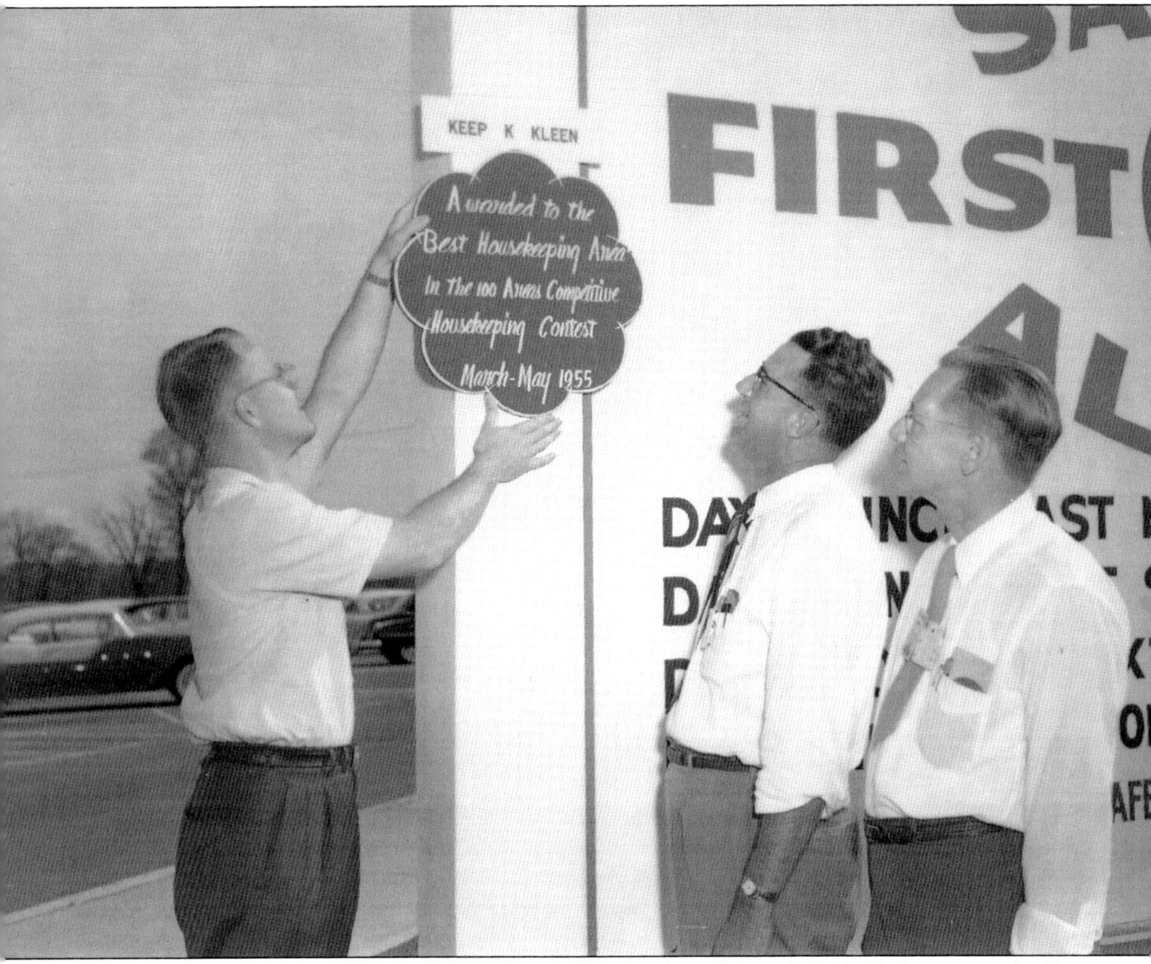

Friendly competitions encouraged safety on-site. In the spring of 1955, K Area won the Best Housekeeping Award during a competition between the five reactor areas. Housekeeping is still an important aspect of maintaining a safe work environment at the Savannah River Site. The placard reads, "Awarded to the Best Housekeeping Area in the 100 Areas Competitive Housekeeping Contest, March–May 1955."

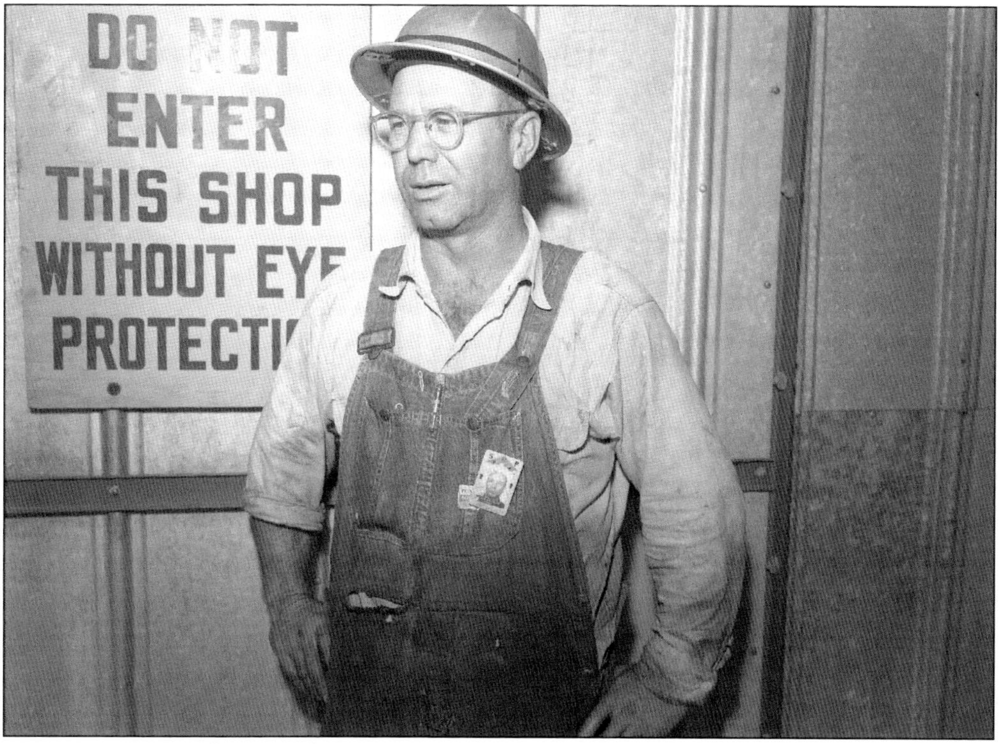

DuPont encouraged site workers to drive safely both inside and beyond the fence. Frequent automobile accidents in the early years lead to the establishment of the Safe Drivers' League, 21,000 employees strong. In a June 1953 *Savannah River Plant News and Views* article, W.H. Sutherland of the Millwright Fabricating Shop in Central Shops and Margaret Cole, from the F Area blueprints department, joined the league by signing the Safe Drivers' Pledge. This pledge, signed by nearly 98 percent of site employees, asked employees to consider the safety of themselves and other families when driving and to contribute to the overall safe work culture at SRP.

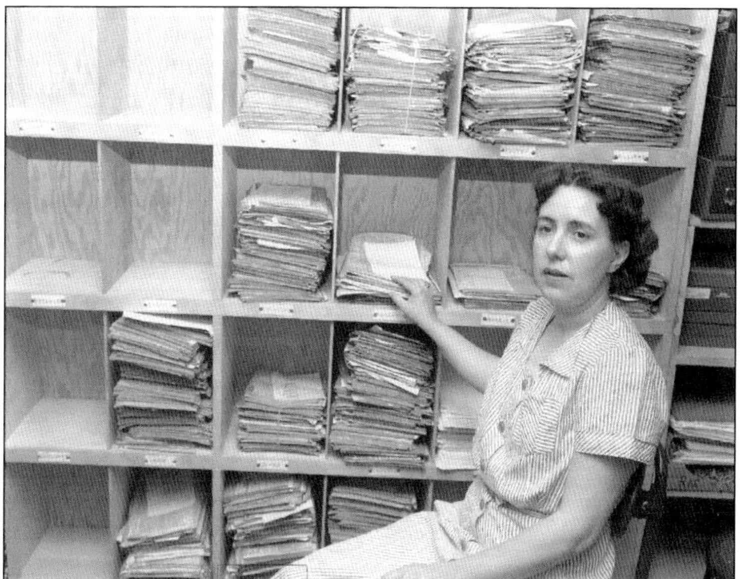

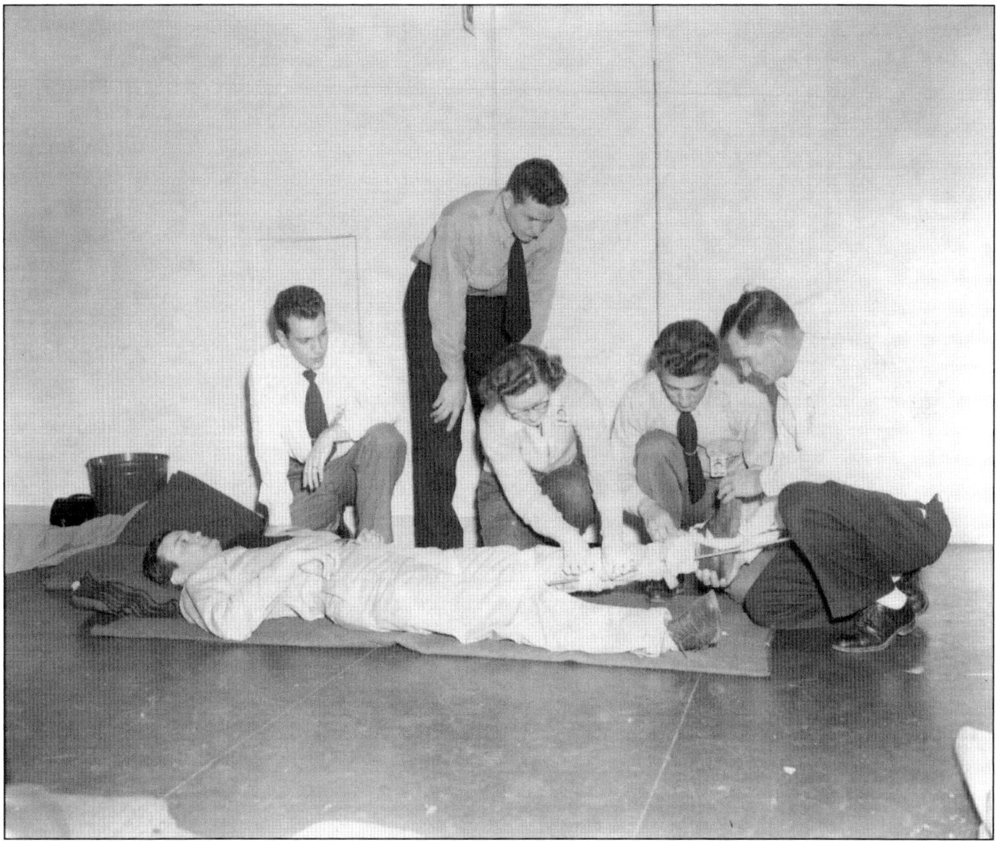

SRP medical provided annual exams, preemployment physicals, and training to keep the workforce at SRP safe, a practice still in place on SRS today. The medical staff also provided first aid training, as depicted here in 1951. In this image, trainees learn to administer a splint on a volunteer. First aid training ensured that employees remained prepared to assist one another in case of injury. This image was captured on February 1, 1952.

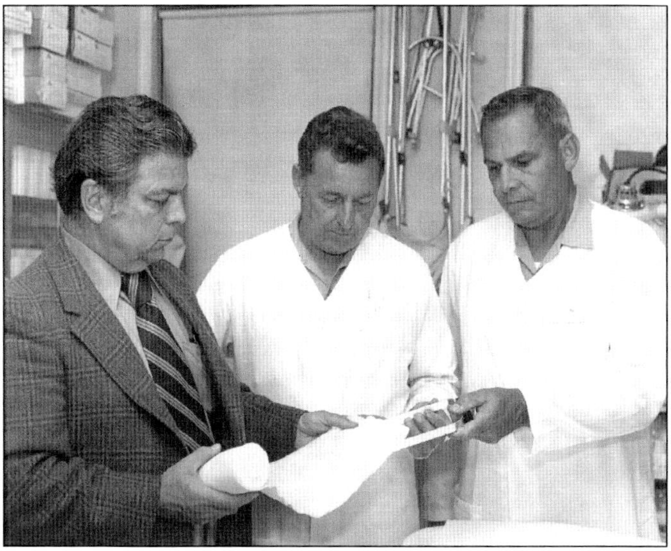

Dr. George Poda (left), who served as Savannah River Plant's medical superintendent for over two decades, shows SRP patrolmen how to apply a splint during an emergency medical technician training class. Because SRP was necessarily isolated from major population centers, it was vital to have trained staff and equipment necessary to perform emergency medical care on-site.

Eight

Community

The influx of new site workers changed the culture, economics, and politics of the surrounding region. New community members formed local clubs, such as DuPont's Supervisory Club; raised funds for a community chest; and became heavily involved in community service and politics. SRP also brought a financial boon to the area. Businesses prospered from the higher salaries of DuPont engineers, with more than 50 new businesses opening in the spring of 1951. These towns received federal grants for updated water purification, new construction of hospitals and schools, and improved police and fire protection. Aiken and Augusta also received a financial windfall to help improve the public school systems, especially to promote science education.

SRP recognized that it needed to facilitate a sense of community among workers. Tens of thousands of people had just arrived in South Carolina and Georgia to work at a nuclear materials facility, where the details of their jobs were kept secret from the public. DuPont strove to create bonds between workers through clubs, family life, and community events. Regional chapters of national professional organizations were created to maintain ties with the national community. The site newspaper helped workers learn about site projects as well as their colleagues' backgrounds. The Operations Recreation Association (ORA) hosted events to encourage site employees to get to know each other through sports and recreation, during which no "shop talk" was allowed. Strong ties developed as plant families set down roots in the local communities and SRP's long-lasting influence spread throughout the region.

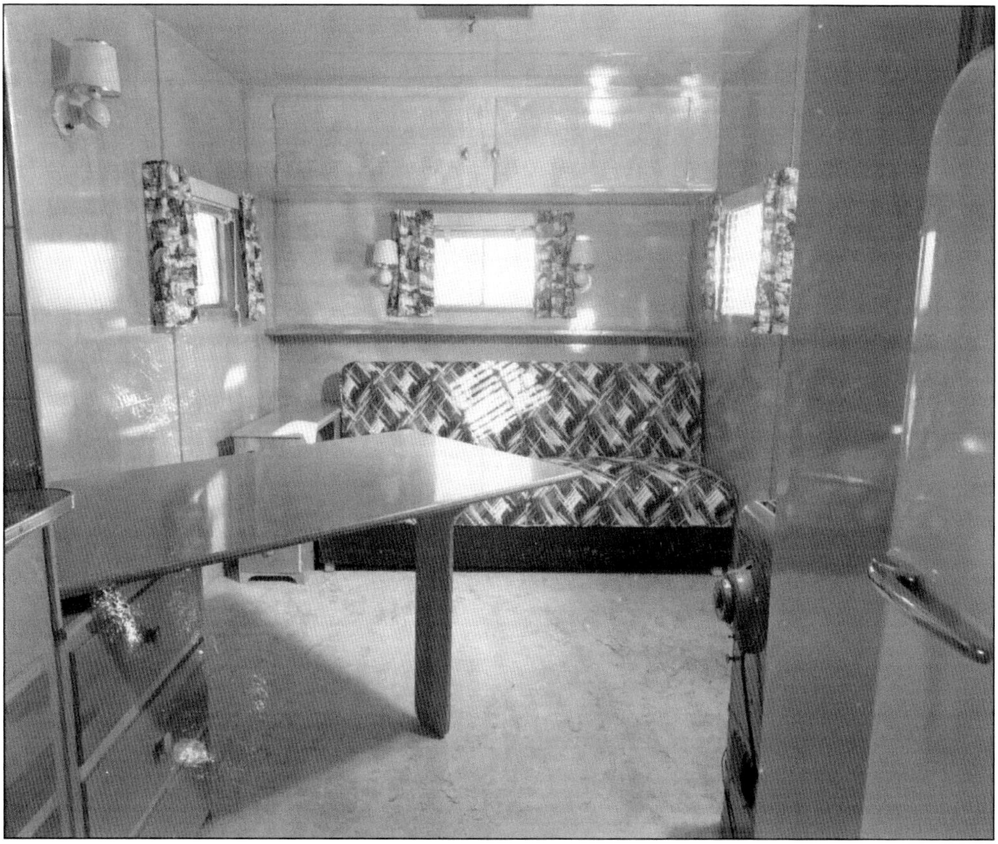

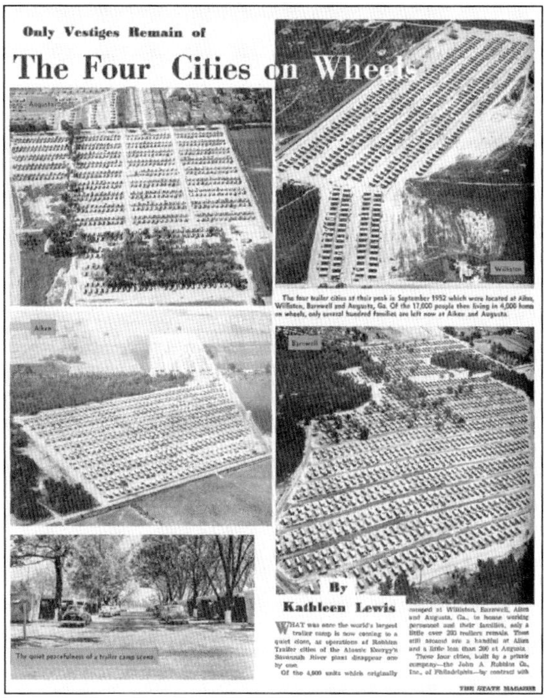

Only Vestiges Remain of

The Four Cities on Wheels

Augusta

Williston

The four trailer cities at their peak in September 1952 which were located at Aiken, Williston, Barnwell and Augusta, Ga. Of the 17,000 people then living in 4,000 homes on wheels, only several hundred families are left now at Aiken and Augusta.

Aiken

Barnwell

The quiet peacefulness of a trailer camp scene.

By Kathleen Lewis

WHAT was once the world's largest trailer camp is now coming to a quiet close, as operations of Robbins Trailer cities of the Atomic Energy's Savannah River plant disappear one by one.

Of the 4,000 units which originally ranged at Williston, Barnwell, Aiken and Augusta, Ga., to house working personnel and their families, only a little over 200 trailers remain. Those still around are a handful at Aiken and a little less than 200 at Augusta.

These four cities, built by a private company—the John A. Robbins Co., Inc., of Philadelphia—by contract with

THE STATE MAGAZINE

The Central Savannah River Area (CSRA) experienced an urgent housing need as the SRP construction force began to move into the area. DuPont's housing office helped ease this problem by supplying trailer homes. Each trailer home was about 26 feet long and included a living room, kitchen, bedroom, and bath. The trailer parks that allowed for family accommodations were established at four park locations. The first location opened in Augusta in the spring of 1952, followed by Barnwell, Williston, and Aiken. The trailer parks closed in 1954 as site construction concluded.

Trailer villages were offered for families and barracks were provided for single men. DuPont contracted with Lyles & Lang Construction of Columbia, South Carolina, to build three *H*-shaped barracks with Homasote siding in Barnwell, Williston, and Allendale. Each of the three dorms could house up to 1,500 men.

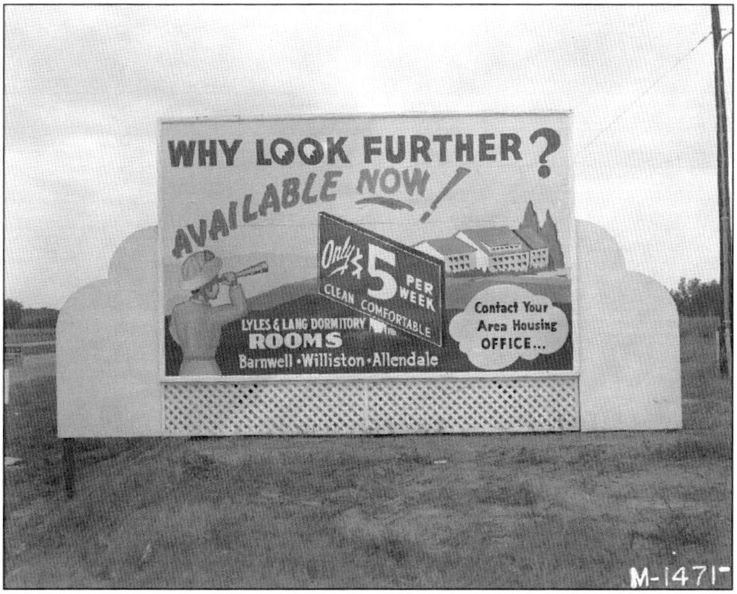

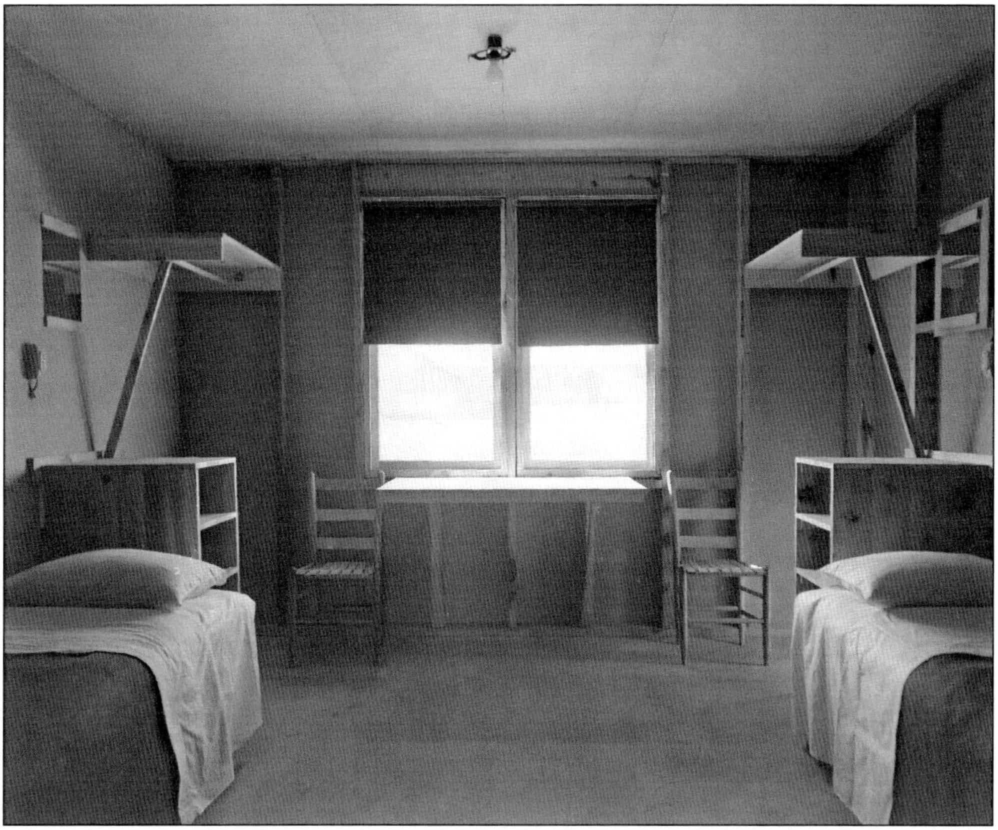

Double occupancy rooms were rented at a reduced rate of $10 per week and included two single beds, two dressers, two mirrors, shelves, a writing desk, two chairs, a space to hang clothes, two linen changes a week, and maid service. After proving unpopular due to location and rudimentary living, the barracks were closed by 1953, less than a year after opening.

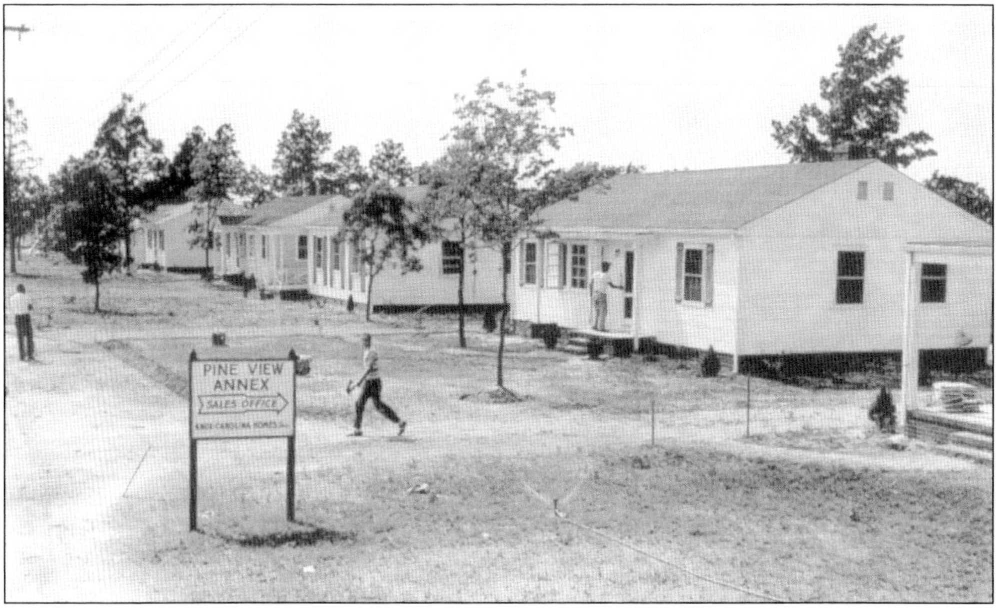

In addition to trailer homes, more permanent housing was developed for the swelling population. Public Law 139, the Defense Housing and Community Facilities Services Act, was passed in late 1951, and a total of 3,225 rental and 625 sale units were built in the region. Two- and three-bedroom units were preferred, with those seeking four-bedroom homes having more difficulty finding space. Between November 1950 and January 1953, a total of 5,465 non-programmed houses were constructed, and "boxlike" houses were laid out on curving streets in subdivisions such as Richmond Hills in Augusta and Crosland Park in Aiken.

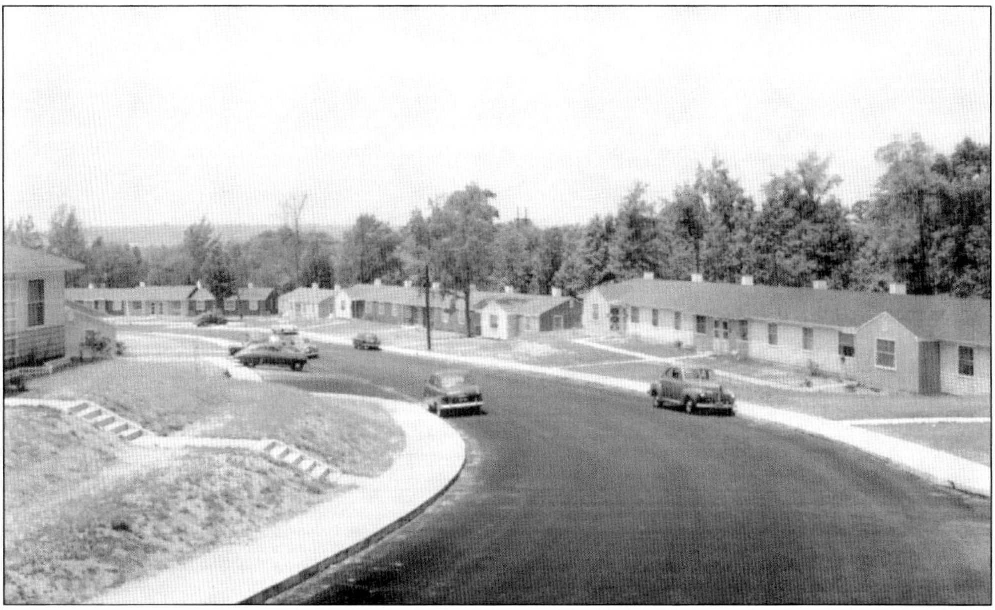

New Ellenton is a town that can trace its origins directly to SRP. Most of the houses moved to the new town from the plant area were placed on the east side of Highway 19. The location was not a great choice from a water-supply perspective, and most buildings without indoor plumbing became rental property for African Americans displaced from the federal reservation. The water-supply problem was not solved until a special congressional authorization in 1953.

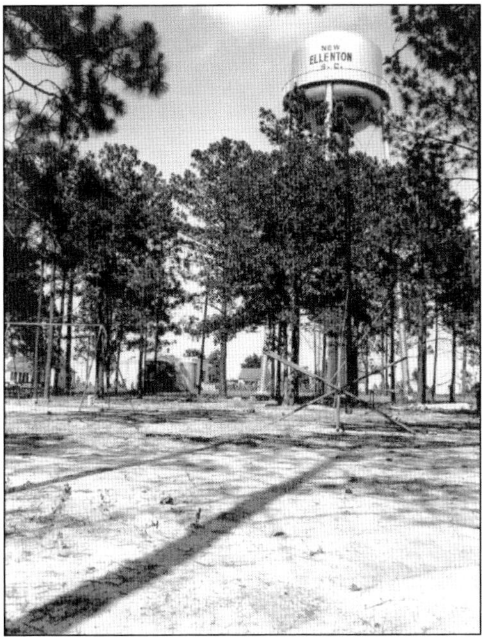

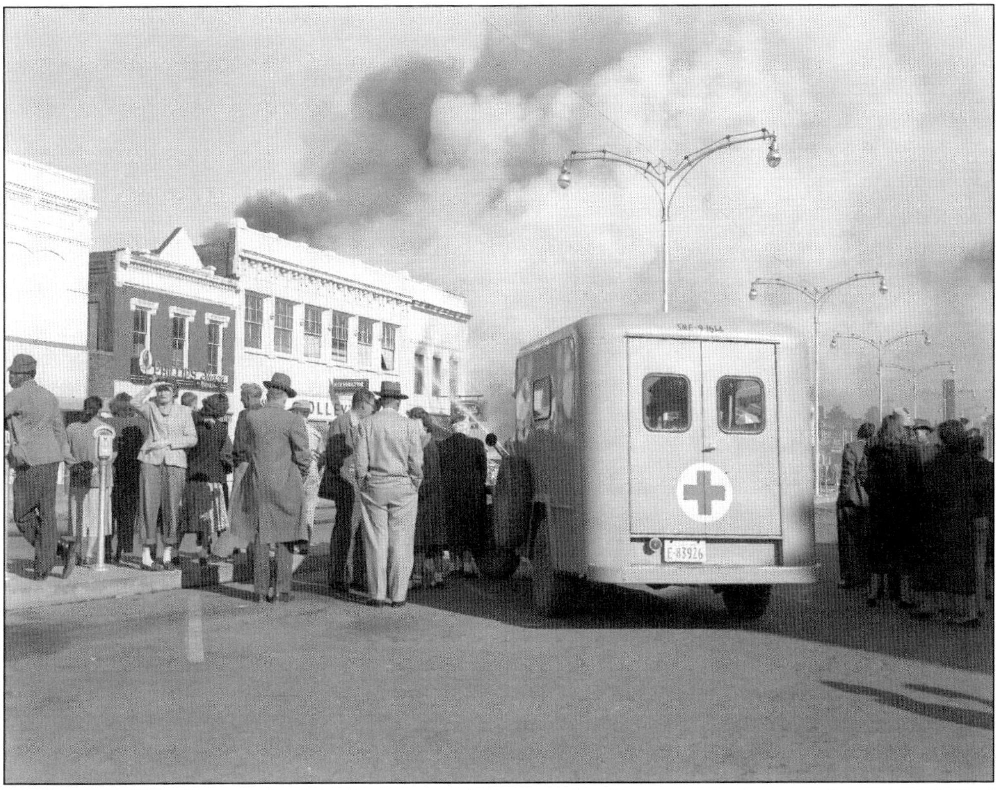

On January 27, 1953, a gas leak in downtown Aiken resulted in an explosion and fire, which killed 10 people. The Jones Electric Co. building was destroyed, and several other structures experienced damage. The SRP sent fire, patrol, and medical crews for support during this emergency. Today, a historical marker stands in remembrance of this accident.

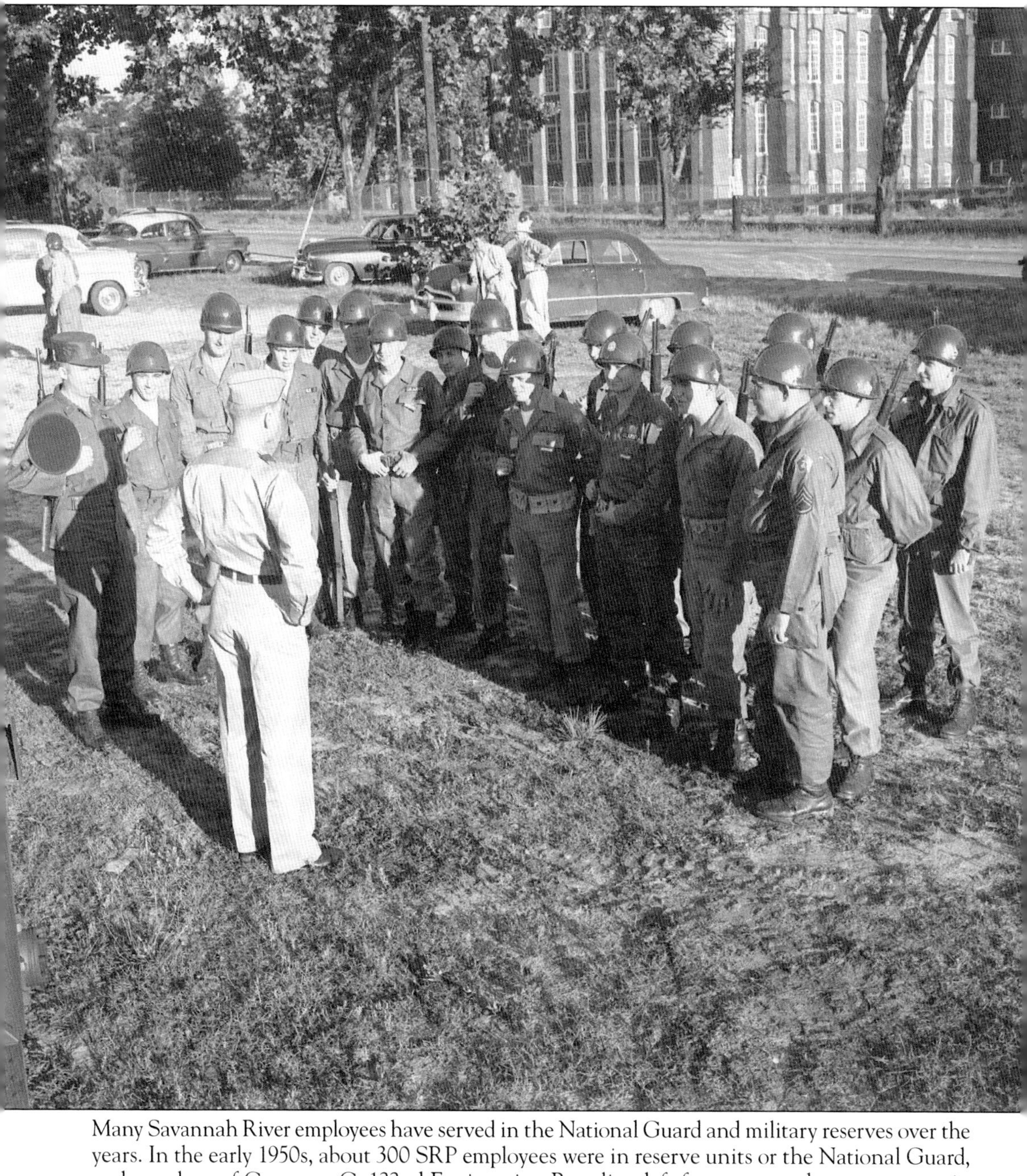

Many Savannah River employees have served in the National Guard and military reserves over the years. In the early 1950s, about 300 SRP employees were in reserve units or the National Guard, and members of Company C, 122nd Engineering Battalion left for a two-week encampment in the summer of 1955.

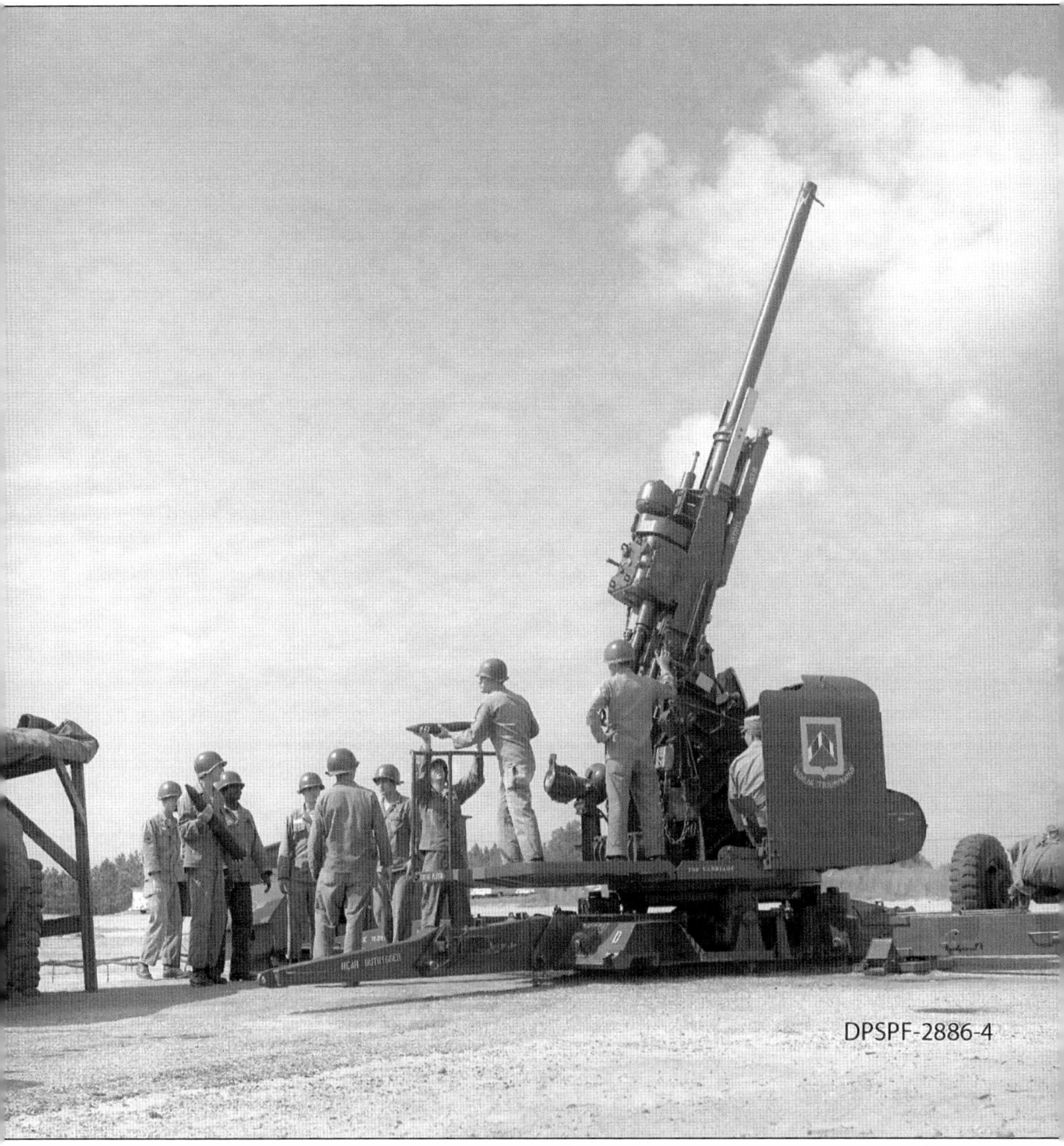

Beginning in 1954, there were plans for three battalions of the Army's Antiaircraft Artillery Command's (ARAACOM) 11th Antiaircraft Group to be stationed at SRP. Original notes in DuPont's scope of work called for eight 90-mm and thirty 75-mm gun sites to be developed. Historical records show that SRP was never threatened by an air attack, and the guns were never utilized. In 1960, the Department of Defense decided to cancel the program.

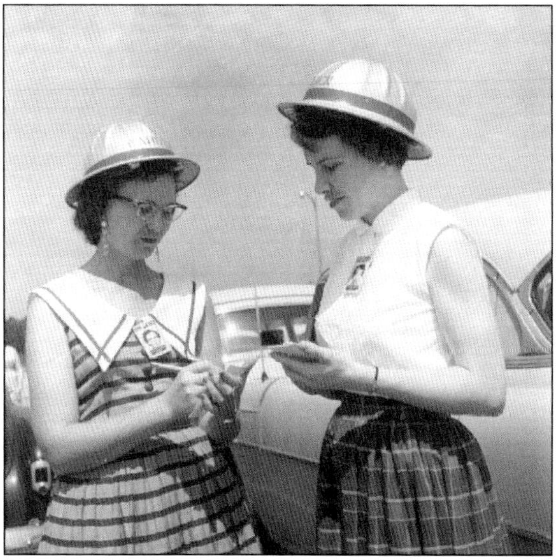

SRP conducted several Civil Defense drills on-site. While the general public could not participate, many plant workers were members of the Civil Defense Corps and completed their roles during this full-scale drill. These two women served as wardens in the evacuation of SRP's administration buildings during a nationwide Civil Defense Operation Alert exercise in 1956.

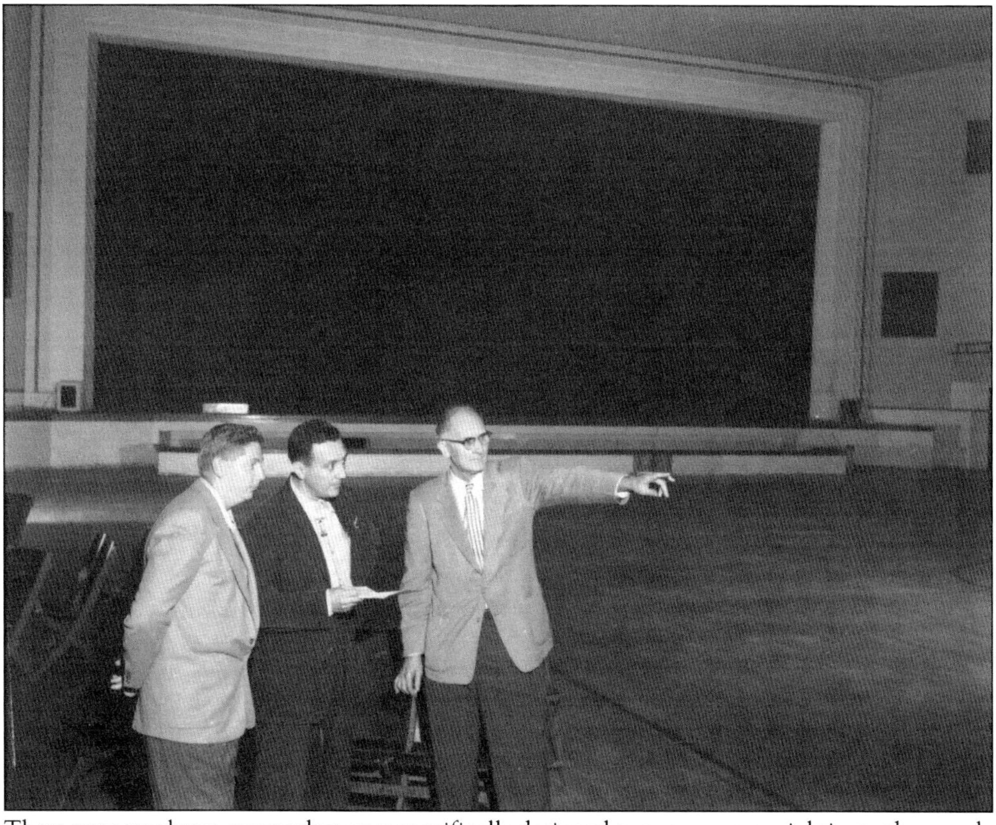

There were employee groups that were specifically designed to encourage social ties to the people and the area. The Operations Recreation Association often organized events such as dances. The annual spring dance in 1955 was held at the Bell Auditorium in Augusta, Georgia. Program chairman Doug Archer, Tony Orsini, and a Bell Auditorium official discuss the final details for the big event during a visit to the auditorium. The plant newspapers would later advertise the upcoming event and share photographs.

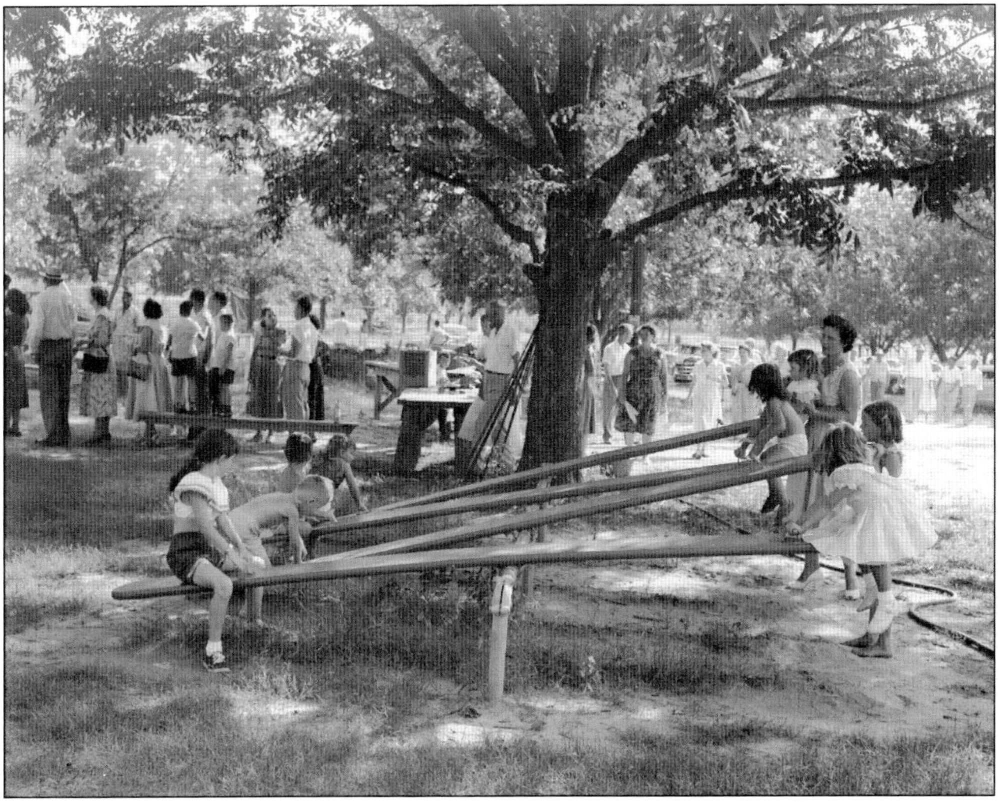

SRP offered three off-site recreation parks, Oak Grove Park near Barnwell, Pine Grove near Johnson's Crossroads, and Pecan Grove in Jackson. The parks were a popular spot for employees and their families to enjoy the weekend and also served as a meeting spot for barbecues and picnics organized by the SRP Recreation Associations established by departments on-site.

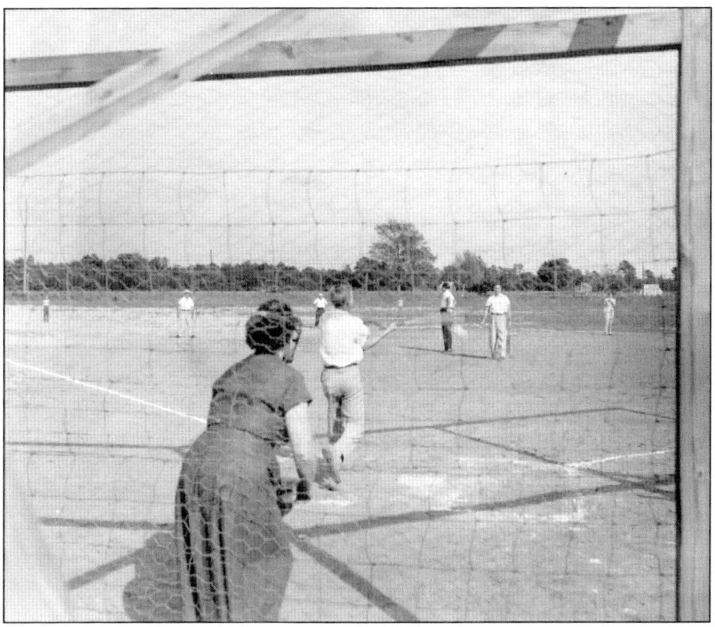

Sports were often a common theme at Operations Recreation Association gatherings. The entire family could play a good game of baseball. It was a fantastic way to meet newcomers, catch up with old friends, and get a bit of exercise. It also provided a bridge into the community as well as opportunities to explore the local recreation venues.

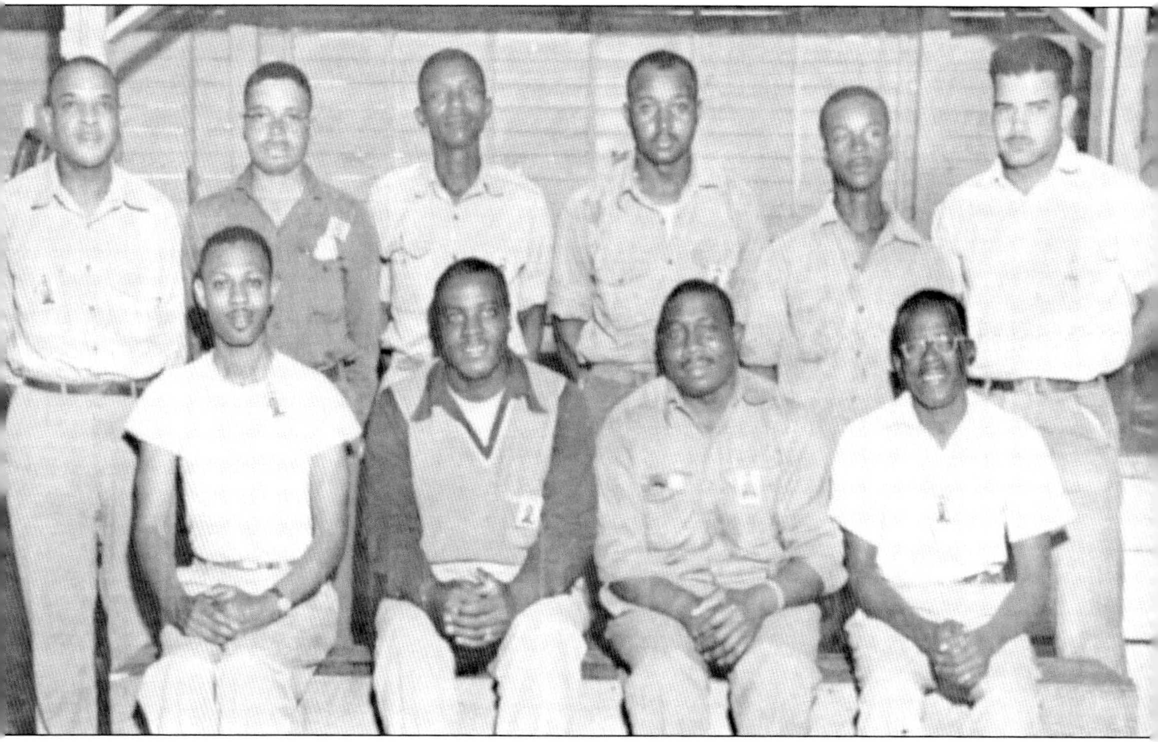

There were initially two recreation associations at SRP; the Colored Recreation Association (CRA) was separate from the Operations Recreation Association and formed in August 1952. The CRA was one of the largest and most active organizations on-site with a peak membership of 3,358 members until it was disbanded and merged with the Operations Recreation Association at the end of 1954. This image features the CRA officers.

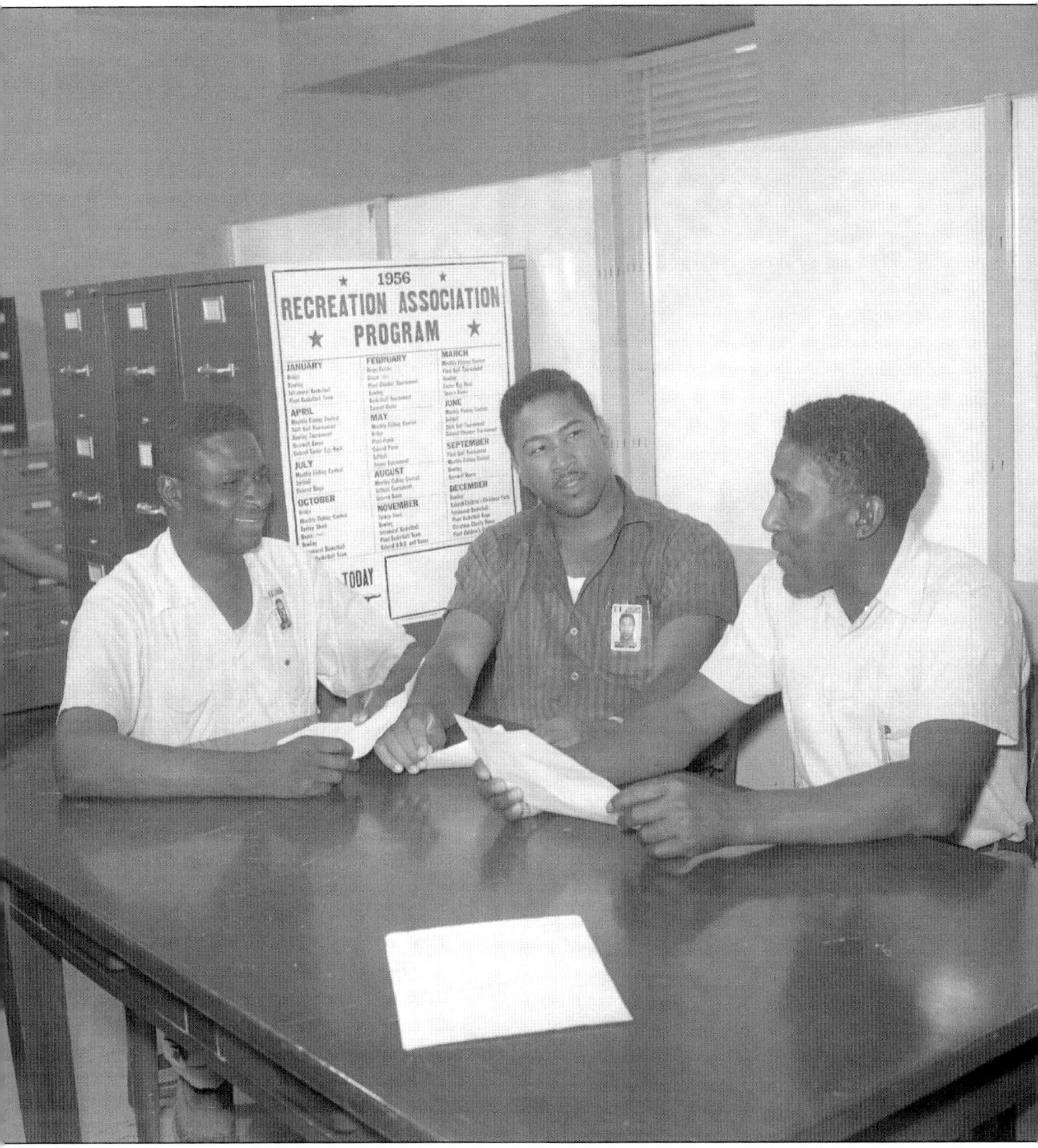

Members of the 1956 Operations Recreation Association (ORA) review plans for a picnic at the Paramount Motel in Augusta, Georgia. The ORA hosted special events on and off-site for employees and their families, such as sports leagues, community gatherings, and summer barbecues. Though the Colored Recreation Association joined with the ORA, separate events were still planned, and venues remained segregated into the 1960s.

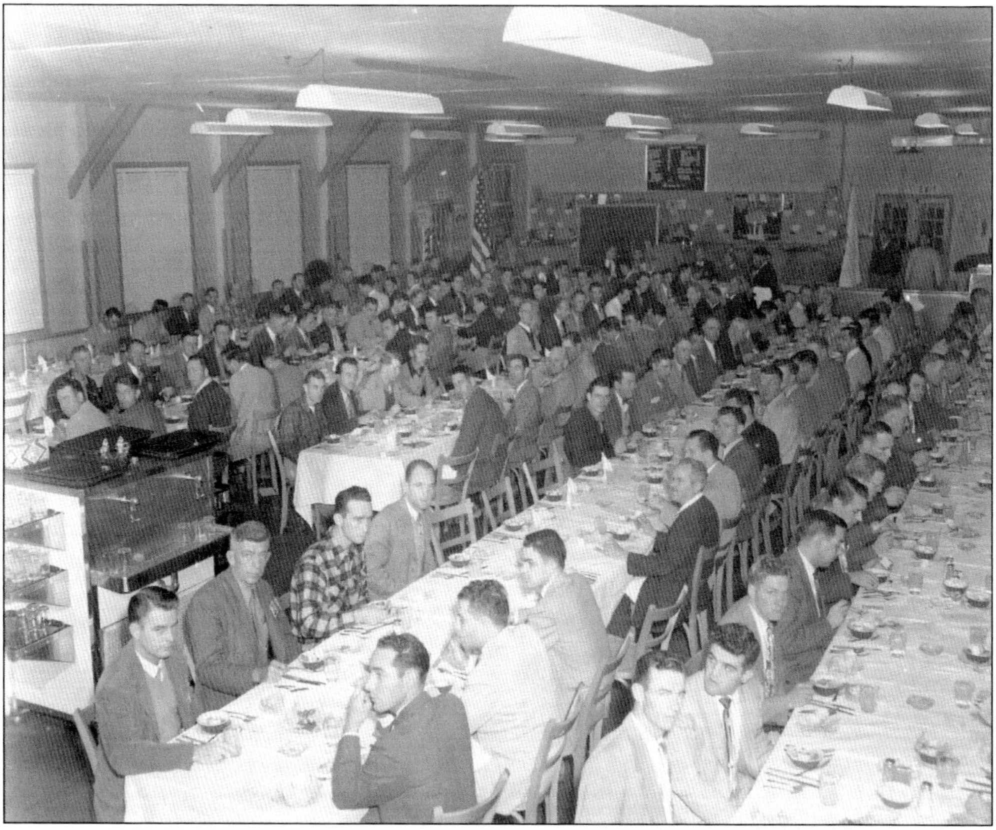

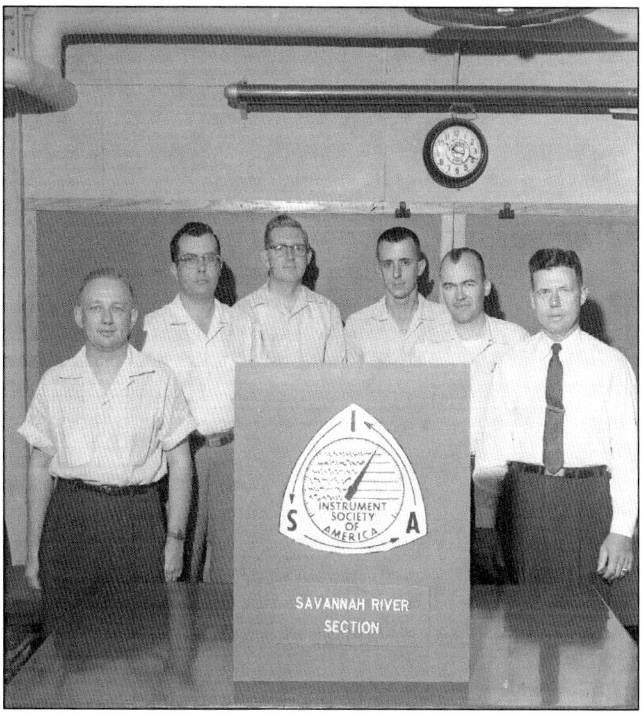

SRP brought many out-of-state engineers and scientists into the Central Savannah River Area (CSRA). This led to new chapters of national professional organizations, such as the South Carolina Association of Engineers, seen at this 1952 meeting (above). In the image at left, members of the SRP instrument department serve as the newly elected officers of the 1957 Savannah River Section of the Instrument Society of America. Other professional organizations include the Savannah River Chapter of the American Society for Metals, chartered in 1954, and the Savannah River Chemical Engineers Club of Aiken and Augusta, organized in 1953.

The SRP Employee Credit Union was first chartered in 1960 to promote thrift among its members and provide reasonable interest loan rates. In later years, the bank expanded off-site. Today, the bank is better known in the community as SRP Federal Credit Union and has over 20 branch locations in South Carolina and Georgia. Pictured are, from left to right, Lena Brown, Rheta Woodard, Vivian Tate, Ruth Carmack, and Mary Sue Beam.

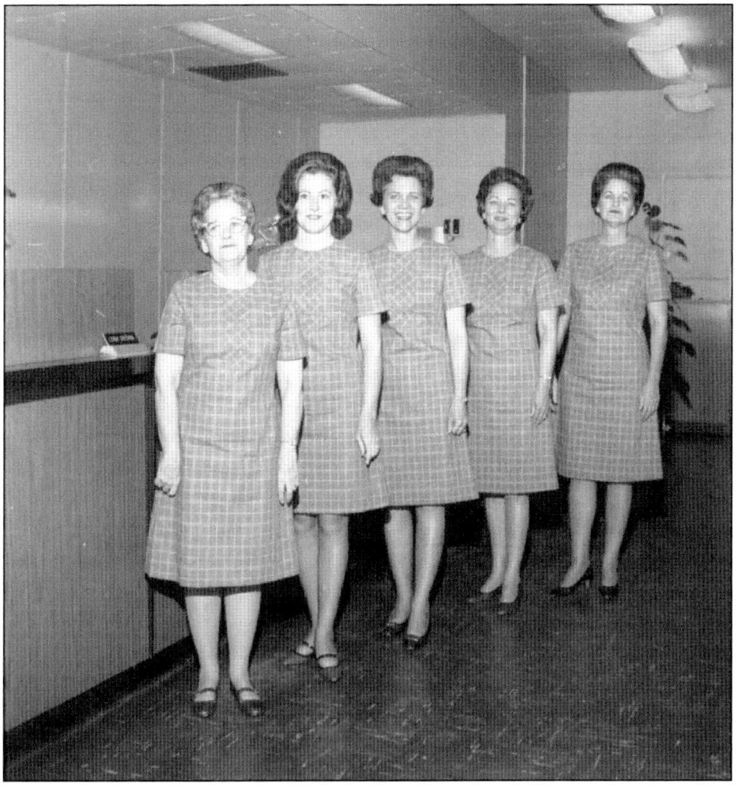

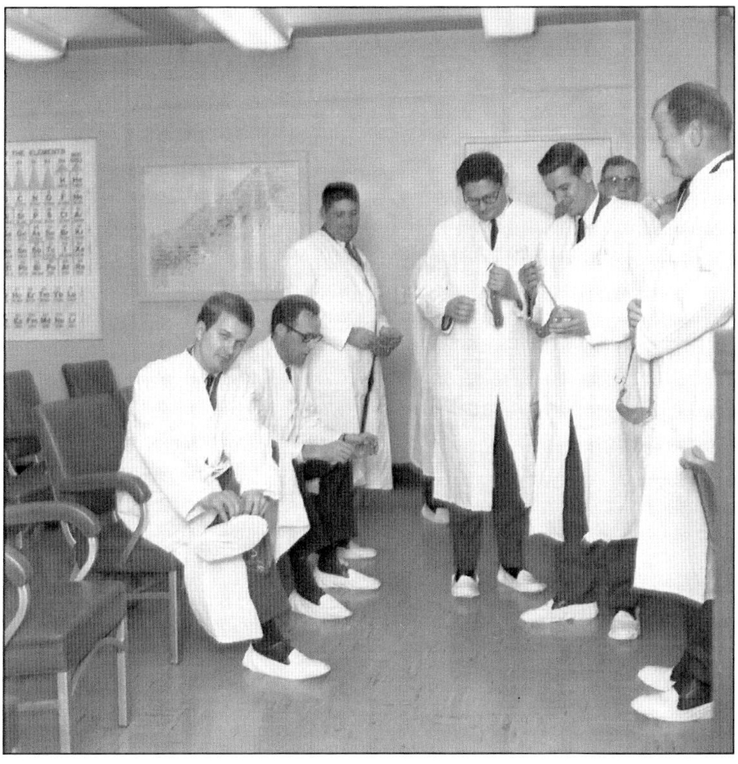

The SRP was closed to the public, but on special occasions, the press was invited to visit. During a 1968 visit to the Savannah River Laboratory, the *Augusta Chronicle* staff dressed in lab coats and shoe covers to tour the nearly completed Isotope Process Development Lab (IPDL). The IPDL looked at developing methods for isotopic heat sources and reflected the growing emphasis on peacetime nuclear products.

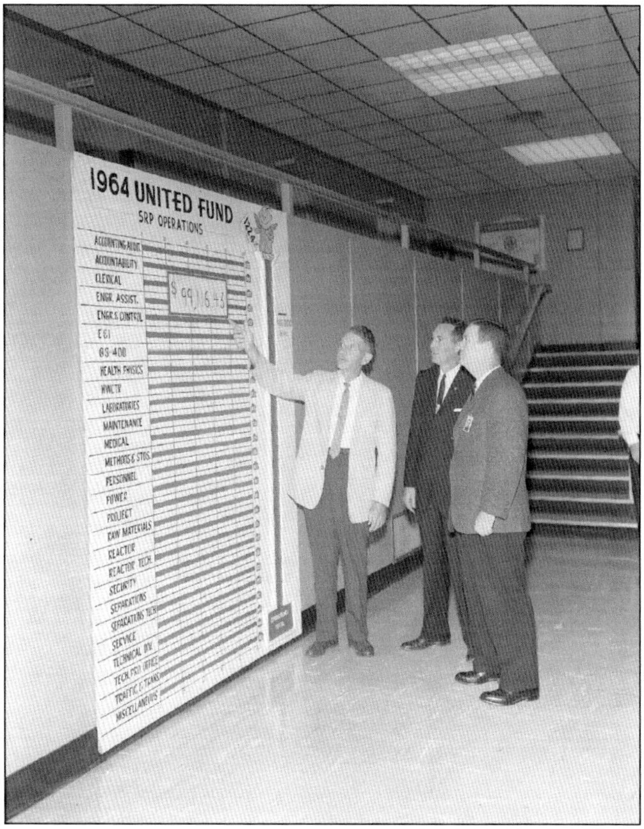

Community giving is a long-standing tradition of Savannah River employees. Each year, a donation goal was shared across the plant, and employees participated in friendly interdepartmental competition to encourage and drive higher donations. Displayed in the administration building, the 1964 campaign for the United Fund, later known as United Way, shows each department meeting and exceeding its goal. Gathered below, the 1978 United Way Committee meets to talk about the campaign goals. SRP employees exceeded the $250,000 goal by almost $70,000. For over 60 years, Savannah River has supported the community through United Way donations and service hours.

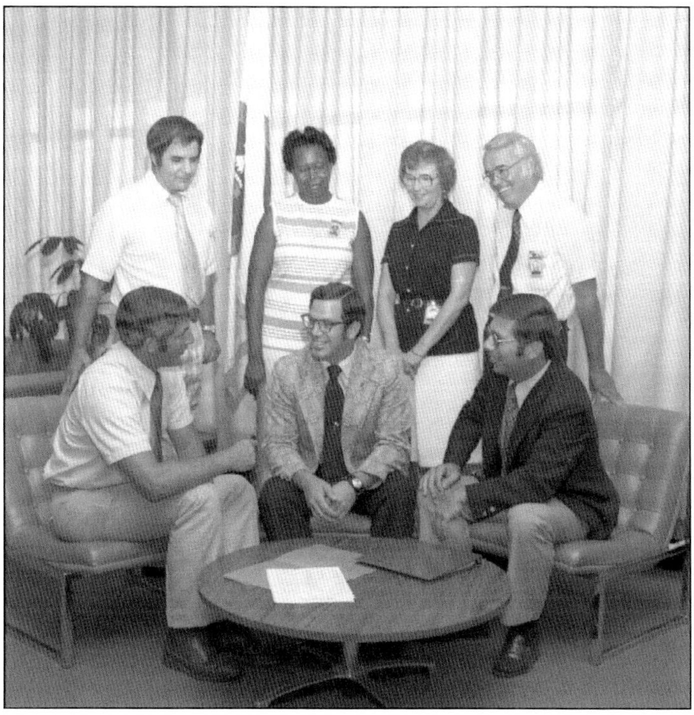

About the SRS Heritage Foundation

Walt Joseph and Dr. Todd Crawford, SRS retirees, founded the SRS Heritage Foundation in 2005 assisted by their energetic spouses, Paula Joseph and Bea Crawford. The foundation has matured, and it now supports the Savannah River Site Museum, which is located in downtown Aiken, South Carolina, and features exhibits on site history and technology and teaches about skills and careers in science, technology, engineering, and mathematics. To learn more about the Savannah River Site Museum, please visit the website www.srsheritagemuseum.org.